Carolina Loyalist

Carolina Loyalist

The Revolutionary War Life of Colonel David Fanning

JOHN HAIRR

McFarland & Company, Inc., Publishers
Jefferson, North Carolina

All photographs and maps are by the author unless otherwise noted.

Library of Congress Cataloguing-in-Publication Data

Names: Hairr, John, author.
Title: Carolina Loyalist : the revolutionary war life of Colonel David Fanning / John Hairr.
Other titles: Revolutionary war life of Colonel David Fanning
Description: Jefferson, North Carolina : McFarland & Company, Inc., Publishers, 2023 | Revised edition of: Colonel David Fanning: The Adventures of a Carolina Loyalist, Averasboro Press, 2000. | Includes bibliographical references and index.
Identifiers: LCCN 2022054791 | ISBN 9781476688671 (paperback : acid free paper) ∞
ISBN 9781476648149 (ebook)
Subjects: LCSH: Fanning, David, 1755–1825. | American loyalists—North Carolina—Biography. | United States—History—Revolution, 1775–1783. | North Carolina—History—Revolution, 1775–1783. | BISAC: HISTORY / United States / Revolutionary Period (1775-1800) | HISTORY / Military / United States
Classification: LCC E278.F2 H35 2023 | DDC 973.31409756092 [B]—dc23/eng/20221122
LC record available at https://lccn.loc.gov/2022054791

British Library cataloguing data are available
ISBN (print) 978-1-4766-8867-1
ISBN (ebook) 978-1-4766-4814-9

© 2023 John Hairr. All rights reserved

No part of this book may be reproduced or transmitted in any form or by any means, electronic or mechanical, including photocopying or recording, or by any information storage and retrieval system, without permission in writing from the publisher.

Front cover images: British Flag © Shutterstock; map of South Carolina and parts adjacent, showing the movements of the American and British armies, 1785 (Library of Congress)

Printed in the United States of America

McFarland & Company, Inc., Publishers
Box 611, Jefferson, North Carolina 28640
www.mcfarlandpub.com

Table of Contents

Acknowledgments	vii
Preface	1
1. Hard Beginnings	5
2. War Comes to South Carolina	13
3. The Whigs Strike Back	22
4. On the Run in South Carolina	29
5. The War Resumes	39
6. The War Shifts North	50
7. Fanning Takes Command	63
8. Elizabethtown and Beatti's Bridge	77
9. Loyalist Highwater Mark	86
10. The Dash to Wilmington	99
11. The Fall of Wilmington	108
12. Abandoned in North Carolina	116
13. The End in the Carolinas	125
14. Exile in Search of a Home	132
15. Triumph and Tragedy in New Brunswick	149
16. A Home in Nova Scotia	159
Appendix A: Sarah Fanning Petition, 1800	173
Appendix B: House in the Horseshoe Battle Damage	175
Appendix C: Places Named for Colonel David Fanning in Canada	177
Chapter Notes	179
Bibliography	189
Index	193

Acknowledgments

In a book of this scope and nature, a writer relies on the kind assistance of numerous individuals to make the project a success. I would like to take this time to acknowledge the help received from numerous people in the United States, Canada and Great Britain.

Staff members of the several institutions and historic sites across North and South Carolina provided access to sites and materials. The late Guy Smith, site manager of House in the Horseshoe State Historic Site in Moore County, North Carolina, during the 1990s, was extremely helpful with field research, tramping with me through some of the most rugged parts of the central part of the state to help hammer out important geographical details where the brutal Tory War took place. He and his assistant, Bill Thompson, provided encouragement to persevere with the research, especially that relating to the history of the Alston House and the history of the Deep River country. A decade after they left, I was fortunate to work with the late Roy Timbs, site assistant Alex Cameron and site volunteer Joe Luck to answer questions about the most famous part of the House in the Horseshoe, that being the holes in the walls—tangible evidence from Alston's brush with Fanning.

Joey Powell and the folks at the Averasboro Press moved forward with the original edition of the biography of Colonel Fanning, and stood strong in the face of the approaching millennial hysteria. Joey also played a key role helping sort out many of the contradictory accounts of the battles of the Tory War by accompanying me on numerous trips across the Carolinas for field research.

Jason Tomberlin of the Louis Round Wilson Special Collections Library at the University of North Carolina at Chapel Hill helped track down digital images from that institution's vast photographic collections. Cathy Taylor-Clifton of the Harnett County Library in Lillington provided valuable assistance obtaining obscure books via the interlibrary loan system.

Lt. Colonel Sion Harrington III of Erwin, former coordinator of the

Military Collection Project of the North Carolina Department of Archives and History in Raleigh, was especially helpful with suggestions on the text of the original version of this book, and of late has taken a keen interest in trying to pin down the exact site of where the Battle of Brown Marsh in Bladen/Columbus County took place. Hopefully the site of this battle can soon be properly investigated by archeologists and preserved for future generations.

The staff at Guilford Courthouse National Military Park were always willing to answer questions about the battle, especially the late Tom Baker, whose detailed knowledge of what went on here during the Revolutionary War period was impressive.

South Carolinians have made several positive steps preserving their Revolutionary War heritage over the years that can serve as an example to other states facing the challenges of trying to preserve history before it is overrun by urban sprawl. The staff at the Ninety-Six National Historic Site nurtured understanding of their unique site which was such an integral part of Fanning's life during the early years of the war. Although there have been outstanding battlefield sites administered by the National Park Service such as the Ninety-Six National Historic Site, Cowpens National Battlefield and Kings Mountain National Military Park, it has only been recently that the State of South Carolina has established an official state historic site to preserve one of the numerous places where the fighting took place in the Carolina Backcountry during the war.

When I was originally researching this book, it was quite a challenge to locate the old roadbed near the ford across the Enoree River where the Battle of Musgrove's Mill was fought back on August 19, 1780. Now, visitors can leave their machetes at home and learn about the fighting that took place here in relative comfort thanks to a state-of-the-art visitor center at the Battle of Musgrove Mill State Historic Site near Clinton, South Carolina. Trails and numerous helpful interpretive panels on the hill where the fighting occurred across the river from the visitor center help illuminate what happened here during the brief but important fight. Hopefully in the not too distant future a similar park and visitor center can be established at another Laurens County locale—Lindley's Fort—a site crucial to the understanding of the early years of the war in the Carolina Backcountry.

No biography of Colonel Fanning would be complete without including an account of the many eventful years he spent in Canada. Fortunately, I was able to secure a scholarship from the North Carolina Writers Network to help underwrite one of my trips to New Brunswick and Nova Scotia to conduct field research in 1996. The network's interest in this project is greatly appreciated.

Several individuals in Canada were helpful in locating material relating to Fanning's days there. Shannyn Johnson of the Canadian War Museum in Ottawa helped track down images of many items which are part of their collection. Staff members of the Public Archives of Nova Scotia were helpful in locating materials in their facility. Rob Gilmore of the Provincial Archives of New Brunswick provided access to the voluminous materials documenting Fanning's legal troubles in New Brunswick. Janet Bishop of the New Brunswick Museum provided valuable assistance in locating documents pertaining to all facets of Fanning's life in New Brunswick. The staff of Fundy National Park explained the nuances of the Bay of Fundy and the unique ecosystem of this part of Canada.

The people of Digby, Nova Scotia, the town where Colonel Fanning lived out the final years of his life, are an extremely friendly lot, and provided much assistance to this writer and his family during visits to their fair town. Hilma Woods and the staff of the Admiral Digby Museum gave much assistance and many valuable suggestions. The museum continues to grow, and is a wonderful place to start a journey back into the past of the Canadian Maritimes.

Of all the people in Digby, none were as deeply interested in this work as was Arnold Trask, a direct descendant of Colonel Fanning. The family stories he has preserved and related concerning his ancestor, as well as the valuable artifacts that he and his family members have passed down for two and half centuries, maintain a living link to the days of the old Loyalists. Mr. Trask coined the name "the Quicksilver Colonel" for Fanning, an apt moniker for someone with the Houdini-like skills to escape almost at will from the gaol at Ninety-Six or any of the other holding facilities of the Carolina backcountry.

Though I never had the pleasure of meeting him face to face, the late Gordon Trask held on to several items belonging to Fanning, including a powder horn Fanning took off one of his adversaries during the fighting in South Carolina. Gordon's widow, Mrs. Barbara Trask, generously shared a photo of the valuable artifact for use in my work chronicling the adventures of the old Loyalist.

To everyone who helped make this project possible, a hearty thank you!

Preface

Several years ago, I authored a book—*Colonel David Fanning: The Adventures of a Carolina Loyalist*, published by the Averasboro Press in 2000. The book was the culmination of a research project I undertook in the early 1990s, which included research trips to the Canadian Maritime Provinces to track down as much information in their local archival repositories about Fanning as possible. I was also hoping to track down any sort of family mementos which might yet remain, being especially intrigued by stories of a bullet extracted after the war from his back that was shown as recently as the early twentieth century as a family curiosity among his descendants near Fanning's final hometown of Digby, Nova Scotia. More traditional research was focused in the British Public Records Office in Kew, England, where study of British military records revealed many forgotten details about military engagements often ignored by historians of the American Revolution.

Many asked at the time why on earth I was wasting so much energy digging up stories about "Scald Head Dave" as he was sometimes known by his enemies in the Carolinas. Interest in the American Revolution had waned with the flurry of activity following the end of the United States Bicentennial commemorations in the late 1970s and early 1980s. But, despite many able historians such as Lindley Butler of Rockingham Community College providing some tantalizing insights into Fanning's wartime activities with the release of his transcription of Fanning's *Narrative* in 1981, as well as Carol Waterson-Troxler's ground-breaking articles about Fanning's misadventures in New Brunswick, no one had yet taken the time to put together a biographical story of the noted Loyalist partisan. The reason for this is because even though two centuries have passed since the Whigs and Tories ended their fighting, one still needs to tread lightly when discussing the brutal conflict, lest one be branded as somewhat unpatriotic.

Most people do not realize just how divided and dangerous the area was back when Loyalist and Whig militias were battling for supremacy across what is now the southeastern United States. The raids and incessant fighting was a true civil war that ripped families apart. Few would have ever thought that those roving bands of Whig raiders would eventually figure out a way to outlast the British government, but these sanguinary affairs not only created a new country in which the Revolutionaries could set up their experiment in a republican form of government but also set in motion changes on a global scale that most geographers and historians seldom stop to examine. The most basic of these was the displacement of thousands of people from their homes throughout the war, climaxing with the Whigs driving off many of their neighbors who hastily gathered their families about them and boarded transport ships for other parts of the King's realm.

The victorious Whigs were not alone in being the source of calamity, as even the British government itself, for whom the Tories had sacrificed so much, compelled thousands of Loyalists to abandon the provinces in East and West Florida, where many had taken the initial steps of getting their lives back together following their tribulations, and abandoning them to the Spaniards when the final peace treaty was signed in 1783. These ripple effects had broad implications which uprooted people all over the world, even as far away as Australia, where the New York Loyalist James Matra's resettlement scheme for providing a safe haven in the Southern Hemisphere for many of his fellow Loyalists was modified for the transportation of convicts to New South Wales.

Since he lived through so many of the events which tore apart the old British Atlantic based empire that was replaced with one more global in scope, the story grew from what I had originally envisioned would be a great adventure story into what became a formal historical study of the Tory War in the Carolinas and the Loyalist diaspora which followed. I found it necessary to try to place events when possible in some sort of context, thus linking them with other actions to provide a more holistic view of what had transpired. I utilized as many primary sources as possible to weed through often conflicting reports to get a better picture of what happened. We are fortunate that Fanning took the time to chronicle his activities during the war; he later compiled several official documents he managed to bring out of the Carolinas, Florida, and the Bahamas for publication in the 1790s.

The original copy of Fanning's *Narrative* has long been lost, believed to have been borrowed by an antiquarian and never returned as promised to his descendants in Nova Scotia. Copies survive, which can be checked against each other for accuracy. Fanning's accounts of battles often give clarity to events that have long been forgotten. But the *Narrative* ends when Fanning leaves the Bahamas headed for his new home in Canada. Unfortunately from Fanning's personal viewpoint, there is a trove of research material in both New Brunswick and Nova Scotia thanks to Fanning's legal troubles. Even though Dr. Troxler published the aforementioned scholarly article in the *North Carolina Historical Review*, which does an amazing job telling the story of what happened to Fanning that led to his exile from New Brunswick, the story of his final three decades in Nova Scotia had by the close of the twentieth century yet to be told by a historian taking the time to dig through the archives and local repositories to separate fact from fiction.

Word spread of my growing manuscript, thanks in no small part to the interest shown by certain members of the North Carolina Writers Network, which generously gave me a research grant to help underwrite one of my trips to Canada. I gave talks and lectures about Fanning's exploits, after which I solicited for any sort of family stories or other such lore to help flesh out the story. Publishers began making inquiries, including several publishing houses no longer in business. The manuscript was finished in 1997.

Even though some might think it a bit dry to go over the minutiae of the book publishing side of the equation, the story of the roundabout way it was finally released for public consumption gives a unique perspective into American popular culture and millennial hysteria. The book was originally contracted as a project with Savas Publishing in 1998 for release shortly thereafter. However, the publisher's concerns about the impending Y2K catastrophe led to several delays. Though we often laugh off such quirks, the delays proved to be very embarrassing, as it took a bit of effort to convince audiences that I did not share such feelings about impending doom. Later—in the year 2000—the world not being engulfed in chaos and anarchy, within the confines of the publishing agreement with the original publishers I released a print run published by the Averasboro Press, which allowed me to keep my speaking agreements, book signings, etc.. The book was well received, but has been out of print for several years. *Colonel David Fanning: The Adventures of a Carolina Loyalist* remains the only book-length biography written about the controversial Loyalist commander, and broke much new ground. Within a decade of the book's release, there was a flurry of books covering various aspects of Loyalist Studies, including works by historian Thomas B. Allen's 2011 book, *Tories: Fighting for the King in America's First Civil War*, and Maya Jasonaff's *Liberty's Exiles*, following in my wake.

More details of Fanning's story have come to light over the past two decades, including both historical and geographical particulars of his and his wife's ill-fated attempt to sail around Florida, many of which I shared with researchers in the *Florida Historical Quarterly* in 2019. Because it is important that Fanning's story remain relevant to scholars of the present era, I felt it was time to release this revised edition with McFarland. Taking the time to read what happened to these folks when civil political discourse ceased and people resorted to violence to settle their disagreements gives us a valuable lesson of the horrors of war and the consequences often unleashed upon the world. By studying Fanning's tragic existence as a lens to negotiate the various events through which he lived, one learns that the old Tory boogieman and his ilk were real people, whose homes and families were once part of the landscape, not just some abstract foreign British Redcoats or Hessian mercenaries from Washington Irving novels, but often friends and neighbors who lost their lives and property in defense of the Royal government under which both sides had lived for generations.

1
Hard Beginnings

Colonel David Fanning was a man who evoked strong emotion from people, both friend and foe alike. To some, he was the personification of evil. The Rev. Eli Carruthers, a historian noted for his Whig leanings, described Fanning as "...a scourge to humanity while living, and a by-word and a name of reproach when dead."[1] Carruthers' bias against Loyalists in general taints his work to the point of making it unreliable, unless one is able to verify his historical accounts of Revolutionary War action in the Carolinas against other sources.

To others, Fanning was the personification of the virtues of the old United Empire Loyalists who had given their all in service to their King. Canadian historian Alfred W. Savary believed Fanning was "...animated by a chivalrous loyalty to his lawful sovereign, and the idea of a 'united Empire'...."[2] Jonas Howe of New Brunswick, another Canadian historian writing in 1890, summed up his views of the controversial Loyalist, stating that "...his career during the revolutionary struggle, as gleaned from the pages of his Journal, proves him to have been a typical Southern partizan of the period—no better and no worse than some who now rank in the annals of the Carolinas as patriots. His exploits as a partizan leader, however, proves him to have been a man of genius, brave and fearless—and had he lived in another land and under other circumstances, would doubtless have won at least a modest meed of honor."[3]

Regardless of how one views the man personally, one thing is clear. Fanning was a tough, resilient, and enterprising soldier, the most successful commander of either side during the brutal Tory War that raged through central North Carolina during the years 1781–1782. He never lost a battle that he commanded, and won renown for capturing the governor of North Carolina. Long after Lord Charles Cornwallis surrendered at Yorktown, Virginia, Fanning remained active in the field. Fanning was a tenacious fighter, in both war and peace. His laurels won on the battlefields in the Carolinas, as well as his troubles in New Brunswick, give ample testimony to this fact.

The Deep River in Randolph County, North Carolina.

The story of the man who made such an indelible mark on the history of North Carolina and Canada begins in south-central Virginia in 1755. In that year David Fanning, Sr., left his pregnant wife and young daughter Elizabeth. He was headed for central North Carolina, searching for land on which to build a new plantation for his family in a fertile region which was just beginning to open up for exploitation and colonization. Tragically, David Fanning drowned in the Deep River in what was then Orange County while engaged in this quest. He left behind not only his wife and daughter but also a son he would never meet.

Whether word of the death of her husband reached Mrs. Fanning before or after the birth of her child on October 25, 1755, is unknown, but the newborn was given the same name as his father. Near the end of his life, David Fanning, Jr., wrote that he was born in "Beach Swamp in the Amelia County in the late Province of Virginia." Several members of the Fanning family lived nearby, including the boy's grandfather, Bryan Fanning, and several uncles.[4]

How odd it is, then, with all of these family members living in the neighborhood, that the widow Fanning should move with her family into North Carolina. Yet she did settle there prior to 1764, for at the January session of the Johnston County Court of Pleas and Quarter Sessions, her children are noted as orphans. David Fanning, "Orphan," was apprenticed to Thomas Leech. Meanwhile, Elizabeth, "orphan of David Fanning," was bound to Thomas Shuttleworth.[5] So before the young David Fanning was nine years old, he had lost both his father and mother. In addition, he was separated from his older sister, and there is no official record or family lore of the two ever meeting again.

For reasons unknown, Fanning's stay with Thomas Leech was brief. At the July term of the Johnston County court he was placed under the guardianship of Needham Bryan, Jr., who was also given the task of teaching the boy to read and write. Fanning's later literary accomplishments and written correspondence give ample testimony to the fact that someone, perhaps Bryan, taught him the basics of reading.[6]

The Bryans were a prominent family in the early history of Johnston County. Needham, Sr., came to the area in 1746 and settled just south of Smith's Ferry along the Neuse River in what is now the south part of the town of Smithfield. He owned thousands of acres of land throughout the county, and served in the Colonial and General Assemblies off and on from 1760 to 1777. He and his family are presumably the ones noted as having been poisoned in the fall of 1777.[7]

Needham Jr., was also active in public affairs. Born two years after his father had settled in Johnston County, the younger Needham held various public offices throughout his life, serving as a justice on the Court of Pleas and Quarter Sessions, as sheriff and as a member of the Provincial Congress in 1776.[8] Bryan was primarily engaged in agricultural pursuits, and it was presumably because of the fact that he needed help with the work on his extensive landholdings that he adopted the young orphan Fanning. Farm life in the eighteenth century was filled with backbreaking work and little leisure, so Fanning's life during his adolescent years was one of toil. But his existence was made even more difficult than that of many of his contemporaries because of the fact that Bryan was a negligent guardian.

Fanning later related that Bryan, "...treated him with great severity and neglect, making him live in the woods to take care of his cattle, and without comfortable food or clothing."[9] Despite such harsh conditions, Fanning remained on the Bryan farm for several years. He learned woodsmanship and became a skilled horseman. He was also introduced to military affairs. Needham Bryan, Jr., was a captain of the local militia unit, which would have given Fanning exposure to the routines of musters and drills. Records show that Fanning was even called up for duty in August of 1771.[10]

One of the most stirring military spectacles the people of Johnston County witnessed prior to the American Revolution came in May of 1771. Governor William Tryon marched with his army up the road from New

Bern headed west to quell the uprising of a group of vigilantes known as the Regulators. Tryon utilized Colonel William Bryan's plantation on the west side of the Neuse near Smith's Ferry as a rendezvous point for the militia units from various parts of the state to join his army. Captain Bryan and his men reported for duty under Tryon at his Uncle William's plantation. On May 3, 1771, the governor reviewed his troops here before marching west. Two weeks later, on May 16, 1771, Tryon's force met and defeated the Regulators at the Battle of Alamance.[11]

During this period of his life, Fanning came down with a disease that left him with his most remembered physical characteristic—his bald, scarred head. He lost his hair as a result of "Tetter Worm" or "Scald Head," names given in the past to a number of eczema-like scalp conditions. Such maladies can today be treated with over the counter antifungal medications, but in the seventeenth century it was much more difficult to contain, so it often left victims disfigured for life. Carruthers noted, "He had also a scald head, or tetter worm, which had been neglected, until it had taken the hair all off his head, except perhaps a little low down about his neck, which had to be cut off; and the smell was so offensive that he never slept in a bed. In fact, he seemed to be so conscious of this himself that he was unwilling, even if he had been permitted, either to eat or sleep with other people until he could get better clothing and cured of his disease. By the kind attentions of Mrs. O'Deniell and the family, he was cured of the tetter, but having lost his hair, he always wore a silk cap on his head under his hat; and, it is said, that his most intimate friends never saw his head bare."[12]

This description was passed down to Carruthers from James Johnson via Archibald McBryde. Johnson was a nephew of O'Deniell and as a youth was present when the young Fanning was residing with the family. "He told McBride that, although he was only eight or nine years old when Fanning came into his uncle's family, he had a distinct recollection of him,— his appearance, condition and deportment; that he was at his uncle's house most of the time that Fanning was there; and that he had often heard the facts related afterwards by his uncle, who was still living at the time when he gave Mr. McBride this information."[13]

The description of the symptoms indicates that the young Fanning suffered from an affliction known as Eczema capitis. This was not a pleasant experience for the boy. "Eczema frequently attacks the scalp," wrote Dr. Milton Hartzell, "particularly in children, and in the careless and uncleanly, and is apt to be of the pustular variety. The hair is often matted together with thick, yellow, greenish or brownish crusts composed of dried serum, pus and blood mixed with sebaceous secretion, which frequently exhale a very disagreeable odor owing to decomposition."[14]

Carruthers' account of Fanning's disfigurement has been embellished upon ever since he wrote it. However, Fanning was far from being the disfigured monster many of these apocryphal accounts portray him to be. Savary, who knew Ross Fanning, the Colonel's son, scoffed at the notion, calling statements, "...respecting Fanning's boyhood and physical idiosyncrasies, given as 'purely traditionary,' such as his being afflicted with 'scald head,' and unfit to sit at table with his fellows or to sleep in a bed, and designed to stigmatize him as a degraded character, belonging to the dregs of society, are evidently unreliable, and of doubtful good faith."[15]

The best surviving account of Fanning's appearance is a more mundane description which was preserved by Jonas Howe. "Colonel Fanning was a man of fine physique, small in stature, but very muscular and in early manhood very athletic. His complexion was florid or sandy and he wore a wig. His early training made him very self-reliant, and caused him also to be exceedingly reckless and passionate."[16]

Regardless of the permanent extent of his disfigurement, Fanning's bout with the scald head coupled with the general neglect he had been suffering induced him to leave the Bryan plantation in search of a better life. Thus, the seventeen-year-old set out on foot and wandered through central North Carolina until he fortuitously ended up at the home of John O'Deniell, "who lived in Orange County, a little below the Hawfield settlement." He was taken in by the O'Deniells, the aforementioned Mrs. O'Deniell curing him of his scalp affliction. Here he was well treated, and he returned the family's generosity by helping Mr. O'Deniell with carpentry work. He stayed with the O'Deniells for over a year.[17]

Unfortunately, we do not know exactly how Mrs. O'Deniell treated Fanning's scald head. Today such maladies can be treated before they get too far out of hand. Dr. Thomas Marryat preserved an interesting recipe for an ointment employed by physicians in the late eighteenth and early nineteenth centuries that included tobacco, tar and calomel. It is interesting to note that even today there are many scalp-soothing shampoos that utilize coal tar as a principle ingredient, but I am not acquainted with any modern shampoos or ointments than employ tobacco. Marryat wrote of his formula, "Scald Head. Let the head be shaved, if it can be performed with any tolerable convenience, and apply the tar ointment, with calomel, rubbing it well in night and morning.

"Take of Tobacco, two ounces, boil in Water, a pint, Till about an ounce is evaporated; then strain, and add a drachm of water of kali. Let a cloth be dipped in this mixture, warmed, and the head be moistened with it each time, previous to the application of the ointment, and the cruel operation of plucking out the roots of the hair will be totally unnecessary." Regardless of the method of treatment, the young Fanning recovered

Fanning's home in South Carolina stood upon the waters of Raeburn's Creek, known today as Rabon Creek, which joins the Saluda River under the backwaters of Lake Greenwood.

from the scald head thanks to the help of the O'Deniells, a fact he never forgot.[18]

When he did finally leave John O'Deniell's, Fanning headed south and settled with William O'Deniell, a "near relative" of John. William lived along the Pee Dee River just into South Carolina, and made his living trading goods with the Catawba. Fanning learned the rudiments of the Indian trade from William, but soon headed west to try his hand at the more lucrative trade with the Creek and Cherokee. He took up residence with Joseph Kellet who lived along Raeburn's Creek (modern Rabon's Creek) in the old Ninety-Six District of South Carolina. This region along the Saluda River Valley with its fertile valleys and forest clad hills, is strikingly similar from a geographical standpoint to the Deep River Valley of North Carolina. Several former residents of the Deep River Country had settled in this part of the colony, so Fanning may have been settling among friends and acquaintances of his late benefactor's.[19]

Since the early days of settlement of the region, the focal point of community activity was at a place known as Ninety-Six, where several trails connecting the coast with the interior intersected. The most important of these trails was the Cherokee Path, which came down out of the Blue

Ridge Mountains and traversed the southern side of Saluda River en route to Charles Town. Ninety-Six was so named because it was believed to be only ninety-six miles via the Cherokee Path to the Cherokee town of Keowee, which stood near present Walhalla, South Carolina.

In 1751 Robert Goudy, who had prospered in his trade with the Indians, purchased two hundred and fifty acres along the Cherokee Path at Ninety-Six and opened a business establishment which became the focal point of trade with settlers and Indian traders in the region. "Goudy built a frontier trading post which prospered and soon rivaled some Charleston merchants in its volume of business," wrote historian Dr. Marvin Cann. "His inventory included goods of every description: cloth, shoes, buckles, thread, needles, glass beads, gunpowder, lead, bullet molds, gold buttons, farm tools, and rum. At his death in 1775, more than four hundred settlers and Indian traders had open accounts at Goudy's store which had become the commercial center for a large backcountry area."[20]

During the French and Indian War a stockade fort was built at Goudy's. The settlers in the area took refuge here during attacks by the Cherokee. Goudy's was also used as a staging area for the expeditions against the Cherokee in 1760 under Sir Jeffrey Amherst and in 1761 by Colonel James Grant.[21]

Following the conclusion of the French and Indian War, in the fall of 1767, the Regulators came into existence as settlers in this region far removed from the seat of government attempted to establish law and order on the frontier. One of their chief demands of the government in Charles Town was a system of courts for the backcountry to administer justice. Thus, as a way of helping address some of the issues raised by the Regulators, seven judicial districts were created in 1769, one being the Ninety-Six District with Ninety-Six as the administrative seat.

To house these circuit courts, a courthouse and jail were needed. The commissioners for the Ninety-Six District selected a site roughly a mile away from Goudy's to erect the official buildings. These were completed by November of 1772.[22] The courthouse was constructed of wood, but the folks built a brick fortress to serve as their jail. The two-story brick building had walls sixteen inches thick, with an upper floor serving as a lookout post and the basement a dungeon for the harder to deal with prisoners. Historian Robert Bass described the structure, "With its base forty feet square and its three stories rising forty feet above ground, it was a veritable fortress. After the election of John Savage as sheriff, it became a fearful bridewell for cattle rustlers, horse thieves and murderers."[23]

Ninety-Six was a bustling frontier village in 1774 when David Fanning moved to the area. A thriving commerce with Indian traders brought a steady stream of customers into Goudy's trading post, and twice a year

The site of where the old Ninety-Six Jail, from which Fanning made so many memorable escapes, once stood, now within the confines of the Ninety-Six National Historic Site.

people from all over northwestern South Carolina came to settle business before the court. Fanning's residence was approximately twenty miles northwest of Ninety-Six, deeper into the wilderness and closer to Indian territory. As a trader, a good deal of his time would have been spent away from home, travelling among the Indians, visiting their towns and pedaling his goods for furs. Then he brought the pelts thus obtained to sell with merchants back among the European settlements. In most instances, Fanning would have transacted his business at Goudy's, but he may have travelled overland to get a better price for his furs from the merchants at Charles Town.

During 1774-1775, Fanning prospered, acquiring twenty horses and six head of cattle. He even constructed some sort of house or cabin on Raeburn Creek, a place of which he was very fond. In the years ahead, especially in times of trouble, he would seek refuge in this home in the wilderness.

2

War Comes to South Carolina

The most popular explanation for Fanning's attachment to the Loyalist cause was preserved by the Reverend Carruthers, who maintained that the reason dated back to an incident which occurred in 1775 when Fanning was on a trading trip with the Indians. While returning from the Indian country, he was ambushed by a party of Whigs who stole all his furs. Robbed of his possessions, Fanning then and there, "swore vengeance on the whole of the Whig party."[1] So says the Reverend Carruthers. However, Fanning makes no mention of this episode in his *Narrative*.

Fanning began his military service during the Revolution not as a Tory partisan but as a young sergeant in Captain James Lindley's company of the Upper Saluda Militia Regiment. Fanning, like many of his neighbors, became caught up in a series of events which plunged the South Carolina backcountry into chaos. To add legitimacy to the shadow government they had formed and given the grand name of South Carolina Provincial Congress, Whig radicals circulated a document around the colony known as the Articles of Association. They hoped to get as many signatures as possible on the document in order to give their revolt a sense of broad support. Several individuals, especially in the backcountry, did not share this revolutionary zeal. One of the most prominent leaders who did not was Colonel Thomas Fletchall, who lived on a plantation along Fair Forest Creek near what is now Union, South Carolina. He was not openly hostile to the Whigs, but he was clearly loyal to the Crown. Even so, Fletchall mustered the Upper Saluda Militia Regiment on July 13, 1775, in order that his men might hear the Association and make their own decisions. Fletchall later noted, "I don't remember that one man offered to sign it." At this particular gathering, the men were introduced to a second set of resolutions which had been drawn up by Major Joseph Robinson. This document, which was received more cordially by those gathered, affirmed their loyalty to the King and expressed their desire to be left alone.[2]

Following this meeting, Fletchall sent the two documents to Captain James Lindley so that he might present them to the men of his company who were not at the meeting on the 13th. Sergeant Fanning spread the word for the men to gather at Captain Lindley's house on Raeburn Creek on July 15, 1775. The exact number of men in attendance is unknown, but loyalty to the King was widespread. "There was 118 men signed in favor of the King, who Declared to Defend the same at the Risk of Lives and Property," Fanning noted.[3]

Meanwhile, tension mounted in the backcountry. On July 12, 1775, a force of Whigs under Major James Mayson, Captain Moses Kirkland and John Caldwell, seized Fort Charlotte on the east side of Savannah River opposite the mouth of Broad River.[4] This post guarded an important crossing into Georgia known as Cowan's Ford. Leaving a token force to hold the stone fort, Mayson and his Whig raiders returned with their booty to Ninety-Six.

Their return to Ninety-Six was far from triumphant. Five days after the raid, two hundred well-armed Loyalists under Robert and Patrick Cunningham marched into Ninety-Six, surrounded the court house, seized the property stolen from Fort Charlotte and incarcerated Major Mayson for the crime. Moses Kirkland, already unhappy at being passed over for promotion, was so

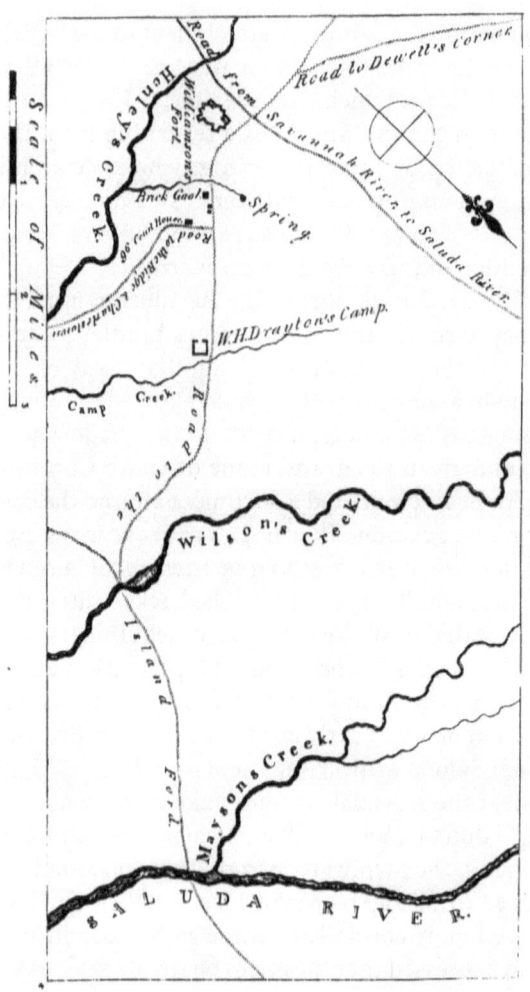

A map showing the area around Ninety-Six, South Carolina, in 1775, which appeared in John Drayton's *Memoirs of the American Revolution.*

impressed with this show of force that he defected. The action lasted until about 9:00 p.m. when Mayson was released and the Cunninghams went home.[5]

In an effort to change the hearts of some of the Loyalists, the Whigs dispatched several individuals into the backcountry to spread propaganda for their cause. Included in this group were William Henry Drayton, William Tennant, Joseph Kershaw, Frances Salvador, Richard Rapely and Oliver Hart. Crowds were gathered under the pretext of holding religious services, a rare treat in the backcountry. Fanning was on hand at one such meeting where Salvador and Rapely harangued about the virtues of the Revolution. Many did not appreciate such a misuse of religion, as Fanning clearly points out: "there was several advertisements set up in Every part of the said District that there was a Very Good prispeteareing minister to call at Different Places to preach and Baptise children."

"But at the time appointed instead of meeting a Minister we all went to meet two Jews by name Silvedsor and Rapely, and after making many Speeches in favor of the Rebellion and used all their endeavors to Delude the people away at last presented Revolution papers to see who would sign them. they were severely reprimanded by Henry O'Neal and many others. It came so high that they had much adue to get off with their lives."[6]

Tennant and Drayton were two of the more successful of these "evangelists," so it fell upon them to appear before a gathering at Colonel Fletchall's at Fair Forest on August 17, 1775. It was a hard audience, for gathered with Fletchall were Robert Cunningham, Joseph Robinson and Thomas Brown. Brown had recently fled his home near Augusta after being assaulted by Georgia Whigs for stating that he did not want to get involved in their struggle. He was beaten senseless, his feet were cooked, and he was ridden out of town on a rail. There is little wonder that following such treatment he should cast his lot firmly with the King, and he was one of the most vocal opponents to Drayton and Tennant's presentation.

The two Whigs were persistent. They tried arguing, persuading, and any other devices they could conceive. But it was for naught, for as Tennant later observed, "reasoning was vain with those who were fixed by Royal emoluments."[7] In an act of fairness, Fletchall summoned his regiment to Fords-on-Enoree on August 23, 1775, so the men could decide for themselves. The turnout was smaller than the earlier meetings, as Fletchall had instructed his captains not to force anyone to show up. Still, a fairly good crowd gathered, and the Whigs got nearly seventy signatures, despite the spirited testimony of Brown, Kirkland and several hardcore Loyalists.[8]

When the Council of Safety back in Charles Town received Drayton's report of the strong Loyalist sentiments, they were alarmed at the prospect of a large-scale civil war. On August 31, 1775, they empowered

Drayton to use whatever means necessary to bring the inhabitants of the backcountry back in line "by eradicating the opposition." By September 11, 1775, Drayton had gathered two hundred and twenty-five Whig militia and established his base at Ninety-Six. From there he dispatched raiders to apprehend the most dangerous Loyalist leaders.[9] Two days later, Drayton took the bold step of issuing a proclamation condemning the actions and motives of the Loyalist leaders. The most ominous portion of this was a warning that he would "march and attack" these enemies of the revolution if they did not cease their opposition.[10]

The proclamation had a most unexpected effect. Instead of intimidating the King's supporters into submission, Fletchall arrived three days after the proclamation was issued at Island Ford on the Saluda opposite Ninety-Six at the head of a Loyalist army over 2,200 strong. Inexplicably, at a time when he held a clear advantage over Drayton, whose force had grown to nearly 1,500 men, Fletchall lost his nerve and would not act decisively against the Whigs. Exasperated, Brown and Cunningham insisted that he be removed from command. Though they were unsuccessful, they did manage to gather eight hundred volunteers for a surprise night attack upon the Whigs, but their plans were spoiled when the river rose and became too high to cross.

The situation became a stalemate, giving Drayton an opportunity to exercise his diplomatic skills by sending word that he was willing to negotiate with the Loyalists. Fletchall, eager to avoid a confrontation, agreed. He ordered his captains to accompany him to the negotiations, and everyone save Brown and Cunningham agreed.

As the respective parties came together on September 16, 1775, liquor flowed freely. Before long, Fletchall, who had taken a few belts to bolster his courage before leaving camp, quickly became inebriated, at which point Drayton introduced terms for a truce. Fletchall was quite accommodating, overly so his men thought, but when the final treaty was completed he compelled his subordinates to sign. All but two, Robert Merrick and Phillip Mulkey, signed the document Drayton had dictated. Thus was consummated the first Treaty of Ninety-Six. Basically, the treaty promised neutrality on the part of the Loyalists, while the Whigs promised to protect the lives and property of those who did not wish to sign the Association. The treaty also recognized the right of the Council of Safety to incarcerate those opposed to the Revolutionary government.[11]

When they heard the news, Cunningham and Brown were indignant. They could not believe that their leader, even in a drunken state, had agreed to such terms, especially when they were on the verge of victory. Many Loyalists refused to acknowledge the document. But before Cunningham could organize opposition, most of the Loyalists disbanded and headed home in disgust.

2. War Comes to South Carolina

Robert Cunningham remained adamant in his opposition to the Treaty of Ninety-Six. In a letter written at Page's Creek on October 6, 1775, he outlined his feelings on the matter to Drayton. He noted that he was, "...as fond of peace as any man; but, upon honorable terms. But, according to my principles, that peace is false and disgraceful from beginning to ending. It appears to me, Sir, you had all the bargain making to yourself; and if that was the case, I expected you would acted with more honour, than taken the advantage of men (as I believe) half scared out of their senses at the sight of liberty caps, and sound of cannon, as seeing and hearing, has generally more influence on some men, than reason."[12]

Such sentiments naturally did not set well with members of the Council of Safety. Thus, it was only a short time before efforts were made to arrest him. He was brought into custody October 23, 1775, by Major Andrew Williamson and sent to jail in Charles Town.

Cunningham's brother Patrick immediately organized a party to ride down the Whigs and liberate his brother. The young Sergeant Fanning was among those who volunteered. Though they were unsuccessful in accomplishing their primary mission, the Loyalists did learn of a plan of ominous proportions—the Whigs were sending a large quantity of powder and ammunition to the Cherokee for use against the supporters of the King.

Cunningham's men scoured the backcountry hoping to intercept the shipment. They found it November 3, 1775, at Mine Creek eighteen miles below Ninety-Six. The shipment was guarded by Lt. Thomas Carleton, cadet Uriah Goodwin, two sergeants and eighteen privates. For some reason, the wagon of ammunition driven by Moses Cotter was riding well ahead of the escort when it was stopped by two of Cunningham's men who asked what was in the wagon. "Rum," was the reply, and soon thereafter Cunningham and the remainder of his force, which Cotter estimated to be a hundred and fifty strong, arrived.

Cunningham rode up to Cotter and said, "I order you to stop your wagon in his majesty's name, as I understand you have ammunition for the Indians to kill us, and I am come on purpose to take it in his majesty's name." Cunningham then jumped on the wagon, removed the cover and exposed the ammunition for all to see. Cotter reported, "then he handed out every keg to his men who were along side the wagon and prepared bags to receive it; after they finished with the powder he, with Messrs. Griffin and Owen, and several others, took out the lead which they unfolded, cut it into small pieces with their tomahawk's, and distributed it among the men."

Soon the escort rode into view. Some of Cunningham's men exclaimed, "There come the liberty caps; damn their liberty caps, we will soon blow them to hell." Violence was averted when Lt. Carleton and his men wisely surrendered. They were made prisoner and marched off to Cunningham's camp, but Cotter was released. He scurried to Ninety-Six and spread the alarm of what had happened.[13]

Shortly afterwards, Cunningham's men brought in Captain Richard Pearis who defected to their cause. He confirmed many of the rumors of the plans to arm the Indians with the ammunition so they could use it against the settlers of the backcountry. Exactly what role Pearis played in the subsequent events at Ninety-Six is uncertain. By his own admission, he did not join the Loyalists until after Cunningham's capture of the powder, but in his Loyalist claim he boasts of being, "appointed by 2200 Loyalists to Command them near 96, with the Assistance of Lt. Coll. Robinson and & Major McLauren." The fact that Robinson is mentioned by eyewitnesses on both sides as the leader tends to dispel this claim as an exaggeration.

Still, even if he was not in overall control, Pearis was considered one of the leaders of the Loyalist group gathering near Ninety-Six, and for good reason. Twenty years earlier, Pearis had won distinction for his exploits in the French and Indian War. He was renowned as the first to enter Fort Duquesne when that post fell in November of 1758. In 1768 he left his home in Virginia and moved to the frontier of South Carolina. His marriage to a Cherokee woman gave him a unique position to act as an intermediary between the Europeans and the Indians in the years leading up to the Revolution. He owned thousands of acres of land in northwestern South Carolina in the region of Paris Mountain. Because of his close relationship with the Cherokee, Pearis was courted heavily by the Whigs, who hoped he would use his influence to gain the Indians' support for the Revolution. But Drayton's arguments were not enough to persuade him to join the rebellion.[14]

Major Andrew Williamson received word of the Loyalists' raid from Major Mayson a few days after the incident. He immediately set to work organizing a Whig force large enough to recapture the ammunition. He hoped to not only awe them into giving up the powder, but to compel them to give up the instigators of the raid as well.[15]

Meanwhile, the Loyalists were gathering once more. With the addition of other companies and new recruits, Cunningham's force grew to 1,890 men. With the Loyalists once more in action, Fletchall decided to join them to take command, but following his actions at Ninety-Six in September, his services were no longer desired by many of his more energetic compatriots. The Loyalists were tactful in dismissing the inept leader who was nevertheless popular with the rank and file. Fanning wrote, "we then formed a Large Camp and Coln. Fletchall Being So Heavy he gave up Command to Majr Joseph Robinson."[16]

Joseph Robinson, like Pearis a native of Virginia, lived on a

2. War Comes to South Carolina

The bed from the road which once led from Ninety-Six to the Island Ford across the Saluda River.

comfortable four-hundred-acre estate he had carved out of the wilderness along Broad River. He owned a large house, barns, sheep, cattle and a fishery on Broad River. In addition to his agricultural skills, he was a man of letters, as he claimed to have owned, "a very valuable Library which he had purchased himself, Law Books & Books in different Languages." Perhaps this is the reason he was chosen to author the "Counter Association" document circulated by Fletchall throughout the backcountry a few months previous. Robinson held the post of "Deputy Surveyor in South Carolina." His duties would have made him thoroughly familiar with the roads, trails and terrain in western South Carolina.[17] Being a man of action, Robinson soon had his force in motion for Ninety-Six.

Williamson was joined by Major Mayson with thirty-seven Rangers at his camp near Ninety-Six, swelling his command to five hundred and sixty-three. With this force, he contemplated a night attack against Robinson, but learned instead that the Loyalists had crossed Saluda River at Island Ford and were moving toward Ninety-Six. A council of war was held, at which time it was decided to set out for Colonel Savage's plantation at Ninety-Six. They felt the cleared ground gave them a tactical advantage with their swivel guns. Marching through the night, they arrived at

Ninety-Six by sunrise on November 19, 1775, ahead of Robinson and his Loyalists.[18]

"At this place, a square of about one hundred and eighty-five yards was taken in, and fortified; as well, as time and means would permit," wrote Drayton. "This was effected in about three hours, by the unrelenting exertions of the men; and a temporary stockade fort was made of fence rails, straw and beeve's hides, with such other materials as were immediately attainable; and by which, curtains of defense were extended from a barn and store to some out-houses; at the distance, of two hundred and fifty yards from the gaol."[19]

At 11:00 a.m., while the work on the defenses was still in progress, the Loyalists arrived. They fanned out to surround the makeshift fort, and took over the court house and jail, both of which provided good cover from Whig bullets. With their dispositions complete, the Loyalists sent word to discuss the situation with the Whigs. Williamson sent Major Mayson and Captain John Bowie to parlay with Major Robinson, Captain Cunningham and Captain McLaurin. The Loyalists were clear in their demands—the Whigs must surrender and evacuate their fort. Williamson stubbornly refused to comply.

That afternoon, two careless Whigs wandered outside the fort and were promptly seized by the Loyalists. Williamson ordered his men to fire, and this was answered in kind by the Loyalists. The two sides continued shooting at one another for the next two days. On November 20, 1775, the Loyalists tried many creative ways to overcome the fort, including starting a grass fire in hopes that it would spread and consume the fort. They also constructed a mantlet. The attackers hoped to utilize this moveable breastwork to advance upon the fort and set it afire, but they were unsuccessful and eventually destroyed the device.[20]

A more menacing foe for the defenders was thirst. Since the beginning of the battle they had been cut off from their water supply in the creek. Early in the siege, Williamson's men set to work digging a well, and on the 21st they struck water.

With the new supply of water, it seemed as though the Whigs had enough food and drink to withstand a drawn-out encounter, but supply problems of another nature were now becoming critical. The Whigs had nearly exhausted their supply of powder. By late Tuesday, their two thousand pounds had dwindled to about thirty. Luckily for the morale of the besieged, the true state of their ammunition was known only to Williamson and one other man.[21]

The issue of the powder shortage left the Whigs in dire straits, but just when they were on the verge of capitulation, an unexpected sight was seen late Tuesday afternoon. The Loyalists "hung out a white flag from the jail" and indicated once again that they wished to discuss terms for surrender of the fort. As before, Mayson and Williamson refused to give up the struggle.

After darkness had fallen, another messenger from the Loyalists approached by candlelight, but this time the bearer was accompanied by Patrick Cunningham. Fifty yards in front of the fort he was met by Williamson, and a long conversation ensued. They finally agreed to take up the matter the following morning at 8:00 a.m.

Next morning the leaders of the respective parties met, and shortly thereafter terms for the surrender of the fort were reached. Besides ending hostilities, this second Treaty of Ninety-Six made some important provisions. The fort was to be "destroyed flat without damaging the houses therein, under the inspection of Capt. Patrick Cunningham and John Bowie, Esq., and the well filled up." Major Robinson agreed to move his men beyond the Saluda River where he could disperse his force or keep it together if he liked. But as events later proved, the most important provision of the treaty was item seven. "Should any reinforcements arrive to Major Williamson or Major Mayson, they also shall be bound by this cessation."[22]

The Battle of Ninety-Six was now over, and South Carolina had tasted its first bloodshed in the struggle for Independence. Each side lost about a dozen men wounded. James Birmingham was mortally wounded and thus has the distinction of being the lone Whig to die in this battle; a "Captain Luper" was the lone Loyalist killed.[23] These men were the first in a long list of men killed in this brutal civil war that had descended upon the South.

3

The Whigs Strike Back

The pandemonium in the backcountry convinced the Whigs that decisive action was necessary if their revolution was to move forward. So on November 8, 1775, the Provincial Congress ordered an all-out attack against the Loyalists. They hoped to dispatch a large force that would intimidate the Tories and convince them of their enemy's resolve.

An army of 2,500 men under the command of seventy-year-old Colonel Richard Richardson was sent to round up prominent leaders and disrupt Loyalist militia musters. As they reached the Congarees, their numbers were swollen by the addition of Whig militia to nearly 4,000 strong. But on November 28, 1775, they received word of Williamson's surrender at Ninety-Six, and of the perplexing item in the ceasefire agreement which bid all reinforcements to abide by the terms of the treaty.

Colonel Richardson convened his officers to discuss their options. They were unanimous in their sentiment of carrying forward the campaign, and had no intention of shackling their revolutionary fervor with a signed treaty. Some did, however, threaten to go home if they were not allowed to put an end to the Loyalists once and for all. Richardson convinced all of them to stay.[1]

Meanwhile, the Loyalists, gaining a false sense of security from their victory at Ninety-Six, were resting on their laurels. Believing they were safe from further Whig incursions because of the treaty, the Loyalists moved off beyond the Saluda and dispersed shortly after the battle. Fanning notes that Robinson, "Ordered the militia to the North side of Saluda River and Discharged them for Eighteen Days."[2]

By December 12, Richardson's men had captured a number of prominent Loyalists, including Captain Pearis and Colonel Fletchall. The corpulent Fletchall was found despite the fact that he had taken refuge in one of his favorite hiding places. "There was also, a large Sycamore-Tree, with a hollow 7 or 8 feet wide, on the north side of Fair-Forest Creek; 2½ miles below Brandon's mills, in which the Colonel occasionally secreted himself … it was in this Sycamore Fletchall was taken."[3]

3. The Whigs Strike Back

A historical marker commemorating the Battle of Great Cane Brake, near Greenville, South Carolina.

This unexpected offensive caught the Loyalists off guard, and the seizure of many of their favorite gathering places disrupted several of the Loyalists' musters, including the one which was scheduled at Hendrick's Mill for Maj. Robinson's forces. Several of the men, including Fanning, heard of an alternate meeting site on Little River out of range of the Whigs. Soon there were three hundred Loyalists gathered there, and they marched to an area along Reedy River known as the Great Cane Brake, which was located within four miles of the Cherokee Boundary, and about ten miles southeast of the modern city of Greenville. Patrick Cunningham, one of the few Loyalist leaders still in the area who had not been incarcerated, was in overall command. They hoped to be reinforced by both Loyalists and Cherokees.

The Whigs' ranks were swelled by the arrival of reinforcements from North Carolina. In addition, another contingent of South Carolinians, this group under Major Andrew Williamson, further increased their numbers. The combined Whig forces advanced as far as the end of the road at Hollingsworth Mill on Raeburn Creek when on December 21, 1775, scouts brought back word of the Loyalists' encampment at Great Cane Brake.

Hoping to take the Loyalists by surprise, Richardson dispatched Col. Thompson with thirteen hundred volunteers to move quickly and strike the Loyalist encampment. Marching through the night, the Whigs covered the twenty-three miles before sunrise the following morning. In the predawn hours, Thompson attempted to move his forces into position to surround the camp, but before he could close the trap a sentinel gave the alarm, at which point the battle began.

Most of the Loyalists were more concerned with fighting for self-preservation than for any strategical considerations. This was especially true of their leader, for at the sound of the guns, Patrick Cunningham bounded onto a nearby horse and rode bareback out of camp for safety. Some claim the Loyalist leader did not take time to dress. "Patrick Cunningham escaped on a horse bareback (and they say without breeches) telling every man to shift for himself."[4]

Many of the men followed his example, though they did not all forget their "breeches," and after only a brief fight the Battle of the Great Cane Brake was over. The Whigs captured a hundred and thirty prisoners and all of the arms, ammunition and supplies of the Loyalists. Col. Richardson reported, "None of our men were killed or wounded, except the son of Col. T Polk, a fine youth, was shot through the shoulder, and was in great danger. Some five or six of the other party, I am told, were killed; happily the men were restrained or every man had died."[5]

The true ordeal of this campaign, however, came at the hands of Mother Nature. The day after the battle, when all the forces were reassembled near Hollingsworth's Mill, snow began to fall and continued unabated for the next thirty hours, covering the ground with two feet of snow. This was very unusual for that time of year in South Carolina, and the men were ill prepared for inclement weather, having left their winter clothing at home. What's more, they did not even bring along their tents. Thanks to this harsh weather, the entire operation was ever afterwards known as the Snow Campaign.

The weather took its toll on the morale of the troops, and many of the frontiersmen, seeing no purpose to hang around any longer, began heading home. On Christmas Day, the North Carolinians who remained were officially dismissed and sent home with, "cordial and hearty thanks." Col. Richardson then headed the remainder of his South Carolinians southeast for the Congaree River.

The march of these men was a grueling ordeal. "I then found the service pretty well done and no possibility of detaining the men longer, the snow then lying on the earth in the smoothest places at least fifteen inches (most say two feet) I marched in the best manner we could downward. Eight days we never set foot on the earth or had a place to lie down, till we had spaded or grubbed away the snow, from which circumstance, many are frostbitten, some very badly; and on the third day a heavy cold rain fell, together with sleet, and melted the snow and filled every creek and river with a deluge of water; but with all those difficulties we reached this place yesterday with the prisoners, whom we have used in the best manner we could."[6]

The Loyalist fugitives of the Battle of the Great Cane Brake fled into the hills and forests of the Blue Ridge, there to face the grueling weather which had descended upon the region. Thanks to his familiarity with the terrain, Fanning was able to make his way to one of the nearby Cherokee towns, where he found refuge from both the Whigs and the weather.[7]

On January 18, 1776, Fanning crossed paths with a detachment of Whigs under Captain John Burns, who promptly made a prisoner of the Loyalist. He does not mention where he was incarcerated, but Fanning maintains he was held for four days. Remaining firm in his convictions, Fanning refused all offers for freedom in return for a Loyalty Oath to the Revolutionary cause, and was finally released after being "Stript" of his property and giving "Security for my future good Behavior."[8]

Fanning remained in the Cherokee country until May when he got word that the Whigs were offering amnesty to those Loyalists who would return to their homes and remain neutral. This seemed to him to be a good opportunity to resume a peaceful existence along Raeburn Creek, so he took them up on their offer and went home.

On June 20, 1776, Fanning was visited by Captain William Ritchie, who represented himself as a Loyalist in need of a guide to the Cherokee country. After much haggling, Fanning reluctantly agreed to guide him on condition that Ritchie tell no one. Ritchie, though, was a Whig, and as later dealings with the Cunninghams would prove out, an unsavory character. On this occasion he left his would-be guide and went straight to the authorities with a fabricated story that Fanning was organizing a Loyalist force to lead on a raid in conjunction with the Cherokees.

The Committee of Safety dispatched Captain John Rogers to apprehend Fanning and bring him into custody. Ritchie's story must have been a good one, as the Whigs took extra precautions not to lose their prisoner, for Fanning was "...thrown into close confinement with three Centinels over me."[9]

Fanning's stay in jail was cut short when the Cherokee, heretofore straddling the fence between the two factions, descended upon the frontier in an all-out attack in favor of the British, who had recently engaged in an unsuccessful attempt to capture Charles Town. The early reports of the Indian raids caused consternation among the Whigs, who were trying to figure out where the next blow would fall. Fanning took advantage of the bedlam to make his escape, and soon was back home on Raeburn Creek. As he was checking about the neighborhood, he soon discovered that most of his Loyalist friends had fled to join up with the Cherokee in

A historical marker near where Lindley's Fort once stood.

their uprising. Those who remained were inclined to go as well, but appear to have been waiting for a leader.[10] Fanning took charge, and soon gathered about him twenty-five men. These he led to Captain Richard Pearis' plantation, or what little there was left of the place. No buildings were standing on his farm, having been burned by arsonists. There, amidst the ashes of Pearis' home, several Indians and Loyalists were gathering in preparation for a raid upon the Whigs.[11]

The target of their raid was an old log stockade on Raeburn Creek known as Lindley's Fort, where nearly three hundred Whig settlers from along Saluda River—men, women and children—had taken refuge from the Indians. The attack was planned for the middle of the night, and it was decided that the Loyalists would dress and paint themselves as Cherokee warriors. One of the ironies of the battle is the fact that the Whigs had taken refuge in an old log stockade on the property of Loyalist Captain James Lindley. Though built sometime prior to the outbreak of the Revolutionary War by persons unknown, it was referred to as Lindley's Fort because it stood upon high ground owned by Captain Lindley overlooking Raeburn's Creek.

The attack commenced at 1:00 a.m. on July 15, 1776, but unbeknownst to the Loyalists, the garrison had been reinforced earlier that evening when

3. The Whigs Strike Back

a hundred and fifty Whigs under Major Jonathan Downs, marching to join Williamson at Whitehall, had stopped to spend the night. Thus, there were nearly four hundred people crowded into Lindley's Fort, while outside were eighty-eight Indians and a hundred and two Loyalists.[12]

The fire of musketry lasted throughout the wee hours of the morning until about 4:00 a.m., when the Indians and Loyalists decided to pull back as no opportunity to storm the fort presented itself. As they began to withdraw and beat a hasty retreat, the Whigs sallied forth and captured thirteen of the Indian-clad Loyalists. The total number of casualties is uncertain. Drayton maintained that the Indians left behind several dead, including "...two of their Chief Warriors." Fanning contradicts these claims, stating that the only Loyalist injury was an Indian chief shot through the hand. The Whigs reportedly lost just one person.[13]

This small engagement at Lindley's Fort played a major role in the Cherokee Uprising in the summer of 1776. Drayton states, "Had the fort been carried, it is not improbable but the disaffected all around, would have joined the Indians, as some had previously done.... This repulse, however, awed the wavering into a peaceable conduct."[14] This Whig victory, coupled with the news of the British defeat at Charles Town, helped silence the discontent in the backcountry and opened the way for a Whig counterstrike against the Cherokee.

The new drive into Cherokee country from South Carolina was led by the newly promoted Colonel Andrew Williamson, and was launched in conjunction with attacks from Georgia, North Carolina, and Virginia. Several Loyalists joined the Whigs during this campaign against what many perceived to be a common enemy. After a series of attacks deep into their territory, the Cherokee were effectually crushed by the fall of 1776, and ceased to be a legitimate military threat to the security of the South Carolina settlers in the Blue Ridge region following the treaty signed at Dewitt's Corner on May 20, 1777. However much they may have been reduced, they remained a menace in the minds of settlers in the area, and Whig leaders exploited those fears for the duration of the conflict.

Following the fight at Lindley's Fort, Fanning fled north into North Carolina. There, for the next eight months, he found anything but peace. "I then left the Indians and pursued my way to North Carolina, where on my arrival I was taken up again and Close Confind but was rescued by my friends three different times after which I made my Escape Good. I then Endeavord for to go home again, and after Experiencing a numberless hardships in the woods I arrived the 10th of March 1777 at Raebuns Creek South Carolina."[15]

His stay at home was a brief one. The very next day he was captured by a Whig force under a Captain Smith, who had Fanning's hands and feet bound before heading for Ninety-Six. After traveling twelve miles, the group halted for the evening. As soon as everyone was asleep, Fanning cut the ropes and stole away into the night. The fugitive made his way back home to Raeburn Creek. He spent the spring and early summer hidden in the woods nearby, relying for sustenance on the benevolence of friends and a group of Quakers.[16]

4

On the Run in South Carolina

While Fanning was hiding in the woods along Raeburn Creek in the summer of 1777, Richard Pearis, the Whig defector who was so active during the fall of 1775, was attempting to raise a force of Loyalists from Fanning's neighborhood to march to West Florida and join the British forces there. He was raising this force despite the fact he had signed "an oath of Neutrality" in September of 1776.

If any man had reason to resume hostilities against the Whigs it was Richard Pearis. Prior to the war he had amassed quite an estate along the Reedy River thanks to his trading activities with the Cherokee. His lands totaled over 10,000 acres, and on these in the vicinity of Paris Mountain he had houses, barns, mills and a trading post. But all of this was put in jeopardy when he changed sides during the fall of 1775.

During the early stages of the Snow Campaign, Pearis was captured and hauled off to Charles Town, where he spent nine months in jail until taking his oath. Upon his return home, he found the place a mass of ruins, burned the prior summer by a group of Whigs under Colonel John Thomas. Pearis' family was carried away by the Whigs, and after a thorough search he found them living with a family in hostile Whig territory. Pearis tried to stay amongst them, but he soon found it necessary to take refuge with Governor Rutledge at Charles Town thanks to numerous threats of physical violence.

Even Rutledge was unable to assure Pearis' safety, as there were constant threats against his life. Exasperated and feeling that he had done everything possible to remain neutral, Pearis headed home to the Reedy River area in the summer of 1777.[1] Once back in a region where Loyalist sympathies were strong, Pearis began raising a body of troops to take to Mobile for British service. Soon he collected four hundred recruits, among them Sergeant Fanning. Unfortunately for their enterprise, there were also a number of spies in their ranks. Soon word got back to the Whigs about Pearis' force, and they took action to end his activities.[2]

In early August the Whigs descended upon a gathering of the

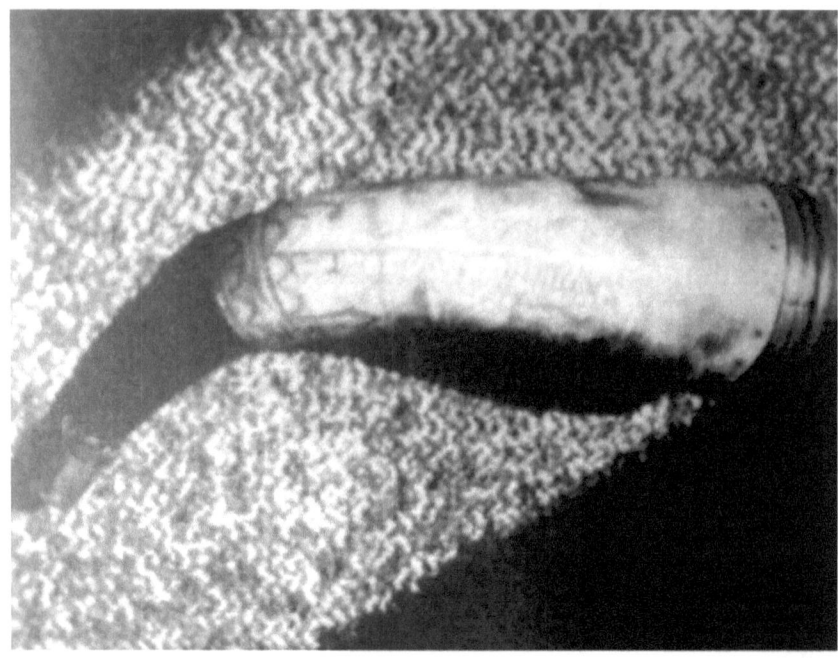

This powder-horn once owned by Colonel Fanning with the name "Samuel Lewis Liet" carved on the side was handed down as a prized heirloom among his descendants to the current owner, Barbara Trask. Family tradition maintains he obtained it during one of his many escapes in South Carolina early in war.

Loyalists on Reedy River, and made a number of them prisoners, including Fanning and Pearis. Realizing that capture meant sure death, the latter escaped on August 5 and headed for the Cherokee settlement with six companions. From there they made their way to the British outpost at Pensacola. There, thanks to the trials and tribulations he had endured in attempting to raise a force for service to the Crown, Pearis was made a captain of the West Florida Militia.[3]

Fanning and those left behind were not so fortunate. They remained locked up (possibly at Ninety-Six) until November, at which point they were tried, "...on a Charge of high Treason for Rising in arms against the United States of America...." Luckily, they were acquitted, for the offense was a capital one. Exonerated, Fanning once again returned to Raeburn Creek, but his return home was delayed when he was cast back into jail to pay rent due for his earlier jail stay. This was assessed after he had already paid £300 to cover the expenses of his confinement.[4]

* * *

4. On the Run in South Carolina

In East Florida, the British were moving forward with plans for an invasion of Georgia. By using a combined force of Native Americans and Loyalists in the northern reaches of South Carolina and Georgia to act in concert with a force of British regulars marching out of East Florida, they hoped to eventually recapture Georgia and South Carolina. The plan was the brainchild of Lt. Col. Thomas Brown, who had earlier gained notoriety because of the abuse suffered at Augusta. He now commanded a group of partisans operating out of East Florida known as the King's Rangers.

The operation was heartily endorsed by the British high command, and preparations were made in the winter of 1778. Loyalist leaders of the Carolina backcountry were alerted to be ready to rise, while supplies and foodstuffs were stockpiled. Brown received intelligence that over 6,000 Loyalists were in readiness, waiting for some show of support from the British government.[5]

Brown dispatched Captain John York into the backcountry settlements to spread the word to mobilize and to guide the militiamen south to rendezvous with the main army. York had been a resident of South Carolina, but little is known of him. He was captured at Great Cane Brake in December of 1775, where he was serving as a militia captain. On a list of prisoners a notation was made stating that he was, "deemed a bad man by both parties."[6]

Fanning reports that York came into his settlement on March 1, 1778, with news for the men to embody. At the subsequent muster, Fanning was elected by his fellow Loyalists to be their captain. "We took a number of prisoners furnished ourselves with horses and marched to Savannah River on the Borders of Georgia 12 miles above Augusta."[7]

Meanwhile, on the Georgia/Florida border, the offensive was moving forward. On March 10, 1778, Lt. Col. Brown led a hundred of his men and ten Indians in an attack on Fort Howe. After swimming the Altamaha River during the night, Brown's men stormed the works at daybreak, capturing the fort, which was subsequently destroyed.[8] Following the capture of Fort Howe, the British offensive self-destructed. Internal bickering between the military and civilian leadership present in East Florida stalled the advance. The initiative was seized by General Robert Howe of the Continental Army, who launched his own attack on East Florida.

In northern Georgia, the Loyalist rising was in full swing. "The trek of the first contingent under leaders named Murphy and Gregory thoroughly alarmed the Georgia Whigs," wrote historian Edward Cashion. "Georgia Governor John Houston informed Congress on April 16 that between five and six hundred marched through the back parts of Georgia on their way to Florida, stealing horses, arms and ammunition as they went."[9]

The passage of such a large group through their territory alerted the

Whigs in Georgia and South Carolina to the impending danger, and they responded by scouring the region hoping to put down any rising while it was still in its infancy. Whether it was fear of running awry of Georgia Whigs or because of the breakdown of leadership among the British, when Captain York met Fanning's band near the Cherokee Ford across the Savannah River he refused to conduct them to East Florida.

York's abandonment of his comrades left Fanning and his cohorts in dire straits. "Capt. York who was our Pilot then Got discouraged and would not Suffer any of the militia to proceed with him back to East Florida except three men; we were then under the necessity of Returning home upwards of 100 miles through the Rebels Country and betake ourselves to the woods as formerly."[10]

York and a small number of men made their way back to East Florida and rejoined the British army, who were then engaged in defending their colony from Howe's attack. The Continentals were also beset with a case of dissension and jealousy among the leadership which adversely affected their ability to fulfill their objectives. This was a repeat of their failed invasion the previous year which resulted in a duel between their two leaders, General Lachlan McIntosh and Button Gwinnett, the latter dying as a result.

Fortunately for the Continentals, there were no duels in 1778, but Howe's army was defeated at Alligator Creek in East Florida on June 30, 1778. His retreat to the north side of the Altamaha ended this futile series of maneuvers on the southern frontier of Georgia for the remainder of 1778. All was quiet there save for cattle raids.

* * *

The success of the raids along the Savannah River brought notoriety to the Loyalist band from Raeburn Creek, and soon the area was swarming with Whigs who were bent on ending their activities. Fanning notes, "...when the Rebels found we were Returned they Raised a body of men for to take us and the space of three months kept so Constant a Look out that we were obliged for to stay in the woods."[11]

Fanning was forced to live off the land, gathering what sustenance he could from the forest around him. He spent almost two months alone in the woods before he came across one Samuel Brown, a fellow Loyalist fugitive with whom he spent the next six weeks. Brown was no ordinary Loyalist soldier. For many years, he had earned a living by preying upon the inhabitants of the Carolinas between the Yadkin River and the Blue Ridge. Eventually he became so successful a brigand that the people of the region nicknamed him "Plundering Sam."

Plundering Sam's hideout along the Catawba River west of Statesville,

North Carolina, was reportedly a repository for the loot taken from his victims. "About fifteen miles west of Statesville, North Carolina, three miles above the Island Ford, there is a high bluff on the western side of the Catawba River, rising three hundred feet high, at a place known as the Look-out Shoals. About sixty feet from the base of this bluff, under an over-hanging cliff, was a cave of considerable dimensions, sufficient to accommodate several persons, but the opening to which is now partially closed by a mass of rock sliding down from above. This cave was the depository for the plunder taken by stealth or violence from the poverty-stricken people in the country for many miles around...."[12]

Fanning makes no mention of how he made the acquaintance of such a notorious character as Brown. Quite possibly he had been a member of Fanning's force which was raiding along the Savannah River. But the two became friends during those trying times in the spring of 1778. Tired of living a primitive existence in the woods, the two men decided in May to head for the settlements along the Green River in North Carolina. There were numerous Loyalists and their sympathizers along Green River, so it was a natural choice for the two weary fugitives.

Nearly a week later, Brown and Fanning parted company—Brown undoubtedly heading back to his lair along the Catawba, Fanning making tracks for the Tyger River country back in South Carolina, where he arrived June 1 and was joined by Samuel Smith. But before this duo could embark on any raids of consequence, they were captured by a group of Whigs commanded by a Captain "Going."[13]

Their incarceration was brief, for on the second night of their confinement they bribed a guard and escaped. Fanning headed for home on a horse he had taken from his captors. This particular horse must have been quite a beast, for the Whigs pursued Fanning to his home in order to recapture it. They even offered to exchange four they had taken earlier from Fanning if he would agree to return it.

A deal was struck, and under a guarantee of safety Fanning set out with his former captors back for the Tyger River. He soon found that his companions had negotiated in bad faith: "...when we had advanced 30 miles we come near to where a Rebel Fort was. I Desird them to Go a little out of the way to avoid it, which they had promised to do, before we proceeded on our Journey one of them laid hold of my horses Bridle and told me to surrender myself a prisoner for they were determined to confine me in the Fort or Carry me to Ninety Six Gaol about 80 miles off.... I therefore after some conversation concluded to Submit for to be Disarmed at the time as they threatened Blowing a ball through me every Instant if I did not surrender."[14]

Once again, Fanning found himself a prisoner, this time confined to an unnamed prison whose only location was given in the abovementioned description as lying on Tyger River "80 miles" from Ninety-Six. The Whigs took no chances losing such a valuable prisoner. They took his clothes and kept a constant vigil over him through the night. Next morning, his feet bound beneath a horse upon which he was mounted, they led their captive before a magistrate.

Upon being released on bail, Fanning returned to the individuals who had so recently bilked him and demanded that they return his clothes and horse, whereupon he was promptly recaptured and taken before another magistrate, this one more sympathetic with their cause. The magistrate committed Fanning to jail. Once again, the Whigs were extremely careful with their prisoner. On the way to jail, Fanning not only had his hands bound, but also was secured by a rope to one of the captors, "a stout fellow," as Fanning described him.

Before they made it to jail, the Whigs stopped for lunch, and locked Fanning and the "stout fellow" in a room. Here their carefulness ended, for they forgot to clear the room of sharp objects. The cunning Fanning soon spied "a pair of hors fleames" lying nearby and awaited his opportunity. The moment soon presented itself, for Fanning's ropemate fell asleep, at which point the wily Loyalist cut himself free and leapt out of a window to freedom.[15]

Following his latest escape, Fanning headed once again for the Green River country between Tryon Mountain and Chimney Rock in southwestern North Carolina. There, he made the personal acquaintance of Colonel Ambrose Mills, whose sympathies were clearly with the King and his followers. Kin by marriage to Colonel Thomas Fletchall (their wives were sisters), Mills lived in what is now Polk County, North Carolina, and seems to have been a supporter of the Loyalist cause from the start of the war. In June of 1776 he was captured by the Tryon County Committee of Safety and forwarded to the Committee of Safety in Rowan County, along with the following testimonial. "With these we send you under gard Ambrous Mills one of the greatest Enemys of our pese in Tryon County a companion of Robinson, and Been lying out in the mountens since before the South Carolina campaign; has held a Correspondence with Camron; has acknowledged himself to have been in the Indian Nations, he Seems Simple but is Subtile and Insinuating and has had Influence enough to pradgudise not only his neighbours but many at a great distance against the Cause of American liberty, in Short his Character is so notorious that we expact that every gentleman in Rowan is acquainted with it and we hope that he will be confind till he has a fare tryel in every article above mentioned and a great deal more can be proved against him when required. For further perticquelers Inquire of Cpt. Cook Commander of his guard;

for fear of a Resque we will not inform you of our own Circumstances but hope Mr. Cook will think to inform you."[16]

Mills spent the summer of 1776 in the jail at Salisbury, where he nearly died. His health wrecked, he signed a loyalty oath to the revolutionary government and was then released September 7, 1776.[17]

When he and Fanning met in July of 1778, Colonel Mills had been laying low. But with an energetic younger companion to help, that was all about to change. The two men decided to raise a force of Loyalists and head south for the British post at St. Augustine, East Florida, there to receive arms, ammunition and other supplies. Fanning maintains that five hundred men reported for duty. Trouble was, not all of them were faithful Loyalists.

Thanks to an informer in their midst, the Whig authorities soon got word of the group Mills was raising, and they dispatched a force to break it up. The Whigs surprised the Loyalists while their forces were scattered, taking Colonel Mills and sixteen others captive. With their prisoners in tow, the Whigs turned and headed east to Salisbury.

Fanning heard of the unfortunate turn of events, and quickly gathered what men he could, which in this instance was fourteen. They set out in hot pursuit, and chased the Whigs for over twenty miles to Gilbert Town, where the Whigs received reinforcements. Now Fanning found himself the object of the chase as he and his men rode west through the night down the road they had so recently traveled.

Next morning, the Whigs continued their pursuit, and ran headlong into an ambush Fanning had laid during the wee hours of the morning. A hot little skirmish ensued and lasted for nearly an hour, at which point the Whigs broke contact and retreated toward the Catawba. Fanning reports that he lost none of his command and did not know about his enemy's losses. Apparently, the Loyalists did not stay on the scene long after the fighting ended.[18]

There is no record of Colonel Ambrose Mills having made it to Salisbury. If he did manage to escape, it was a stroke of luck, as he would not have fared well on his return appearance before the Rowan Committee of Safety. Had the Whigs gotten hold of him, there is little doubt that he would have had a date with the hangman in 1778.

Their enterprise spoiled, Fanning and his fellow Loyalists dispersed. At this point, it appears that he had grown weary of the war and its constant raids and the incessant fighting. So, instead of once more returning to Raeburn Creek, he headed northwest across the mountains to the settlements on Holston River. Somewhere high in the Blue Ridge, he ran across three men in that wilderness of forest-shrouded mountains who would deny him his opportunity for peace. One of the group recognized the lone traveler, but kept the news a secret. He offered his hand in friendship, and as Fanning went to shake it, he was seized. Once again, David Fanning was a prisoner, and, as before, he was headed for the gaol at Ninety-Six.

The ride across the mountains back to South Carolina must have been quite an ordeal for the prisoner. His hands were bound behind his back, and his feet tied together underneath the horse's belly. In this condition he rode the trails over a hundred and fifty miles back to Ninety-Six.

Upon his arrival, Fanning was placed in the confines of the now familiar gaol at Ninety-Six, where he remained for seventeen days. During that time he had been smuggled "two files and a knife," which were used to saw through the bars of the cell. Fanning escaped through the hole thus created, and headed home for Raeburn Creek.

Fanning hid out in the woods for some time, living a very primitive and spartan existence. Eventually, he was convinced that he could make peace with the Whigs via Captain Robert Gilliam. Fanning set up a meeting, and the two got along so well that they continued their dialogue with clandestine meetings in the forest. Their meetings went on for more than a month, but came to an end when Gilliam resorted to trickery, seized Fanning's rifle and captured him; "he presented my Rifle to my Breast and told me I was his prisoner or a Dead man. I was under the necessity to surrender and carried me again to my old Quarters at Ninety Six."[19]

When Captain Gilliam arrived at Ninety-Six with his prisoner on October 11, 1778, he presented the jailer with a familiar face. Many times he had tried to hold the elusive prisoner, and each time Fanning managed to get away. The authorities at Ninety-Six were determined that he would not get away again. Fanning was "stripped entirely naked," then chained in the middle of the floor of a room, "thirty feet square, forty five from the ground the Snow beating in through the Roof with 4 Grates open day and night." The authorities at Ninety-Six must have been confident that their prisoner was secure. But they were wrong.

On the night of December 20, 1778, Fanning was able to get rid of the irons. He then proceeded to borrow some clothes from another inmate, fashioned them into a sort of rope, crawled through a window the bars of which he had loosened on a previous stay, and lowered himself to the ground. The rope snapped about halfway down, and Fanning fell to the ground. Though unhurt, the noise of the landing awakened the jailer, who alerted the guards of the post. The fugitive eluded his pursuers, but in the process was injured "by a fall."

Once again free, the wounded man headed home for Raeburn Creek. But his taste of freedom was short-lived. Three days after his return home, the Whigs arrived and once more captured Fanning and took him back to Ninety-Six. The jailer took extra steps to make sure the prisoner did

4. On the Run in South Carolina

not escape again. Injured, naked, chained to the floor of an open room with wind and snow blowing in through the open windows, Fanning spent a very miserable time. After eleven days, he managed to work the chain loose from the floor and was able to move about the room. The jailor took pity on him and did not attempt to tie him back down, but the iron chain was left around the prisoner's leg in what was hoped would be a deterrent to future escapes.

Ever resilient, on the night of February 13, 1779, Fanning once more escaped from the gaol at Ninety-Six. First, he removed an iron bar from the window of his cell. With this iron bar he pried a plank out of the floor which left a hole through which he dropped to the ground level. Finding the door secured, he proceeded to the chimney where on a previous stay he had loosened some of the brick. With the help of another prisoner, Fanning opened a gap through which the two men crawled. Once again, he had broken out of the gaol at Ninety-Six.

They may have been free, but they were not safe. Naked in the cold February night, the fugitives first procured transportation by absconding with a couple of horses tethered near the gaol. After travelling a short while, the escapees stopped at a house along the road for much needed supplies. The sight must have bordered on the comical: two naked men on horseback riding up in the middle of the night, one with a large chain dangling from his leg. What the inhabitants of this house thought of the sight has unfortunately not been recorded, but Fanning and his companion did manage to obtain clothes and weapons.

The Whig authorities scoured the countryside for their escaped prisoners. The fugitives eluded capture by staying in the woods, but it was only a short time before Fanning's less resilient companion was retaken. Next day, Fanning was surprised by a group of Whigs, and though he managed to escape, he lost his weapon.

Soon thereafter, with a price of "seventy silver dollars and 300 paper ones" on his head, Fanning was ambushed by a party of sixteen men. Despite being shot twice in the back, he managed to evade capture. After riding a dozen miles, he dismounted, set his horse free and took to the woods on foot. For the next eight days, Fanning remained in the forest, subsisting off what he could scavenge. All the while, his wounds were becoming infected.

Finally, he was reunited with his horse and rode off to a home of a friend who lived nearby. His haggard and forlorn appearance gave him the look of a man beyond death. It was only after a good deal of coaxing that he convinced a young lady of the house that he was not a ghost.

Fanning described his predicament at this low point in his life. "I looked so much like a rack of nothing but skin and bones, and my wounds had never been dressed and my clothes all bloody. My misery and situation was beyond explanation, and no friend in the world that I could depend upon."[20] The person at whose house Fanning found refuge did in fact prove to be a friend. Here, he rested, was fed and had his wounds treated. One of the bullets he received in the back was extracted, but the other he was destined to carry until it was removed many years later in Canada, where it was shown as a curiosity well into the twentieth century. "The bullet received by Colonel Fanning in the encounter related was," wrote historian Jonas Howe in 1890, "after many years of suffering, extracted during his residence in New Brunswick, and is now in the possession of his great-grandson, Fanning Smalley of Digby."[21]

In a sense it is unfortunate that Fanning did not record the name of this particular friend in his *Narrative*. Yet in all likelihood he left the name out to shield his benefactor from Whig retribution.

* * *

While Fanning was busy being locked up and escaping from Ninety-Six, many of his Loyalist neighbors had ridden off with Colonel James Boyd, who raised a sizable force of Loyalists from both Carolinas. Boyd embarked on a project similar to Captain York's, and hoped to lead his recruits back to Florida, but he was killed and his little army defeated at the Battle of Kettle Creek, Georgia, on February 14, 1779. Had Fanning not been incarcerated and/or on the run, he in all likelihood would have been a part of Boyd's little army, and may have shared the fate of his old commander, Captain James Lindley, who was captured at the Battle of Kettle Creek. Lindley and several of his comrades were taken back to Ninety-Six, tried, convicted and executed by Whig authorities.[22]

* * *

Word soon reached the Whigs leaders at Ninety-Six that Fanning yet lived. Exasperated, they drafted a letter which gave him an unrecorded number of days to turn himself in, or else eight of his friends would be incarcerated and their lands confiscated. Fanning claims that he received the notice after the deadline had passed, and upon reporting this to the Whigs his friends were set free. Their property, however, was not returned.

About a week later, upon the urging of his friends and comrades, Fanning accepted a "conditional pardon" which in effect stated that he would be left alone if he stayed out of the war. Furthermore, he occasionally had to guide Whig parties through the backcountry of the Carolinas.[23] A tired and wounded Fanning accepted this offer.

5

The War Resumes

David Fanning lived at peace, if his Loyalist Claim made in 1787 is accurate, "for 12 months and 12 days." He even claims in his *Narrative* to have been offered a company in the Continental Army. How different history would have been had this man accepted and commanded a company under Daniel Morgan or Francis Marion.[1] Instead, Fanning remained true to his convictions and declined the offers. He lived at peace on his farm on Raeburn Creek until the spring of 1780, when the war caught back up with him, and forces beyond his control drew David Fanning back into the fray.

With the conquest of Georgia in 1779, the British set about subjugating the next state to the north. On May 12, 1780, Charles Town fell to the British, and soon the King's forces were in control of virtually the entire state. At the instigation of leaders such as Major Patrick Ferguson, the Tories were instructed to report for duty to the King, and more importantly were given an opportunity to mete out revenge on their Whig tormentors.

Like many of his Loyalist neighbors, Fanning took this opportunity to rejoin the action. In the middle of May he teamed up with one William Cunningham to raise a force to lead into battle. This was long before Cunningham set about a series of particularly violent raids for which he earned the nickname "Bloody Bill." Fanning and Cunningham had followed similar paths, the latter having served throughout the numerous campaigns in the backcountry at such places as Ninety-Six and Fort Charlotte, while Fanning had once served under Patrick Cunningham, William's cousin. There was one major difference which separated the two men—William had been a Whig supporter during the early days of the Revolution.

Like many of his fellow Whigs, Cunningham lost faith in the cause and became a Loyalist. Naturally, this did not set well with his Whig comrades, but none took greater offense than Captain William Ritchie, the character Fanning had met earlier in the war. Upon hearing of William's defection, Ritchie paid a visit to Cunningham's lame brother, John, whom he murdered.

William Cunningham got word of this deed while in Savannah, and immediately set forth for the Ninety-Six area to exact revenge. Horseless, he made the trip on foot, and by the time he reached home, he found that Captain Ritchie had struck again, this time mistreating his father. Cunningham quickly set out in pursuit of Ritchie, and found him at home at leisure. Cunningham took little pity on his Whig antagonist, mortally wounding him before their encounter was finished.[2]

Fanning and Cunningham gathered a small group of men about them and set out to capture Colonel James Williams, an inveterate Whig who was described by Loyalist Lieutenant Anthony Alaire as being "a very violent, persecuting scoundrel." A former member of the Provincial Congress, Williams was serving as colonel of the Whig militia in the Ninety-Six District. He lived at Mount Pleasant on Little River south of the present town of Laurens. The two Loyalist leaders must have reasoned that capturing such a high-ranking prisoner would make a good impression on Captain Pearis, who returned to the area with his West Florida Loyalists and was directing the Loyalist activities in this region of South Carolina.[3] Williams was able to elude capture on this occasion thanks to a timely warning. But he was nearly apprehended. "Coln. Williams got notice of it and pushed off and though we got sight of him he escaped us," Fanning recalled.[4]

Soon thereafter they took their men to Pearis' camp, where Fanning was ordered to ride about through the countryside spreading the news that the British were once again in control of the region and it was time for those loyal to the King to report for duty. Fan-

This monument commemorating the Battle of Musgrove's Mill stands near the bridge over the Enoree River in Musgrove Mill State Historic Site, near Clinton, South Carolina.

ning rode his circuit and rejoined Pearis at Ninety-Six on June 11, 1780. The Loyalists had recaptured this crucial outpost the day before, "without firing a shot."[5]

Shortly after the fall of Ninety-Six, the Loyalists bagged two very important prisoners, General Andrew Williamson and Colonel Andrew Pickens. Williamson was the highest-ranking Whig official left in the state after Governor John Rutledge had fled north to Philadelphia following the fall of Charles Town. Pickens was an influential leader of the Whigs in the Ninety-Six region and a resilient fighter.[6]

Pearis was very lenient in his dealings with his former antagonists, paroling some of the most inveterate Whigs of the area. Some of Pearis' comrades thought he was too lenient, and voiced their displeasure to Cornwallis.[7] Soon Colonel Alexander Innes of the South Carolina Royalists arrived in Ninety-Six and began directing operations for establishing order in that part of the backcountry. He placed Lieutenant Colonel John Harris Cruger in charge of the outpost at Ninety-Six, a key spot in Cornwallis' strategic line of outposts garrisoned across South Carolina.

Encouraged by the successful pacification of the South Carolina backcountry, Loyalists in southwestern North Carolina began to stir. Cornwallis urged them to remain peacefully on their farms, lay in their crops and await his arrival in Charlotte at which time he would give the word to embody. But the Loyalists were impatient. Lieutenant Colonel James Moore returned to his home near Ramsour's Mill in western North Carolina and began spreading the news of the British successes in South Carolina. By June 10, 1780, forty men had gathered together for possible service, but Moore told them of Cornwallis' directive to lay low. But word spread fast, and within three days two hundred men gathered together. At this meeting there was another British officer present, Nicholas Welch, who impressed the crowd with more tales of British deeds. Within a week, their ranks had swollen to over 1,300 men, many of whom were unarmed.

The Whigs of the region were fast mobilizing to quash this Loyalist uprising in its infancy, and forces under the direction of General Griffith Rutherford were converging on Ramsour's Mill. On June 20, 1780, Colonel Francis Locke with approximately four hundred Whig militia surprised the Loyalists. Following a sharp engagement in which a hundred and fifty men were killed or wounded, the Loyalists fled, leaving the Whigs masters of the field.

Lieutenant Colonel Moore escaped capture and made his way back to the British camp at Camden. He was nearly court-martialed for disobeying orders and prematurely raising the Loyalists. The effect of his defeat was more far-reaching than the mere number of killed or wounded, for it

Much of the action for the Battle of Musgrove's Mill took place along this old road leading to the ford across the Enoree River.

made the Loyalists upon whom Cornwallis was counting for support wary of reporting for duty in the future.[8]

The Loyalist forces at Ninety-Six were consolidated under the command of Robert Cunningham, who now held the rank of general. At this point, thanks to his intricate knowledge of the countryside, Fanning was once again put to work scouting through the western portions of the Carolinas.

Save for a few minor skirmishes, this period of duty was uneventful for Fanning until the middle of August, when he and fourteen of his followers united with the Loyalist forces consolidating under Colonel Alexander Innis at Musgrove's Mill on the south side of the Enoree River. A strong body of Loyalists under Colonel Daniel Clary maintained a post at the mill guarding a strategic river crossing, and Innis halted there as he marched with his detachment of Provincial regulars and Loyalist militia en route to join Major Ferguson, who was at that time encamped several miles to the east at Winn's plantation in what is now Fairfield County.[9]

The arrival of Innis' force was opportune for the British, as at that very moment a large contingent of Whig militia was bearing down on Musgrove's Mill from the north. This force, numbering about two hundred and fifty strong, was made up of South Carolinians under Colonel James Williams, Georgians under Colonel Elijah Clarke and North Carolinians under Colonel Isaac Shelby. These men, who jointly managed the operation, were part of Colonel Charles McDowell's army encamped at Smith's Ford on the Broad River and had volunteered for what they knew would be a hazardous and grueling trek. There were claims that these men's patriotism was fortified for undertaking such a dangerous mission in the first place by the possibility for financial gain. A rumor was circulating about that there was some sort of treasure chest destined for Ferguson waiting at Musgrove's Mill.[10]

At sunset August 17, 1780, the Whigs set out on their raid. Marching through the night, they travelled through thick forests and passed over numerous watercourses en route to their objective. By dawn, the Whigs were on a ridge within a mile of Musgrove's Mill. Shelby sent out scouts to reconnoiter the Loyalists' position, their having crossed the Enoree at Head's Ford approximately a mile above the mill. They scouted the camp undetected, but ran into a Loyalist patrol on the return trip just west of the ford on Cedar Shoal Creek. A brief, hot fight ensued in which one Loyalist was killed and two wounded, while the Whigs lost two men wounded. Two members of the Loyalist patrol were able to make it back to the mill and spread the alarm that Whigs were in the vicinity.

When members of the Whig patrol returned to the main army atop the ridge, they told their leaders the news of their having been detected. The Whig commanders quickly realized that the element of surprise was gone, but they also knew that neither men nor beasts were in any shape to outrun the well-rested Loyalists. Furthermore, intelligence gained from some local residents reported that Innis had recently arrived with his aforementioned force from Ninety-Six.

Their only option, therefore, was to throw up defensive works to await an attack. Hastily the men piled logs, dead trees and anything else they could use as a barricade onto their makeshift breastworks. When the works were completed, the Whigs took up position behind them, with Clarke's men on the left, Williams' in the center and Shelby's on the right. A force of horsemen, about forty in number, waited on the flanks, while Clarke kept forty riflemen in reserve.[11]

The Loyalists on the south side of the Enoree remained oblivious to the activities taking place on the hill across the river. They were no doubt on their guard thanks to the encounter with the Whig patrol, but must have dismissed this group as inconsequential as they made no efforts to track them down.

Since the British were seemingly ignorant of their enemy's position and true strength, the Whig leaders devised a plan to draw the British into

An interpretive display marking the location where the final phase of the Battle of Musgrove's Mill took place.

range of their position atop the hill, hoping to catch them off guard in a surprise ambush. In order to draw the British across the river, Shelby dispatched Captain Shadrack Inman, who had a part in the plan's formulation, forward with twenty-five men to attack the British and then retreat to the north side of the river and up the hill. Meanwhile, the remainder of the army was to remain concealed behind their brush piles until the pursuing British were within fifty yards, at which point Shelby would fire his gun as a signal to the others to open fire.[12]

Captain Inman and his men rode forth to provoke the British into a fight. They crossed the Enoree, briefly skirmished with the Loyalists, then fell back across the river. The sounds of drums, bugles and shouted orders indicated that Innis had taken the bait, and it was only a short time before they were seen crossing the river in force. Inman continued his retreat up the hill, the British in hot pursuit, until the Georgians halted two hundred yards short of their comrades atop the hill. At this point they turned, feigned an attack on the center of the British troops, then turned and ran.

The British steadily advanced up the hill, with the Provincial regulars in the center and the Loyalist militia on the flanks. Seeing the Georgians fleeing before them, they marched onward, confident of success.

Sensing victory, the British were shocked when two hundred rifles rang out from behind the piles of brush fifty yards in their front. Up to this point, Innis and his fellow commanders were still ignorant as to the extent of the force confronting them. The British lines faltered briefly, but order was restored and the attack continued. On the right flank the Loyalists and regulars were halted at the breastworks, but on the left they broke through and pushed the Whigs back with bayonets. Clarke threw his reserves against the British right flank, but the onslaught continued.

Just when the British were on the verge of victory, Innis fell to the ground severely wounded, shot by William Smith from the Watauga settlement who exclaimed, "I've killed their commander!" This was the second wound Innis received, as he is reported to have taken a shot in the neck and thigh, the latter bullet breaking the bone. He was quickly conveyed to the rear.[13]

At this point the Provincial regulars, not the militia, began falling back. The reason for this was in no small part due to the fact that most of the British leaders were either killed or wounded. At first, they retreated in good order, with the militia also falling back, but when about halfway back to the river, order was lost and a precipitate flight to the rear commenced.

During this retreat, several hand-to-hand struggles ensued. In one of these Captain Inman was slain. Draper noted, "He received seven shots from the Tories, one, a musket ball, piercing his forehead. He fell near the base of a Spanish oak that stood where the modern road leaves the old mill road, and where his grave was still pointed out but a few years since."[14]

Draper also preserved a colorful account of the closing scenes of the battle. "Many of the British and Tories were shot down as they were hastening, pell-mell, across the Enoree at the rock ford." After they were fairly over, one, not yet too weary to evince his bravado, and attract attention for the moment, turned up his buttock in derision at the Americans, when one of the Whig officers, probably Brandon or Steen, said to Golding Tinsley: "Can't you turn that insolent braggart over?" "I can try, responded Tinsley, who was known to possess a good rifle, when, suiting the action to the word, he took prompt aim, and fired—and sure enough turned him over, when some of his comrades picked the fellow up, and carried him off."[15] The battle ended with the Whigs returning to their position atop the ridge on the north side of the Enoree. There they intended to rest and regroup before renewing the action, some contemplating a stroke for the stronghold of Ninety-Six itself.

There are several casualty figures given for the Battle of Musgrove's Mill, and nearly all contradict one another, though all place the Whig casualties unbelievably low. Dr. Henry Lumpkin, prominent South Carolina historian, came up with the following figures based on various accounts. "The British casualties in the hard-fought little action at Musgrove's Mill were 63 dead, 90 wounded and 70 captured, some 50 percent of the effectives engaged. The American loss was negligible, only 4 dead and 8 or 9 wounded."[16]

Fanning reports that, following the battle, he and his fellow Loyalists retreated a little over a mile before stopping. That night, Captain Abraham de Peyster marched them back to Ninety-Six.[17]

As stated earlier, Shelby, Clarke and Williams were contemplating a strike for Ninety-Six. But before they were able to rest from their exertions at Musgrove's Mill, a message from Colonel McDowell arrived informing them of Gates' defeat at the hands of Cornwallis at Camden on August 16, 1780. Gates' army was decimated, and General Caswell was advising the Whigs in northwestern South Carolina to save themselves. McDowell was hoping to regroup at Gilbert Town in North Carolina.

The Whigs did not take long to decide that the best course of action was a hasty flight out of harm's way. The prisoners were distributed among the men, three Whigs guarding one prisoner, the three men sharing the task of letting the prisoner ride along on their respective horses. The trek north was a test of endurance, and they barely eluded capture as a detachment under Major Ferguson pursued them to a spot south of North Tyger River, arriving in the vacated camp thirty minutes after the Whigs departed.

The British broke off pursuit at the campsite south of North Tyger River, but the Whigs were ignorant of the fact. They travelled through the night, not stopping until they had crossed into North Carolina. They had covered over a hundred miles and won a victory in a fierce battle in two days.

Draper noted, "It was a remarkable instance of unflagging endurance, in the heat of a southern summer, and encumbered, as they were, with seventy prisoners. No wonder, that after forty-eight hours of such excessive fatigue, nearly all the officers and soldiers became so exhausted, that their faces and eyes were swollen and bloated to that degree that they were scarcely able to see."[18]

The defeat at Musgrove's Mill and the failure to liberate the prisoners was the only blemish in what was a banner three days for British arms. Cornwallis had won an astounding victory at Camden, decimating the Continental Army under General Horatio Gates.[19]

On August 18, 1780, Banastre Tarleton and 160 men surprised Colonel Thomas Sumter's camp at Fishing Creek, routing the Whigs. Sumter barely missed capture, and fled the scene without his coat, hat or saddle. The Whigs suffered severe damage—a hundred and fifty killed and wounded and over three hundred men captured. In addition, they lost many valuable supplies. The British had sixteen killed and wounded.[20]

5. The War Resumes

Shortly after de Peyster returned safely with his command to Ninety-Six, Fanning was ordered back to scout in the mountains along the border with the Cherokee. He continued this until Captain Pearis ordered him to ride throughout western South Carolina to spread the word to all Loyalists who were home to report for duty.

While carrying out this latest assignment, on October 2, 1780, Fanning ran across the camp of Major Ferguson and his force of Loyalists at Gilbert Town. Here he saw many of his friends and comrades, including Colonel Ambrose Mills. Little did Fanning realize that after he departed the next morning, he would never see many of these friends again.[21]

On October 7, 1780, Ferguson's army was crushed at Kings Mountain by a group of mountaineers who have since been dubbed "the Overmountain Men." Ferguson and nine hundred of his eleven hundred men were dead or captured.[22] For Ferguson, it could have been a banner day. He was close to the protection offered by the main British army of Lord Cornwallis and had, unbeknownst to Ferguson, been promoted to Lt. Colonel.

Almost immediately following the battle, Whig depredations began. Some of the Loyalists were shot after they had surrendered. Upon finding the body of Ferguson, many of the Whigs proceeded to urinate on the corpse as a sign of disrespect.

The Whigs did not remain long on the field of victory. They divided up the prisoners and withdrew toward the north before the arrival of Cornwallis and "Bloody Banastre" Tarleton. On the night of October 14, at a place known as Bickerstaff's, they stopped their hasty retreat long

Fanning narrowly missed being with Ferguson at Kings Mountain.

enough to indulge themselves in a drunken orgy of vengeance. Ten Loyalists were hanged and more scheduled, until the murder finally became too much for even Colonel Campbell to bear, and he ordered the festivities to end. Among the dead was Fanning's friend from the Green River country, Ambrose Mills.

A quick-thinking Loyalist who was scheduled to dance from the hangman's noose told Colonel Campbell that, in gratitude for sparing his life, he would share a secret. Banastre Tarleton and his hard-riding dragoons were in hot pursuit, he had been told, and would very shortly liberate the prisoners. With this bit of knowledge, the festivities at Bickerstaff's ended, and the "Overmountain Men" hurriedly departed for the safety of their mountains. Many of the prisoners were marched north to the Moravian towns.[23]

Another stroke of good fortune came to the Whigs at a place known as Shallow Ford of the Yadkin in North Carolina. Colonel Gideon Wright of Surry County had gathered a sizable army of Loyalists estimated at between 300 and 900 men from northwestern North Carolina. He was heading south to unite with the main British army at Charlotte. After stopping at Richmond, then the county seat of Surry, he and his party moved south.

On October 14, 1780, after crossing the Shallow Ford of the Yadkin in what is now Yadkin County, Wright's Loyalists were attacked by a group of Whigs from Surry County and southwestern Virginia under the command of a Captain Cloyd. In the heated engagement, the Loyalists were driven back across the Yadkin, with fifteen killed and four wounded. The Whigs had one killed and one wounded.

Captain Cloyd and his men had won an important victory. Not only did this help keep the morale of the Loyalists in the region low, Cloyd's win also deprived the Loyalists under Wright of the opportunity to inadvertently surprise the column marching north with the prisoners from Kings Mountain.[24]

The fortunes of the Loyalists from beyond the Yadkin River never recovered from the disaster at Kings Mountain. Combined with the setbacks at Shallow Ford and Ramsour's Mills, Kings Mountain proved to be particularly damaging to their morale. Even worse, the British had incurred heavy casualties in their attempts to hold the Carolina backcountry. Dr. Lumpkin writes, "From July until December 1780 the partisans in South Carolina alone had inflicted on the British and Loyalist forces a loss of 1,200 killed and wounded with 1,286 captured. The American guerrulla fighters had sustained during the same period 497 killed or wounded and 320 taken prisoner. The men of the South had inflicted three times the number of casualties on their enemy as they suffered themselves."[25]

5. The War Resumes

Despite the resources expended, the British had little to show for their efforts in the Carolinas. Blunders and rotten luck plagued the British to the point where they were now in a worse predicament than they had been in the spring. With this in mind, it is easy to understand why the Loyalists in the Carolina backcountry were becoming demoralized.

6

The War Shifts North

The four-month period between October of 1780 and February 1781 were trying times for those South Carolinians loyal to King George III. An incursion by General Thomas Sumter toward Ninety-Six, thwarted only by the timely arrival of Tarleton's forces and an indecisive fight at Blackstocks Ford, caused much consternation among the Loyalists of the region. Adding to their apprehensions was another incursion, this one from the west under Colonel Elijah Clark and Lt. Colonel James McCall, whose forces were defeated on December 11, 1780, along Long Canes Creek.

The most menacing of these attacks came in the form of a force of Continentals and militia under General Daniel Morgan, who had advanced into South Carolina in late December and was encamped along Pacolet River on Christmas Day. Loyalist militia forces were converging for a strike on Morgan, but he hit first, striking a contingent of two hundred and fifty Loyalists marching up from the southeastern portion of the state. Lt. Colonel William Washington, leader of Morgan's cavalry forces, caught up with these Loyalists near the present town of Clinton at a place called Hammond's Store on December 29, 1780. The Loyalist forces were decimated, with a hundred and fifty killed or wounded and forty men captured.[1]

Next day, December 30, Colonel Joseph Hayes was dispatched by Lt. Colonel Washington with approximately a hundred men to capture a Loyalist stockade outpost known as Williams' Fort. When the Whigs arrived, Hayes immediately demanded the fort's capitulation. General Patrick Cunningham, commanding the Loyalist forces inside, asked for time to consider the request and was given five minutes. The Loyalists used this time to sneak out the back door of the stockade and hide in the woods.

Such a bold stroke within fifteen miles of Ninety-Six garnered the attention of Cornwallis, who dispatched Tarleton to break up Morgan's activities and clear the northwest region of South Carolina of "rebels." This action led to the Battle of the Cowpens, in which Daniel Morgan and his small army of Continental soldiers and Whig militia crushed Tarleton's

6. The War Shifts North 51

The Buffalo Ford across the Deep River.

veteran British troops. Following the disastrous defeat at the Battle of the Cowpens on January 17, 1781, Cornwallis decided that the time for decisive action against Nathanael Greene and the Whigs in North Carolina had come. So the British headed north in a chase that would take them clear across the province.

Setting out in pursuit of Morgan, the British army trudged along at a snail's pace. Realizing that he would never catch up with the fleet Americans, especially now that he was devoid of the fast-moving troops lost at Cowpens, Cornwallis took the bold step of converting his entire force into light troops. On January 25, 1781, at Ramsour's Mill on the South Fork of the Catawba, the British army destroyed all but the most essential of their supplies.

Encumbered now with only their weapons and packs, the British hoped to run down the main American army under General Greene. Thanks to a skillful retreat, the Americans were able to elude the British all the way across the state until they were in a relatively safe position behind the Dan River.

Unable to bring his antagonist to bay, Cornwallis marched his weary troops east to Hillsborough, North Carolina. There, on February 27, 1781, amid much fanfare and a twenty-one-gun salute, the Royal Standard was raised and a proclamation read calling on all of His Majesty's subjects to report for duty, preferably with their own weapons and provisions.

* * *

The defeat at Cowpens threw the Loyalists of South Carolina into further disarray. Many lost heart and scampered to Charles Town to be closer to the protection offered by the garrison of British troops there. When fugitives from Cowpens came calling on General Robert Cunningham, he refused to call out his Loyalist militia troops. Perhaps he was worried about becoming the target of the next Whig attack.[2]

Fanning was well aware of the problems these setbacks presented to the Loyalists. He noted, "The Rebels after this Begin to be numerous and troublesome and little or no Regulation amongst us."[3] Since there were no bold leaders willing to take the field in South Carolina, Fanning followed the action north.

Thus in the winter of 1781 Fanning returned to North Carolina where he headed for the Deep River settlements. What compelled him to take up residence along the Deep River is unknown. Several of his neighbors down in the Raeburn Creek settlement in South Carolina had moved out of the Deep and Haw River area. Perhaps he was going to stay with friends or family members of South Carolina comrades. He may have even had some family members of his own there. Remember, his father had drowned in the Deep River, ostensibly hoping to build a new plantation.

Carruthers gives an interesting account of Fanning's first days back in North Carolina: "…he had his residence on or near Deep river, and about the mouths of Brush and Richland creek, where, remaining for a few weeks *in cog*, he took up his lodgings sometimes under the open canopy of heaven, but oftener in the humble dwelling of John Rains, who afterwards became a major in his corps, and one of his most efficient men."[4] Fanning remained "in cog" until he was convinced that Cornwallis was serious in his intentions of subduing North Carolina. In the middle of February 1781, Fanning went public and began circulating an "Advertisement" for recruits to join Lt. Colonel John Hamilton's Royal North Carolina Regiment, a regular British army unit composed mainly of Loyalists which was part of Cornwallis' command.[5]

Carruthers maintains that Fanning's first public appearance came on a Sunday morning at an unspecified church. As services ended and members were filing out, they saw Fanning sitting astride his horse under a tree in front of the church. He addressed the parishioners, whom he had been informed were sympathetic to the Loyalist cause, and reminded them of the unfair treatment they had received from Whig authorities. Fanning also made mention of the unjust Confiscation Acts which had deprived many of them of their property. The speech was successful, and many of those present agreed to fight for the King.[6]

Fanning did more than make speeches to gain the confidence of his new neighbors on Deep River. One of his first acts was to hunt down a noted horse thief in western Chatham County. Charles Shearing had been sentenced to death for stealing horses back in 1779, and would have been hanged at Hillsborough for his crime had he not been pardoned by a special act of the legislature.[7] Shearing did not learn his lesson with his brush with death and remained obnoxious to his neighbors until the winter of 1781. Ever fearful of revenge, he would not even sleep in his house lest he be surprised and captured. Instead, he had fixed himself a hiding place in the corncrib where he figured that no one would think to look for him. There is no record of the exact reason for Shearing's gaining the ire of Fanning. Regardless, the Loyalist veteran of so many raids in the upcountry of South Carolina was now out to exact retribution for his offenses. On a dark night, Fanning scoured the house and outbuildings of Shearing's farm but could find no trace of the man. Finally, almost as an afterthought, he checked the corn crib, and upon peering through the cracks could make out the figure of a human.

Fanning stuck the barrel of his gun through the crack and fired. No sounds of agony came from within, so Fanning departed without opening the crib and checking. Had he done so, he would have discovered that Shearing was gravely wounded—the bullet had ripped a hole in the man's neck—but he was not dead.

As soon as Fanning was gone, Shearing crawled out of his hiding place and managed to travel eight miles to his neighbor Cornelius Tyson's house, where he was nursed back to health. This brush with death taught him a more lasting lesson than his brush with the hangman's rope at Hillsborough, and Charles Shearing ended his reprehensible conduct against the people of southwestern Chatham.[8]

Fanning was not the only person in central North Carolina actively recruiting troops for the British. There were several others raising forces of Loyalists throughout the area, and most of these scattered Loyalists were under the direction of Dr. John Pyle, who lived over in northern Chatham near Cane Creek. Pyle had been an active Loyalist from the earliest days of the war, receiving a Colonel's commission from Governor Josiah Martin in 1775. Pyle participated in the Moore's Creek debacle, was captured, escaped, and then took the Loyalty Oath to the State and posted a bond guaranteeing his future good behavior in December of 1776.[9]

When Cornwallis moved into the area, but just prior to his raising the Royal Standard at Hillsborough, Fanning left Dr. Pyle's place at Cane Creek, where the latter had been assembling a large body of Loyalists for service. Fanning returned to the Deep River, recruiting troops and disarming Whig sympathizers along the way. By February 22, he had embodied enough men to warrant his return to Cane Creek where they would be turned over to Pyle. Fanning had also managed to bag a few prisoners, as he writes, "...I took two Rebel officers prisoners and several soldiers."[10]

Meanwhile, Pyle's forces had swollen to the point where he was now ready to present his little army to Cornwallis at Hillsborough. By the 23rd, his four hundred untrained and ill-equipped men were ready to move forward and rendezvous with Tarleton's cavalry, who were to escort the Loyalists back to Hillsborough.

On the 24th, Pyle's forces were headed up the road to their meeting with Tarleton. Late in the day, two of his men encountered a cavalry force attired in green jackets and plumed helmets. They sought out the leader of this force, whom they believed to be Tarleton, and reported that Pyle's men were only a short distance away. The green-clad cavalry commander sent one of the men back to Pyle requesting that he move to the side of the road so that his own men, much fatigued, could move unhindered to the camping site.

The Loyalists concurred, and took up a position off the road as the green-clad cavalry passed, the latters' sabers drawn in salute. Just as the leader reached Dr. Pyle, sounds of battle were heard coming from the rear of the column. At this point, Pyle discovered that he had been fooled. The commander of this cavalry force was not Banastre Tarleton but was instead his nemesis, Colonel Henry Lee of the Continental Army, at the head of Lee's Legion.

A gruesome ordeal followed in which the surprised Loyalists were attacked by what they perceived to be friends. In the brief encounter, at least ninety-three Loyalists were killed, and an unknown number wounded. Most of the Loyalists were captured, though several managed to escape by hiding in the woods. Even the hapless Dr. Pyle, though wounded, eluded capture by fleeing and hiding in a nearby pond. The Continentals lost only one horse. This brief melee was dubbed Pyle's Massacre by the British, but is best remembered by its more colorful name—Pyle's Hacking Match.[11]

Fanning and his band of raw recruits rode upon the scene shortly after the action was finished. "I then Directed my march to the place where I left Coln Pyles and came within a little Distance of the Dragoons that had cut him up when I was informed of his misfortune by some of his party that had fled, we then separated into small parties and took to the woods for some time."[12]

Further troubles awaited the Loyalists. On the night of March 4, 1781, a Whig cavalry patrol under Captain Joseph Graham raided a British patrol. Tarleton dispatched a force to overtake these raiders. The British caught up with a body of horsemen and attacked them, but in the darkness did not learn that they were actually attacking a body of Loyalists coming in to join Cornwallis.

Graham recalled, "...upwards of one hundred cavalry was sent up the road after us, and at 11 o'clock at night met a company of Tories coming in to join them; not doubting that it was the party which had defeated their picquet, they instantly charged them and considerable slaughter was made before it was discovered they were friends." This mistake, coupled with Pyle's Hacking Match, had disastrous consequences on the British ability to lure large numbers of Loyalists into their ranks. Graham continued, "Those small affairs did more to suppress toryism in the South than anything that had before occurred. A few days before at Pile's defeat, they had been cut up by Lee's men and ours, when they thought it was their friend Tarleton, in the present case they were cut up by the British when they thought it was Americans. It is not known that any of them joined the British afterwards"[13]

For the next three weeks, Fanning and a small band of followers— probably less than thirty—stayed away from the center of action between the two opposing forces under Cornwallis and Greene. The climax of the two armies' cat and mouse game came on March 15, 1781, at Guilford Courthouse, where the tired, worn-out British army soundly defeated the Continentals after a hard-fought battle. But Cornwallis, forced at one point to shell his own men who were locked in a bitter hand-to-hand melee with the enemy, wrecked his tired and depleted army in the process, leaving him in no position to finish off his adversary. Greene retreated his army, taking refuge behind defensive works nearby at the Speedwell Furnace on Troublesome Creek, waiting in vain for a British attack that never materialized.

Many have suggested that Fanning was present at Guilford Courthouse, but in his *Narrative* he states that he was not there, but was instead on that very day involved in a minor action with a Captain Duck, who managed to catch the Loyalist band unaware and made off with their horses and arms. Undaunted, Fanning and three of his comrades went in pursuit and retrieved fourteen of the beasts. He unfortunately gives no clues as the exact location of where this action took place. They returned to their encampment, and within a week Fanning had assembled twenty-five men. With these recruits he set out to join up with Cornwallis's army bound for Cross Creek. On March 22, 1781, their camp was situated near Dixon's Mill in present Alamance County. A late season snow that blanketed the ground had coincided with the arrival of the British, and ever after the community has been known as Snow Camp.[14] The young Loyalist partisan must have been quite surprised with what transpired at Dixon's Mill, for there he visited with none other than Cornwallis himself. "On our arrival his lordship met us and asked me several Questions Respecting the situation of the Country and disposition of the people.—I gave him all Information in my power...."[15] Following their conversation, Fanning deposited his twenty-five recruits with the British army, then returned to Deep River to gather more men. His tale of a personal encounter with the British chief no doubt helped his recruiting efforts, for over the course of the next day he gathered seventy men.

Before they could make their way back to Cornwallis, who by March 24, 1781, had moved his army and was encamped at Chatham Court House, they ran awry of a party of "Rebel Dragoons." No match for an organized force in their present condition, Fanning ordered the men to disperse into the woods until the dragoons passed. Soon the coast was clear, and he caught up with the British army at Ramsey's Mill.

Ramsey's Mill, located on the Deep River a short distance above its confluence with the Haw, was a hive of activity those two days in March of 1781 when Cornwallis was there. With his army encamped in a large field nearby known as Glasscock's Old Field, the British commander dispatched foraging parties through the surrounding countryside to bring in much needed supplies. The British were also busily constructing a bridge across Deep River so the troops and wounded could cross the river without getting wet.

Greene was close at hand, so as soon as the bridge over Deep River was complete, the British headed out for Cross Creek, where Cornwallis was expecting to find reinforcements and a supply depot established by Major James Craig operating from Wilmington. The stop at Cross Creek would not only mean the British would gain valuable materials, but it would also give them ample opportunity to halt, rest and regroup. In addition, the region around Cross Creek was renowned for its Loyalist sympathies, so Cornwallis hoped recruits would flock to join his battered army.[16]

So on they trudged through northern Cumberland by Barbecue Presbyterian Church. A day before they arrived at their destination, the British army was joined by a Loyalist who had been forced to seek refuge in the forest. His plight was similar to that of Fanning during the earlier days of the war back in South Carolina, as well as numerous others who remained loyal to the King. An eyewitness described the man thus: "He had scarcely the appearance of being human; he wore the skin of a racoon for a hat, his beard was some inches long, and he was so thin, that he looked as if he had made his escape from Surgeon's-hall. He wore no shirt, his whole dress being skins of different animals. On the morning after, when this distressed man came to draw his provisions, Mr. Brice, the deputy master-general of the provincial forces, and the commissary, asked him several questions. He said that he had lived for three years in the woods, under ground; that he had been frequently sought after by the Americans, and was certain of instant death whenever he should be taken; that he supported himself by what he got in the woods; that acorns served him as bread; that they had, from long use, become agreeable to him; that he had a family, some of whom, once or twice in a year, came to him in the woods; that his only crime was being a loyalist, and having given offense to one of the republican leaders in that part of the country where he used to live."[17]

The scene which greeted Cornwallis when he arrived at Cross Creek must have been bitterly disappointing. There were no supplies awaiting the British army there. Major Craig had sent a letter to Cornwallis explaining the impossibility of safely transporting materials up the Cape Fear, but Cornwallis had not received the news until it was too late.[18]

To further add to Cornwallis' disappointment, the Loyalists around Cross Creek did not flock to join the British. This scene was sadly reminiscent of the reaction to the populace at Hillsborough, and prompted the British commander to later write Lord Germain, "From all my information I intended to have halted at Cross Creek, as a proper place to refresh & refit the Troops, and I was much disappointed on my arrival there to find it totally impossible: provisions were scarce, not four days Forage within twenty miles, & to us the navigation of the Cape Fear River to Wilmington impracticable for the distance by Water is upwards of an hundred miles, the breadth seldom above a hundred yards, the banks high, & the Inhabitants on each side generally hostile."[19]

The one bright note to the situation was the news that Greene had broken off pursuit at Upper Little River. The forces of Colonel Lee had been hot on the trail of the British army, but had been ordered to veer south to form a junction with General Francis Marion in South Carolina. Meanwhile, Greene was marching off to the southwest, also headed for South Carolina.

This left Cornwallis with little to fear save minor raids from Whig partisans who were more nuisance than threat. Based on these developments, he ordered his army to continue its course to Wilmington for supplies. Meanwhile, he dispatched several of his Loyalists back into their settlements for recruits, and told them to be ready for the coming campaign as soon as his troops were reoutfitted.

Fanning states that his men had lost their mounts on the march to Cross Creek. Whether they were lost to the enemy or requisitioned by the regular British forces is not specified, though the latter is the more plausible explanation. At any rate, Fanning and his followers headed back for the Deep River settlements. "...as we had lost most of our horses we Determined to Return to Deep River, and join his Lordship when on his way to Hillsborough."[20]

This return to the Deep River settlements put Fanning right in the path of Greene's army marching to South Carolina. The Continentals were heading along in a random fashion, stopping to harass Loyalist sympathizers and relieve them of their personal property. Fanning notes that he captured eighteen of these individuals.[21]

Before leaving the region, General Greene made note of the turmoil between Whigs and Loyalists during this period which would prove to be the early stages of a period of intense military activity in Revolutionary North Carolina, often known as the Tory War. "Nothing but blood and slaughter has prevailed among the Whigs and Tories, and their inveteracy against each other must, if it continues, depopulate this part of the country."[22]

Fanning's success against these raiders drew numerous Whig forces from around the state into his area who were trying to end his raids. Their absence from home, however, presented opportunities for Loyalists in other regions to spring into action, especially those in Cumberland and Bladen counties. Soon there were Loyalist bands operating throughout the eastern half of the state, thanks in no small part to Fanning.[23]

As activity began to die down toward the end of April, Fanning and his followers felt more at ease. Most of his force had dispersed in the face of the Whig onslaught and returned to their respective homes, while only a handful remained in the field with Fanning. But there was little rest for this small Loyalist band. In early May of 1781, as his group of eight men were lying about a friend's house over near Deep River, Captain John Hinds and a party of eleven men were riding hard to surprise them. News of their coming reached Fanning just as Hinds arrived, and the Loyalists were pinned down in the house. As the Whigs approached the house, the Loyalists burst out with guns blazing, and made a successful dash for the woods. In the fray they managed to kill one of the Whigs and capture several horses and firearms. The Whigs in turn managed to capture two men whom they promptly executed.[24]

The execution of these two men outraged Fanning and his followers, who set about planning their revenge. This was the first in a long line of brutal encounters between Fanning and the two men who would prove to be his bitterest enemies in this stage of the fighting—Colonels John Collier and Andrew Balfour of the Randolph County Whig Militia, who were Hinds' superior officers and responsible for the execution. There is no record explaining the inveterate hatred these men had for the King's

6. The War Shifts North

supporters, but these two men were the most vindictive adversaries the Loyalists in central North Carolina faced, and were responsible for numerous atrocities, many of which were answered in kind by Fanning.

Over the next couple of days, Fanning gathered a dozen of his followers, and on May 11, 1781, set an ambush for Collier's force at the Buffalo Ford across Deep River in southwest Randolph County. After waiting two hours, Fanning's scouts reported that a portion of Collier's crew had been delayed in reaching the river because they were engaged in pillaging a Loyalists' house three miles away.

Seeing an opportunity to catch his enemy in a disorganized state, Fanning set off to attack them. Fanning gives the meagre details of the ensuing fight. "I instantly marched to the place and Discovered them in a field near the house. I attacked them Immediately and kept up a smart fire for half an hour, during which time we Killed their Capt. and one private on the spot, wounded three of them and took two prisoners besides 8 of their horses well appointed and several swords, this happened on the 11th of May 1781."

Unfortunately, the exact spot of this encounter three miles from the Buffalo Ford is now unknown. This is also true of the several encounters in the days following, including a raid the next day in which the Loyalists inflicted five dead and three wounded, and captured three prisoners. Most intriguing was the encounter with a group of Whigs "30 miles off..." which Fanning's force surprised after a night march and a ten-minute battle. "We Killed two of them and wounded 7 and took 18 horses well appointed."[25]

Fanning returned to Cox's Mill to rest and wait for his next opportunity to strike. Shortly thereafter he captured two Whig soldiers who told of the approach of a baggage train escorted by light cavalry from General Greene's outpost at Camden, South Carolina. The column was under the command of Colonel Guilford Dudley of Cumberland County. Dudley was the commander of the contingent of North Carolina Militia in General Greene's army, and had served with distinction at Hobkirk's Hill on April 25, 1781. Discharged by General Greene on May 10, Dudley and his men were headed to Hillsborough to disband. Their route took them right into the hands of Fanning.

Upon hearing of Dudley's approach, Fanning and his men headed south to intercept the column. At an appropriate place, which traditionary accounts place somewhere within the bounds of modern Montgomery County, the Loyalists hid in the woods on both sides of the road. His ambush set, Fanning took one man and rode ahead to scout for the approach of Dudley.

A mile and a half down the road, he found what he was looking for. Problem was, the Whigs spotted him as well, and a chase ensued. "I then wheeled my horse and Returned to my men," wrote Fanning. "when I came within a hundred yards of them Dudley and his Dragoons was nose and Tail, and snapped their pistols several times."

When the Whigs came upon the ambush, the Loyalists open fire. Now the roles of hound and hare reversed, and the chase headed south down the road. After two and a half miles, the Loyalists came upon the Whig baggage train, valued at "1000 sterling," but Dudley and his men did not stick around to guard it. With such valuable property in his hands, Fanning called off the pursuit, gathered up the booty and returned to Cox's Mill.[26]

The baggage belonged mainly to Colonel James Read, a member of the Continental Army. General Greene wrote a letter to Governor Ashe asking if would be possible for the state to reimburse Read for his losses. "Lt. Col. Dudley on his return had the misfortune to lose the Colonels baggage in crossing the Country from Pedee to Haw River," wrote Greene. "These losses fall very heavy upon the Colonel as he has been long in the Continental service and of course has suffered greatly in his private fortune."[27]

Ambushes such as this one held a strategic advantage to the British in that the lines of communication between General Greene's forces in South Carolina and the Whig forces in Hillsborough and Virginia were interrupted. In an effort to steer clear of the Loyalists' territory along Deep River, the Whigs usually chose the more circuitous route to Hillsborough or Halifax by veering west through Charlotte, Salisbury and Guilford Courthouse. This added nearly a hundred miles to the journey.[28]

Fanning set up his main base of operations at Cox's Mill. The name of this place was given to both the actual mill near the mouth of Mill Creek on the west side of Deep River in Randolph County below the present town of Ramseur, as well as the surrounding community. In addition, Harmon Cox operated a mill across the river on Millstone Creek. This creates no small amount of confusion when trying to identify the place.

The original Cox's Mill had been founded by William Cox (Harmon's father) back in 1760. The mill was a prominent place in the central portion of North Carolina, especially during the Regulator troubles when William's son, Harmon, escaped the hangman's rope thanks only to a pardon from Governor Tryon. After the death of William in 1767, the mill was taken over by another son.

Fanning had close ties to the Cox family. His former neighbor and military commander in South Carolina, James Lindley, was William Cox's son-in-law. Captain Lindley had been executed two years earlier at Ninety-Six thanks to his prominent role during the campaign which ended in the Loyalists' defeat at Kettle Creek, Georgia.

The nature of Fanning's base at Cox's Mill is uncertain. Many militia groups utilized mills as convenient muster grounds. Whether Fanning and his men fortified the mill house or erected a stockade nearby is uncertain.[29]

On June 8, 1781, Fanning received intelligence that Collier and Balfour were gathering a large force ten miles away for an attack upon the Loyalists. Seizing the initiative, Fanning and 49 of his men immediately departed to attack the Whigs that very night.

The element of surprise was lost when one of Fanning' guides was captured, so the Whigs were ready. An especially vigilant sentinel fired upon the attackers when the Loyalists were within "thirty steps of them."

Alerted, Balfour, Collier and their 160 men put up a spirited defense during the night battle which lasted four hours. With the approach of morning, Fanning ordered his men to fade back into the woods. He had lost one killed and six wounded. Whig casualties were unrecorded, but the attack thwarted their offensive. Unfortunately, the exact location of this night fight is a mystery.[30]

The Loyalists' successes in the Deep River country brought them once again into the spotlight of Whig authorities, and soon another effort was launched to scour the area and rid the region of the Tory menace. By mid–June, the country was again filled with Whigs, including forces under Collier and Balfour. Colonel Dudley was also back, this time at the head of, "300 men from Virginia." Dudley undoubtedly was relishing the opportunity to make up for losing his baggage to Fanning.

During this escalation of Whig activity, Fanning noted that the Whigs "...took a negro man from me and sould him at public Auction amongst themselves for 110 pounds."[31] The fact that Fanning would have a slave with him seems odd at first glance, as there would be little for the man to do. Fanning never mentions allowing escaped Whig slaves to take advantage of Lord Dunsmore's Proclamation of 1775 granting them freedom if they served militarily in the King's forces. The fact is the man in question was a valuable piece of Colonel Fanning's psychological warfare arsenal. Records show that Fanning kept a conjurer with him from time to time. Among the enslaved African Americans, the conjurer was a very important and much feared person. A holdover from African tribal days, conjurers/medicine men and their "magic" were feared by many of the African Americans of the era who still believed in the supernatural powers of these individuals. By correctly utilizing one of these people, Fanning could intimidate the African Americans friendly to the Whigs for accessing valuable intelligence about their master's activities.

With the area now swarming with Whigs, Fanning decided that the most prudent thing for his force to do was disperse and await an

McPhaul's Mill and Tavern was an important rendezvous point for Loyalists operating in the vicinity of Little Raft Swamp.

opportunity to rise again under more favorable circumstances. This was a popular tactic among the Loyalist partisans, and was especially effective against armies composed of militia forces whose terms of enlistment were very short. Fanning therefore headed for the seclusion offered by the wilderness of the Uwharrie Mountains, and patiently waited for his next opportunity to strike. But not all of his comrades shared his enthusiasm.

Down in Bladen and Cumberland counties, Colonel Thomas Robeson was discussing a cessation of hostilities with colonels Hector McNeill and Duncan Ray, prominent leaders of the Loyalists among the Highland Scots. The latter two gentlemen are the ones who came up with the idea for a truce. Sadly, nothing ever came of these talks, and the Whigs and Tories continued an internecine contest which escalated as time passed.[32]

7

Fanning Takes Command

When the Whig offensive finally died down, the Loyalists were able to leave their hiding places in the woods and gather together. But when they reconvened, there was dissension in the ranks, and the problem would not go away until one question was solved: who was in charge? Up to this point, the various Loyalist commands in North Carolina operated pretty much independently. On the occasions when more than one command was present, Fanning was usually considered to be in charge, provided of course, that he was among those present. But there were those present of equal rank who questioned Fanning's authority.

Most vocal among the opposition was Captain William Elrod, who commanded a contingent from Rowan County. Very little firsthand information about this man has survived. We know that he lived in Captain Cox's District in Rowan County and had his taxes doubled in 1778.[1] The Reverend Carruthers was able to dig up some interesting facts about him. "Elrod appears to have been a man of true courage, and would sometimes do a generous act," he wrote. This was quite a compliment for a Tory coming from Carruthers. He continued, "Elrod ... lived in the Forks of the Yadkin, where Colonel Bryant had control; and as he carried on his operations mostly in that region, up and down the river, we know very little about him. He was a young man, and lived in a small log house with his mother. With a few men he rallied round him at his call, he was very enterprising and efficient in the service of the King. He was not properly a marauder, or mere freebooter, for he had a nature which, if circumstances had permitted, would have raised him above such a course."[2]

One day in late June, Elrod arrived at a Loyalist gathering in the Deep River area and began spreading rumors that Fanning was trying to enlist them all in the British Army as part of Col. Hamilton's Royal North Carolina Regiment. Elrod then pulled out one of the leaflets Fanning had distributed earlier in the year when he was indeed recruiting for Cornwallis' army. Many of the rank and file believed Elrod, and wanting no part of the

This structure was the original Chatham County Courthouse captured by the Loyalists during Fanning's Raid in July of 1781. The above photograph was taken by Ben Dixon MacNeill in the 1920s (North Carolina County Photographic Collection #P00001, North Carolina Collection Photographic Archives, University of North Carolina–Chapel Hill).

regular army they quickly headed for home. By the time Fanning arrived, hardly any remained.

At this point, Fanning asked the field officers present to vote on who should be in command. "I then declared I never would go on another scout, until there was a field officer," he said. In an instant, Fanning was elected to command. Still not satisfied, he instructed that the issue should be voted on by all the men. A large group of Loyalists gathered soon thereafter, and the outcome of this election was the same. Those present then signed a petition to the commanding officer of the British garrison at Wilmington asking that their choice for a leader be approved.[3]

Petition in hand, Fanning headed off for Wilmington with a small band of followers. Once there, he presented the document to Major James Craig of the 82nd Regiment, the man in charge of this post. Craig had been able to convince Colonel Nisbet Balfour of the importance of maintaining a British presence in North Carolina and was thus able to remain in Wilmington after Cornwallis had moved on to Virginia. Craig knew that evacuating the town would cause long-term damage to the British war effort in North Carolina and would further erode the people's confidence in the British government's resolve to protect them. Memories of the sufferings meted out by the Whigs following the farcical Moore's Creek campaign of 1776 was still fresh in people's minds.

He also realized the potential value of the Loyalist partisans to the

British military effort. By employing these troops in raids against Whig leaders and communications, he could erode the inhabitants' confidence in the Whig's ability to govern, capitalizing on the disaffection many of the inhabitants already felt with the Whig government. Key to this part of his strategy was that in order to convince the Loyalists to come out for the King he also had to show them that they would be employed in operations near their homes and not shipped off to the north to win the war there.

Craig expressed his confidence in being able to successfully prosecute a campaign in North Carolina in a letter to Balfour dated May 28, 1781. "I am pretty confident even with what force I have I could encourage and support them so as to become Masters of the Country & disarm the rebels...."[4] Craig's enthusiasm won the argument and he was allowed to remain, but material support for his operation was lacking. General Greene's operations in South Carolina and Cornwallis' campaign in Virginia were a constant drain on British manpower. Thus, reinforcements Craig needed to hold Wilmington while he rode forth with his own troops to support the Loyalists and exploit his foothold on North Carolina did not materialize. Still, with the meager contingent of his 82nd Regiment, Major Craig was able to carry out a remarkably effective campaign in North Carolina.

The British had done well to place an officer of Craig's caliber in command of such an exposed and vital outpost. A native of Gibraltar and son of a noted Scottish jurist, Craig had entered the army at the age of fifteen as an ensign in the 30th Regiment. After studying at several military schools in Europe, Craig had worked his way up to captain of the 47th Regiment when he was wounded at Bunker Hill in the opening days of the war.

He partook of several prominent battles, including Trois Rivières, Ticonderoga and Freeman's Farm. One biographer noted, "...he distinguished himself so much in the early part of Burgoyne's advance upon Saratoga, that the general sent him home with dispatches announcing his early successes. For this he was promoted major without purchase into the newly raised 82nd Regiment, with which he sailed for Nova Scotia."[5]

With his headquarters set up in Wilmington, Craig looked to the rest of the defenses of this vital port. In addition, he moored prison ships in the river and established a prison yard for the prominent Whigs rounded up by his Loyalist partisans. This structure was the infamous "Bull Pen," most widely known as "Major Craig's Bull Pen."[6]

It is unfortunate that Fanning did not pen his personal observations of such an individual as Major Craig. Years later, one of Craig's comrades left us the following description. "In person he was very short, broad and muscular, a pocket Hercules, but with sharp, neat features, as if chiseled in ivory. Not popular, he was hot, peremptory, and pompous, yet extremely beloved by those whom he allowed to live in intimacy with him; clever, generous to a fault, and a warm and unflinching friend to those whom he liked."[7] There was a world of difference between Fanning and Craig. One was a well-educated career soldier, while the other was a backwoodsman with no formal education. Yet despite their differences, the two men seem to have formed a good relationship.

Major Craig was impressed with Fanning, and on July 5, 1781, granted the petitioners from the Deep River country their wish. Captain David Fanning became Colonel David Fanning of the Loyal Militia of Randolph and Chatham Counties. As a symbol of his authority, Fanning was given a red coat and a new sword.[8] Fanning remained in Wilmington for more than a week, discussing various matters of strategy with Craig and formulating a rough outline of a future plan of operations.

The following episode might have given Major Craig an idea of the type of person to whom he had just given command of the Randolph and Chatham Militia. The small group of Fanning's partisans which had accompanied him were encamped near a group of British regular troops on the grounds of the brick home "Belvidere." The two forces shared a nearby spring as a common water source.

One day, as was wont to happen, differences arose between some of the Loyalists partisans and the British regulars. The three particular Loyalists involved in this altercation were arrested and placed under guard in the British camp.

Word soon got back to Fanning that the British held three of his men. Fanning promptly placed three British soldiers under arrest in the Loyalist camp, and then sent word to his captives' commanding officer that they would be released when the militiamen were free. Indignant at such a breach of authority, the British officer stormed with his sword in hand to Fanning's camp, burst into his tent and asked for the person responsible for arresting the British soldiers. Fanning answered that he was the guilty party, at which point the British officer took a swing with his sword at Fanning's head.

Agile and "lithe as a Bengal tiger," Fanning avoided the blow and soon had his new sword so recently received from Major Craig pointed at his antagonist's chest. If the British officer continued, Fanning pointed out, he would be skewered. Fanning repeated his assertion that the prisoners would be released as soon as his men were free. His demands were soon met.[9]

Fanning departed Wilmington and was back in the Deep River country by July 12, where he immediately set about the task of reorganizing the Loyal Militia. He called a general muster at Cox's Mill, and on July 16 began issuing commissions and establishing some sense of order to his command.

Nearly a hundred and fifty men reported for duty at this muster.

Problem was, only about a third of them were sufficiently armed. Fanning kept fifty-three, then sent the rest home and put them on notice to be ready to report when he called for them. With this force of fifty-three men, Fanning set off on his first raid as Colonel of the Loyal Militia of Chatham and Randolph.

The same day the Loyalists were mustering at Cox's Mill, the Whigs were gathering at Chatham Courthouse, now known as Pittsboro. The highlight of their gathering was to occur on the morrow, when a group of those loyal to the King were to be tried and executed. Fanning planned to spoil their fun.

Late in the evening of July 16, the Tories left Cox's Mill and by 7:00 a.m. on July 17 were at the courthouse, which stood on a hill on the south side of Robeson's Creek on the site now occupied by Horton Middle School. When Fanning's men burst into the courthouse, only one or two individuals were present. They informed Fanning that when the court adjourned the day before, everyone went home and were supposed to report back by 8:00 a.m. that morning. Fanning ordered his men to fan out and cover all of the approaches into town and capture anyone headed in. By 9:00 a.m., the Loyalists had gathered fifty-three prisoners, which included the Whig militia officers, some Continentals with their captain, plus various county officials.

Prisoners in hand, Fanning departed Chatham Courthouse and headed back to his base at Cox's Mill. Of the fifty-three taken, thirty-nine were paroled, but he kept the ones "...who I knew were most Violent against Government." These he planned to hand over to Major Craig.[10]

With about fifteen picked men, Colonel Fanning departed for Wilmington, keeping off the well-traveled path in order to elude Whig pursuers. The going was slow, as only a few of the prisoners were mounted, so it took until July 22 to reach John McPhaul's Mill and tavern on Little Raft Swamp, near the community of Antioch in what is now Hoke County. Once there, he was able to obtain enough horses for the rest of his entourage, possibly thanks to Colonel Elder Hector McNeill, who frequently used McPhaul's Mill as a base.

Before departing McPhaul's Mill for Wilmington, the captives wrote a note to Governor Thomas Burke outlining their plight and that of the Tories. In all likelihood, the note was drafted under the watchful eye of Colonel Fanning.

> "Sir:—On Tuesday last we were captured at Chatham Court House by a party under the Command of Col. David Fanning, which party we found consisted of persons who complained of the greatest cruelties, either to their persons or property. Some had been unlawfully Drafted, Others had been whipped and ill-treated, without tryal; Others had their houses burned, and all their

property plundered, and Barborous and cruel Murders had been committed in their Neighborhoods. The Officers they complain of are major Neal, Capt. Robertson, of Bladen, Capt. Crump, Col. Wade and Phil Alston, the latter a day or two ago a few miles in our rear took a man on the road and put him to instant Death, which has much incensed the Highlanders in this part of the County. A Scotch Gentleman the same day was taken at one MacAfee's Mill and ill treated. He is said to be a peaceable and inoffensive man, in name we do not know. He lives in Raft Swamp. Should be happy if he could be liberated. Notwithstanding the Cruel treatment these people have received, We have been treated with the greatest Civility and the utmost respect and politeness by our Commanding Officer, Col. Fanning, to whom we are under the greatest Obligations, and we beg leave to inform your excellency that unless an immediate stop is put to such inhuman practices we plainly discover the whole country will be deluged in Blood, and the innocent will suffer for the guilty. We well know your abhorrence of such inhuman conduct, and your steady intention to prevent it. All we mean is information. We expect to be delivered to Major Craig in Wilmington in two or three days, entirely destitute of Money or Cloathes. How long we shall remain so, God only knows. All we have to ask is that the perpetrators of such horrid Deeds may be brought to tryall, that prisoners may be well treated in future."[11]

The document was signed by Gen. Herndon Ramsey, Joseph Hine, Matt. Ramsey, W. Kitchin, John Birdsong, James Williams, Matthew Jones, Thomas Scurlock, James Herndon and M. Gregory. Simon Terril was paroled to deliver the message to the governor.

As soon as they acquired horses, the group made good progress and were in Wilmington by the 24th. Fanning turned over the prisoners and paid his respects to Major Craig, whom he presented with a set of rules he had drawn up for the conduct of his militia forces. The major approved them, and agreed to have copies drawn up for distribution.

From the wording of a letter Major Craig sent to his superiors in Charles Town on July 30, 1781, it appears that Fanning's feat at Chatham Court House was the genesis of a plan to capture the leading Whig figures of North Carolina. "One of my Tory parties under a Colonel Fanning who is exceedingly active, surprised a few days ago the whole heads of Chatham County to the number of thirty-six who were assembled in the Courthouse to draft men. He paroled twenty-four but brought down twelve of the worst here, one of whom observed he had beheaded the County. A few such strokes would be of great service."[12]

Fanning's stay in Wilmington on this occasion was brief, however, as he hastened back to the Sandhills. The Loyalists in the region were upset over the murder of Thomas Taylor, alluded to in the aforementioned letter. Taylor lived on the south side of Bear Creek in southwestern Chatham

Kenneth Black Cemetery, Southern Pines, North Carolina.

County, and appears to have uttered some sort of comment which antagonized Alston as the Whig party passed by his house in pursuit of Fanning. John Carroll and John Kendrick, both of whom were leading contingents of Alston's force, testified later to a special committee of the House of Commons which was investigating the matter. They stated that Taylor "...had long been and continued to be an Enemy to this State, and was actually guilty of misprision of Treason a few minutes before, if not at the very instant he fell into the recontre with Colonel Phillip Alston."[13] Exactly what the nature of the argument was is unknown, but the murder of Taylor created much furor amongst the Loyalists, and would haunt Alston for years to come.

When Fanning arrived at Cross Hill near the present town of Carthage, he received the details surrounding yet another murder of a Loyalist. This time the victim was his good friend Kenneth Black. Black had been killed in cold blood by Whig ruffians under the command of the notorious Colonel Alston. It was a brutal and senseless crime which, coupled with the murder of Taylor, Fanning could not allow to go unpunished.

Kenneth Black, who lived near what is now Southern Pines, had been an ardent Loyalist since the earliest days of the Revolution. He had even provided a place to stay to the famed Scottish heroine Flora MacDonald in the days following the confiscation of the MacDonalds' property thanks to the part played by her husband in the Moore's Creek fiasco.[14] Fanning had

House in the Horseshoe, Moore County, North Carolina.

chosen to stay at Black's house while en route to Wilmington with some of the prisoners bagged at Chatham Courthouse. Carruthers recounts that Fanning and his men were "very kindly entertained" by Kenneth Black.[15]

Next morning, Fanning's group headed onward, with Black serving as guide for part of the way. The Colonel's horse injured a leg and could not continue on the long journey, so Black exchanged mounts with him and then headed back toward home. On the way back, at Ray's Mill Creek, Black ran into Alston's party riding in pursuit of Fanning, hoping to liberate the prisoners. Black attempted to flee, but the injured horse was not fast enough. Soon, some of Alston's men were within pistol range, and let out a volley, striking Black.

Wounded, Black managed to travel about two hundred yards further, at which time he fell face down in the mud. Carruthers describes what happened next. "When they came up they smashed his head with the butt of his own gun, and when begging for his life."[16] Their victim dead, Alston's men turned and continued after Fanning's party. A short distance later, he called off the chase and camped for the night.

Next morning, while headed back to his home in the Horseshoe Bend of the Deep River, Alston stopped by Kenneth Black's to inform Mrs. Black that her husband was dead. He even admitted that it was his own men who had done the deed, "for which he expressed much regret." So much "regret," in fact, that upon hearing that two old men, Hector McNeill and John Buchan, were nearby building Black's coffin, he rode over and paid them a visit. Alston accused old Hector of harboring a runaway slave, and on that pretense drew his pistol, put it to the old man's head and pulled the trigger. "Snap" went the hammer, but the weapon misfired. Alston tried two more times, each with the same result. His murderous tendencies stymied for the time being, Alston ordered McNeill taken prisoner and stated that he would hang him if the slave was not returned in a couple of days.[17]

This was the gist of the story which greeted Fanning on his return to the area. Hearing that Alston was at his home near Deep River, Fanning gathered together the men he had immediately available—twenty-five all totaled—and set out to put an end to Alston's depredations. "…I was determined for to make Example of them for behaving in the manner they had done to one of my pilots by name Kenneth Black," is how Fanning put it.[18]

They departed late on Saturday, July 28, 1781, and rode all through the night. They crossed Deep River upstream from Alston's at Dickerson's Ford, and by dawn had taken up a position around the house. The sentries which Alston had posted at the two gates of the fence surrounding his house were asleep. One set was taken prisoner; the other group of sentries awoke and sounded the alarm. Soon, all the Whigs were awake and firing out of the doors and windows of the Alston House. The fight lasted for over three hours, with the Tories unable to leave their cover behind the fence and charge across the yard, the Whigs trapped in the house with no place to go. At one point, a British officer identified as McCoy by Carruthers stood to lead a charge. He was immediately shot through the heart as soon as he cleared the fence.[19]

Another British officer later identified by Archibald Murphey as Captain Andrews was killed as he stood to get a clean shot. "During the fight," wrote Murphey, "Captain Andrews , a British officer, who had accompanied Fanning from Wilmington, climbed up the fence, that he might shoot with more effect through a window of the house. As he stood on the fence, one of the men in the house shot him through the head."[20] Weary of playing the game of taking potshots at one another, and perhaps more importantly concerned that Whig reinforcements would soon be on the scene, Fanning decided to put an end to the encounter once and for all. Spying an oxcart loaded with hay nearby, he ordered some of his men to take it up, set it afire, then push the vehicle against the house, the object being to burn the house down around the Whig defenders.

At this point, Alston's wife, Temperance, decided enough was enough. Rising from the bed she had occupied since the fight began (the children were hidden in the chimney, which was deemed by the Alstons to be the safest spot inside the house from flying bullets), she strolled outside with a

Damage to the House in the Horseshoe was extensive. Bullet holes remain to this day.

white flag. She called out to Fanning that her husband and his companions would agree to surrender if Fanning agreed to spare their lives. Impressed by the bravery of Mrs. Alston, Fanning granted her request.

The fighting at the Battle for the House in the Horseshoe was over. In the course of the affair Fanning reports two killed and four wounded out of his force of twenty-five. Whether this includes the two officers Major Craig sent out to observe the Loyalist activity in the central part of the province, who were killed in the melee, is unknown. Of the Whigs, whom Murphey asserts numbered between twenty-six and thirty men, Fanning claimed to have killed four and "wounded all the Rest except 3." Fanning paroled the prisoners that day as agreed, keeping a copy of Alston's parole which was dated July 29, 1781. He included a transcript of this in his *Narrative*, and, thanks to this, it is possible to accurately pinpoint the date of the battle.[21]

Many might argue that, based on the total number of people involved, this was more of a skirmish whose impact on the overall outcome of the course of the Tory War was negligible. This conclusion, however, is far from accurate, since Fanning neutralized the ever-active Alston and his Whig raiders, thus taking them out of action for the next several months.

7. Fanning Takes Command

This would prove especially critical following the upcoming raid on Hillsborough and the Battle at Lindley's Mill, as the Loyalists had a relatively safe avenue to take their valuable prisoners for deposit into Major Craig's Bullpen in Wilmington. If Alston had been active, his horsemen no doubt would have liberated Governor Burke and the other prisoners as the Loyalists were crossing the Deep River at Dowd's Mill while Fanning lay critically wounded and their strike force was under the command of younger and less experienced leaders.

The Loyalists' concerns over Whig reinforcements proved to be well justified. While the fighting raged, a party of Whig horsemen later identified by Murphey as belonging to "Captain Duck" lay just across Deep River within sight of the fray, but made no attempt to cross. Perhaps they were afraid to take on the notorious Fanning, or more likely, they felt Alston was getting his just deserts.[22]

With all of the post-battle details taken care of, Fanning headed for his base at Cox's Mill, and there sent the men who had been with him in the morning's fight home to rest for the evening. There was no rest, though, for the Loyalist leader, as he soon heard of a wagon loaded with a precious cargo of salt which had passed by early that morning. After a hard ride of sixteen miles, Fanning and eight of his compatriots overtook the wagon and captured it with little resistance. They returned with their valuable prize to Cox's Mill the next morning.

Back at his base, things were far from quiet. Captain Rains, who had been left in command, was under attack. The Whigs broke off the engagement as soon as Fanning arrived on the scene, then sent in a flag of truce with terms for the Loyalists' surrender. Fanning replied that he was willing, "...to make peace with the Sword."[23] The Whigs gave the matter thoughtful consideration, but it wasn't long before they decided it was time to retreat.

The Loyalists were glad to see the attackers leave, but the indefatigable Fanning took the offensive. His scouts soon brought back word that the attackers were not numerous, and had fallen back on a much larger Whig contingent consisting of about four hundred troops under Colonels John Paisley and Andrew Balfour. The Whigs were encamped about two miles above Cox's Mill at a place identified as Brown's plantation.

Fanning's forces could not have been greater than a hundred and fifty, as many of his men were ranging through the countryside bringing in supplies and recruits, but this numerical disadvantage did not discourage him. Fanning sent word to the Whigs that he wished to "...determine the matter by force of arms."[24] He also complained to them of the ill treatment some of his men had suffered when captured by the Whigs and warned of dire consequences if they persisted. Colonel William O'Neal of the Orange

County Militia sent word back, "that wherever they met me they would fight me, but not by an Immediate apoint."[25]

On that, Fanning decided that the present lack of confidence on the part of his antagonists warranted an immediate bold response. He and his men, though greatly outnumbered, rode forth to the attack, but when they arrived at the enemy's camp they found it deserted. Soon they learned that the Whigs were heading with all possible speed to Salisbury.[26]

With his only considerable foe along the Deep River headed off toward the Yadkin, Fanning took the opportunity to rest his weary men. By August 11, with ammunition low, he determined to take a part of his force to Wilmington for supplies. En route, he planned to raid a few of the more prominent Whigs in the Cape Fear Valley, and drop in on the merchants at Cross Creek.

Captain Richard Edwards with his men from the Orange County Loyalist Militia remained behind to weaken the confidence of the people of the central portion of the state toward the Whig government. Details of their operations are sparse. Writing from Hillsborough on August 20, 1781, Armond Armstrong informed Governor Burke, "Edwards and his Company came Three days ago on the other side of Haw River, with an Intention, it's said, to plunder this Place. This is sworn to by a certain Thomas Rickitt, who is made Prisoner; also that they intend breaking up Guilford and this Court. They are not so much charged with Plundering as disarming, and, as they say, informing the People. And what is somewhat Strange, altho' the General Complaint is that there is no Arms to oppose them, they seldom fail of finding Arms in every House they go to. They have at present an uninterrupted Command between Deep and Haw River."[27]

Things had not been quiet around Cross Creek. The Scottish Loyalists had been stirred to action by a number of things, including the overzealousness of local confiscation officers and murderous raids by Alston, Colonel Thomas Wade and their ilk. Now the Scots were moving, and on August 14 they took a play straight from Fanning—they captured a county court while it was in session.

On this occasion, Colonel John Slingsby coordinated the efforts of colonels Hector McNeill, Duncan Ray and Archibald McDugald as they descended upon the county court and merchants at Cross Creek. They captured the court house, which stood near the site of the present Cumberland County Library off Maiden Lane in Fayetteville. Ironically, and quite involuntarily, Fanning saved a number of the Cumberland officials when the Tories took the court house. Historian Malcolm Fowler relates that Captain Alexander Avera of the Whig militia from near the modern Erwin area, got wind of the impending attack. Fowler continues, "Mounting his swiftest horse, he galloped down the King's Highway on the east side of the river, crossed the river at Beasley's Crossing above Fayetteville and pounded into Cross Creek.

"He unceremoniously dashed into the courtroom, bawling: 'Gentlemen! Hear me! Fanning is on his way here to take you prisoner.'

"It is said that never before, or since, has the Cumberland Courthouse cleared so quickly and completely. Despite Avera's warning, several of them were captured before they could get out of town. Avera was among those who escaped."[28]

The Scottish Loyalists under Slingsby took possession of Cross Creek for several days and used it as a base from which to raid the Whigs in the surrounding countryside. They captured a great deal of the Whigs' supplies, and enacted vengeance on their enemies, especially those like Thomas Hadley who were particularly cruel and overzealous in prosecuting their confiscation duties.

So when Fanning arrived in Cross Creek on August 16, 1781, the Loyalists were in control of the town. Fanning's stay was brief. On August 17 he was joined by Major Samuel Andrews with a contingent of the Bladen Loyalist militia. The combined forces crossed the river at Campbellton and took up the march toward Wilmington along the east side of the Cape Fear.

In Bladen County, near the present community of White Oak, they came upon the home of Captain Peter Robeson, a prominent Whig leader. The Loyalists quickly put Captain Robeson's house to the torch. Across the river they spied the home of Robeson's brother, Colonel Thomas Robeson. A detachment of Fanning's men was dispatched across the Cape Fear and soon Col. Robeson's house met the same fate as his brother's.

Fanning and Andrews continued with their raid down the east side of Cape Fear. After seven days of raiding, they were safely inside the British lines at Wilmington. Here, Fanning turned over the prisoners he had collected to "Capt. Leggett, then commanding." Captain John Leggett of the Royal North Carolina Regiment was Craig's second in command. He owned land along Rockfish Creek in Cumberland County, and had served the Loyalist cause since the Moore's Creek campaign, where he was captured. He spent most of the war in prison, but since the fall of Charles Town had maintained an active role.[29]

While the Loyalists under Fanning, Edwards, Ray, Slingsby, Andrews and McNeill were on the rampage in the upper Cape Fear Valley, Major Craig sallied forth from Wilmington to mount his own campaign through southeastern North Carolina. He took along a force of two hundred and fifty regulars and nearly a hundred Tories, and hoped to gain volunteers along the way.

Following a proclamation reminding the inhabitants that they were all British subjects and those eligible should report for duty with Loyalist units, Craig departed Wilmington on August 1 headed with his men into Duplin County. At Rock Creek, east of the modern town of Wallace, Col. James Kenan's five hundred men attempted to halt the British advance. After a spirited contest, the Whig militia ran low on ammunition and then fled.[30] The British remained in Duplin for about ten days, raiding Whig farms throughout the present Sampson/Duplin area. Many in the region repaired to the King's Standard and by the time Craig was ready to continue, his Loyalist component had risen to three hundred.[31]

Craig headed his little army toward New Bern, which the British occupied on August 19. Along the way they met with only minor resistance, thanks in part to an order from Governor Burke to General Alexander Lillington not to risk a battle.[32] The British remained in New Bern two days before heading up the Neuse River to Bryan's Mills, where a Whig detachment under Colonel James Gorham was defeated. Thanks for this victory was due in no small part to the liquor which some of Gorham's cavalry had found and quickly disposed of. Thus inebriated, they were not in position to protect the flank and Gorham was forced to retreat across the river.[33]

Craig's forces spent the night there at Bryan's Mill and used it as a base to set out on raids to destroy Whig property nearby. At some point during the night he got wind of a rumor which put General Anthony Wayne at the head of a contingent of Continental soldiers heading down from Virginia intent on defeating the British raiders. Believing this report, Craig ordered his men to turn south and carry out the campaign toward Wilmington. The force encamped at Richlands on the New River on the 25th, and continued south to Wilmington, stopping to destroy some of the vital salt works along the coast. Major Craig and his men were safely back at the British base at Wilmington by September 1, 1781.[34]

8

Elizabethtown and Beatti's Bridge

Equipped with an adequate supply of ammunition, Fanning and his followers parted company with Captain Leggett on August 26, 1781, and headed back up the King's Highway along the west side of the Cape Fear. They camped for the night somewhere in lower Bladen County between Elizabethtown and Wilmington.

On the morning of August 27, the Loyalists continued their journey and were soon at Elizabethtown, where Fanning saw a troubling site: "...on my arrival I found Coln. Slingsbee of the Loyal Militia of Bladen County—with a number of paroled Rebels—in his camp."[1] Slingsby, who had coordinated the capture of Cross Creek two weeks earlier, had fallen back with his portion of the Bladen Militia to what was considered safe territory in lower Bladen, while Colonel Elder Hector McNeill and his Highlanders headed into western Bladen around McPhaul's Mill. McDougald and Ray had moved off with the Cumberland militia into northern Cumberland.

Thanks to his two successful mercantile operations—one at Cross Creek and the other in Wilmington—Slingsby had formed many friendships with his Whig neighbors before the war. He had once even served on the Wilmington Committee of Safety and was responsible for blocking the channel of the Cape Fear to British incursions in November of 1775. Slingsby, though, could not stomach an open break with the British government, and resigned from the Provincial Congress in April of 1776, breaking all ties with the revolutionists. He apparently lived at peace among his former compatriots until Major Craig occupied Wilmington, at which time Slingsby was made colonel of the militia for Brunswick and Bladen counties. On many occasions, Slingsby used his position of authority to help a Whig friend. But Slingsby's kindness was his undoing.

There is no record of whether Fanning and Slingsby discussed the upcoming campaign, or if instructions were given for a rendezvous in the interior of the province at a later date. Fanning records that he merely warned Slingsby of the dangers of keeping so many members of the opposing army in his camp, even if they were just "paroled Rebels." Whatever

Tory Hole Park in Elizabethtown, North Carolina.

rapport transpired must have been brief, for Fanning and his cohorts soon parted company with Col. Slingsby and headed for McPhaul's Mill.

The misfortunes which befell the Tories at Elizabethtown on the night of August 27, 1781, are shrouded in myth and uncertainty. Sadly, there are no firsthand accounts of the episode known to exist. The nearest thing to a firsthand account includes a sentence from a pension claim filed over forty years after the war by a Whig participant, Musgrove Jones, as well as a few lines in Fanning's *Narrative*. The latter were merely secondhand reports gained from both fugitives of the encounter and reports of a relief party that arrived on the scene too late to help.

The known facts behind the Battle of Elizabethtown are simple enough. A Loyalist outpost at the Bladen County seat was surprised on the night of August 27, 1781. This sudden attack resulted in much consternation among the Loyalists but few casualties. Most accounts agree that there were less than twenty total, but among the dead was the Loyalist commander, Col. Slingsby.

Fanning believed that in the dead of the night the paroled Whigs he had warned about used concealed arms to treacherously attack their captors. He wrote the following observations. "I disapproved of keeping them [Whig prisoners] there and told him I thought it imprudent and unsafe, the Event proved so, for that night they having arms Concealed fired upon

8. Elizabethtown and Beatti's Bridge

his camp and wounded him mortally and five Captains also were wounded some of which died afterwards of their wounds."[2]

The earliest extant Whig account of the action was penned in November of 1784 when William Dickson of Duplin County wrote a letter to his cousin Robert in Ireland in which he chronicled several events occurring in southeastern North Carolina during the Revolutionary War, including two sentences chronicling the affair at Elizabethtown. After noting that "Maturine" Colville, Bladen Loyalist commander, was murdered earlier, Dickson gives details of his successor. "He was succeeded in command by Col. John Slingsby, who headed the troops embodied, about 400 at Bladen Court House. Colonel Brown, with about 150 of the Whigs, surprised him in the night, slew Colonel Slingsby and two of his captains and some of his men, and retreated without any loss, and returned in the morning where he found only the slain and some of the wounded, the rest having fled and made their escape."[3]

For several years after this, the story was embellished and retold several times until it became a part of the folklore of the people living in the Cape Fear Valley. In the winter of 1843–44, A.A. Brown, editor of the *Wilmington Weekly Chronicle*, became interested in the events surrounding the Battle of Elizabethtown. "No notice of the battle was found in any history of that period. We understood that there was an imperfect relation of it published in a Federal paper twenty-five or thirty years ago," he wrote. Not satisfied, Brown addressed a letter to "…a distinguished gentleman of Bladen," asking for information. Brown received his reply, a lengthy letter which he published in his paper in February of 1844. This account is the one which has been copied by subsequent historians, namely John Wheeler and the Reverend Carruthers.

Since this letter from 1844 forms the basis of all subsequent accounts of the Battle of Elizabethtown, it is interesting to note the sources conscientiously chronicled by the "gentleman of Bladen." "The foregoing narrative was detailed to me by two of the respective combatants, who now sleep with their fathers; the substance of which I have endeavored to preserve with all the accuracy a memory not very retentive will permit. A respectable resident of Elizabethtown has recently informed me that he was a small boy at the time of the battle and lived with his mother in one of the houses to which the Tories repaired for safety; that he has a distinct recollection of the fire of the Whigs, which appeared like one continuous stream. Documentary evidence I have none."[4]

In this account, one reads the full details of the band of Whigs under Robeson and Brown, who forded the Cape Fear with rifles overhead, stealthily took up a position west of town, and attacked, driving the Loyalists into a defile ever afterward referred to as "the Tory Hole." This is also where the mysterious Colonel "Godden," Slingsby's mythical fellow commander, was introduced into the story. "In the death of Slingsby, the Tories were deprived of an officer whose place it was difficult to fill; but few were equal to Godden in partisan warfare."[5]

It should be noted that Godden is mentioned nowhere in the Colonial Records or the British Public Records, nor any other contemporary source. Surely such a master of partisan warfare should have captured somebody's attention. Thus, it is difficult, if not downright impossible, to piece together what actually happened to Colonel Slingsby and his Bladen Loyalist Militia at Elizabethtown that fateful night of August 27, 1781. This episode spawns much conjecture, but one thing is certain. Until a firsthand account of the Battle of Elizabethtown comes to light, the story behind this Loyalist disaster in Bladen County will remain a mystery.

On the afternoon of August 27, 1781, Fanning and his troops continued on their way and arrived at McPhaul's Mill by the 29th. There they stopped to rest, hoping to gain news from other Loyalists active in the area who utilized this place as base for their activities. The aforementioned Colonel Elder Hector McNeill often encamped at McPhaul's Mill.

Two days passed at McPhaul's Mill before news of McNeill's whereabouts reached Fanning, and unfortunately it was not good news. McNeill and a force of about seventy Scotsmen had stirred up a proverbial hornet's nest over in Montgomery County by raiding Richard Fanning's Mill on Little River, taking a number of Whig prisoners. Most of the captives were under the command of Colonel Thomas Wade of Anson County, and Wade was now in hot pursuit of McNeill. Wade's force numbered around four hundred, and he was expecting to be reinforced at any time.[6]

As soon as Fanning heard of McNeill's predicament, he sent word to the old Scotsman offering his assistance if needed; "…in three hours I Received for answer he would be Glad for to see me and my party…" wrote Fanning.[7]

McNeill was at that time about eight miles west of McPhaul's Mill about one-half mile from a place known as Beatti's/Beattie's Bridge, which spanned Lumber River just upstream from the spot where today US Highway 401 crosses that watercourse near the small town of Wagram. For many years the bridge across this point on the river was known as Gilchrist Bridge. "For years Beattie's Bridge was the main causeway on upper Lumber River, being the only crossing that was always passable, it became a strategic point for the Whigs and Tories," wrote Governor Angus McLean. "An adjacent island, large enough to quarter equipment and afford protection for a large body of troops, added another distinct advantage to the place. Besides this, the heavy traffic in stores and produce, the dense swamp, the wretched condition of the road, and the narrowness of

8. Elizabethtown and Beatti's Bridge

Beatti's Bridge crossed Lumber River near where the old US 401 bridge crosses the river at Wagram.

the passageway made it an easy base from which to forage and otherwise harass the enemy."[8]

Fanning gathered a hundred and fifty-five of his men and headed for Beatti's Bridge through the night with all speed. As the sun was rising, he found Colonel McNeill encamped about three miles from Beatti's Bridge, with scouts out keeping track of Wade's movements. Wade was reported to have crossed Lumber River and encamped on a hill which was identified by Governor McLean as "...on the identical spot where old Montpelier Church now stands in Hoke County." The church the governor used as a landmark is no longer standing and its congregation has since relocated on the opposite side of the river in Wagram. The site of Wade's encampment would have been on the hill over which US 401 passes on the east side of the river, near the intersection with Hilltop Road.[9]

Fanning listened to all of the reports which McNeill's men were able to give him, then quickly formulated a plan. Wade's men were encamped on the hill with a thick swamp in his front and Lumber River in his rear. He had thrown out his men into line of battle facing the swamp since his skirmishers had tangled briefly with those of the Highlanders. He was expecting an attack at any moment. There was only one way across the swamp, a "crossway" which was apparently unguarded. Fanning directed his men to cross the swamp along the "crossway" two abreast, and when they emerged on the western side, his troopers were to quietly turn to the right and take up a position all down Wade's line. Since he was outnumbered nearly two to one, Fanning resorted to a stratagem which would hopefully inflate his numbers in the eyes of the enemy. "When formed my little party I left great Vacancies in order to appear as numerous as possible and to prevent the turning my flank."[10]

McNeill's men, meanwhile, were to cross the swamp and turn left, passing around Wade's right flank and taking up a position overlooking the approach to Beatti's Bridge. There he was to sit and monitor the progress of the battle. If Fanning's men were in danger of being defeated, McNeill was to attack Wade's right flank and rear. If all went well, however, McNeill's Highlanders were to cut off Wade's retreat by securing Beatti's Bridge. Thus, Fanning hoped not only to defeat his numerically superior adversary, but to totally eliminate them as an effective fighting force.[11]

By 11 o'clock, September 1, 1781, the Loyalist horsemen were nearly in position, having crossed the swamp (Fanning being the first across) and proceeded down Wade's front as instructed. Before they had covered the total distance to Wade's left flank, however, one of the Loyalists fell from his horse and the shock of his landing caused his weapon to fire. This gave the alarm to the Whigs, who fired a volley which brought down eighteen of the Loyalists' horses. The action was now on.

Fanning ordered his men to dismount and form a line of battle. They began firing methodically and advancing uphill, all the while the red-coated Fanning directing them. The terrain proved to be an advantage to the Loyalists, as the hill upon which Wade formed his line had little vegetation save a few scattered pines. In addition, the hill was just steep enough to provide cover for the advancing Loyalists—if a Whig stood to get a clear shot, he made of himself an easy target, while most shots from Wade's men passed harmlessly over their enemies' heads.

As the battle raged, Fanning was riding up and down the Loyalist lines between the two forces, urging his men on and directing the advance. "Dressed in rich British uniform, he rode between the lines during all the fight, and gave his orders with the utmost coolness and presence of mind. It is strange that he had not been selected by some of Wade's men, as he was at the close of the fight not twenty yards distant from them."[12] Wade's men stood their ground until the Loyalists were within twenty-five yards of their lines. At this point, the Whigs broke and ran, fleeing toward Beatti's Bridge and Fanning's well-laid trap.

McNeill had placed only a token force at the bridge which was quickly swept aside by Wade's fleeing men, who continued their flight across

Lumber River toward safety. Fanning arrived on the scene, and with what forces he could gather pursued the fleeing Whigs for seven miles until he was finally forced to admit that they had escaped.

The Loyalists were victorious. Two hours of hard fighting had resulted in the defeat of a numerically superior force with a loss of only five wounded and five dead horses. This is even more remarkable when one realizes that the victory was won solely by Fanning's hundred and fifty-five men, as McNeill's seventy men were in reserve behind Wade's right flank, and few of the Highlanders saw action at the bridge itself.

The Whigs' losses were extensive. Fanning noted, "we pursued them 7 miles and took 54 prisoners 4 of which died that night. On our Return we found 19 Dead and the next day several Came in and surrendered all of which were wounded, and we had Reason to suppose the several died in the Swamps by accounts Received from those who Came in afterwards."[13] Though stunning, the victory was not a total success. It was well within the power of the Loyalists to have totally crushed Wade's force, but despite Fanning's best directives, the Highlanders had failed to cut off his avenue of retreat across Beatti's Bridge.

Why had McNeill failed? Carruthers places the blame on a lack of communication between Fanning and McNeill. He also mentions the fact that the Highlanders refused to serve under Fanning. The latter reason was an aversion which materialized after the war, when it was expedient to distance oneself from Fanning and his actions. As for a lack of communication between McNeill and Fanning, the fact that McNeill's men were where they were supposed to be and put up a token struggle discounts this hypothesis.

Governor McLean, however, notes the most plausible explanation. "It is quite probable, too, so local historians say, that if Colonel Hector MacNeill had obeyed orders and moved promptly, Colonel Wade's whole force would have been captured before they escaped over the bridge. But there seems to have been good reasons for the Tory commander's dilatory action: his own brother 'Red' Alex MacNeill had joined the Whigs and was a captain in Colonel Wade's command, and a number of his own men's relatives were among the revolutionary forces. Therefore, Colonel Hector MacNeill delayed the attack in order to give his brother opportunity to escape or defend himself. When he was at last ready to attack, his half-hearted and lukewarm actions had helped the Whigs so much that they were not only able to resist capture, but to escape easily over the bridge."[14]

That afternoon, the Loyalists regrouped and took stock of what they had won. "Besides a few wounded we took 250 horses most of which were loaded with effects they had plundered from the friends of Government," wrote Fanning, "and as I had formerly ordered that whoever found concealed goods of any kind Should hold them, I also ordered that Every man should Keep that he had taken that day."[15]

Following the division of booty, the Loyalists began taking care of the prisoners. Most of these were paroled, except for thirty of the more troublesome ones who were turned over to Major Craig in Wilmington. When the Loyalists began sorting out the prisoners they had taken, they discovered that one Joseph Hayes had fallen into their hands. Hayes was recognized by Captain Elrod as the same person who had recently raided his house on the Yadkin and assaulted members of his family. With little deliberation, Hayes was sentenced to be hanged for his crime.

The rope was tied to a convenient tree limb, and the noose secured around the prisoner's neck, who was sitting upon the back of a horse. The signal was given, the horse bolted, and Hayes dangled at the end of a rope. Hayes hung for fifteen minutes, at which point he was cut down from the tree. The Loyalist surgeon examined the prisoner, and to the amazement of all found the condemned man to be clinging to life. The surgeon quickly asked Elrod for permission to resuscitate the prisoner, which was given, and soon it was evident that Hayes would survive.[16]

When the action and post battle activities finally came to an end, Fanning headed with his men for their familiar grounds at Cox's Mill on Deep River. They halted for the night near Little River, where they were rejoined by the detachment that had been sent back to Elizabethtown to assist Slingsby. This party had been too late to intercept the Whigs, who had quickly dispersed with their loot.[17]

En route to Cox's Mill, Fanning's scouts brought in Thomas Dougan, colonel of the Randolph Whig militia, who had been sent by his comrades to spy out the situation among the Tories. After a brief trial, Fanning sentenced Dougan to death. At this point, several of Dougan's friends and neighbors who happened to be serving in Fanning's Loyalist militia from Randolph came to their neighbor's defense, stating that he was "…an upright man, and a friend to his country; and those who differed from him in opinion as to the combat in which they were engaged, abated neither their esteem nor affection for him."[18]

The entreaties had little effect upon Fanning, who ordered that the sentence be carried out. Amid tumult and uproar, Dougan was placed on a horse, his hands secured and a rope placed about his neck. At this point, one of Fanning's subalterns, whose name has unfortunately not been recorded, stepped forward and told Fanning in no uncertain terms that he would shoot Fanning if Dougan was hanged.

With a potential mutiny on his hands, Fanning proposed a compromise—he would allow forty of his most loyal and faithful followers to vote on Dougan's fate. This decision was agreed upon, and while the condemned man sat on the horse with a noose about his neck, the Loyalists had a plebiscite. When the votes were tallied, it was a close call, but Fanning's "bloodthirsty" band had decided to spare the life of Thomas Dougan. He was quickly removed from the makeshift gallows and treated as a regular prisoner of war. Dougan was sent to Wilmington, where he nearly perished once again at the end of a hangman's rope. But he was, again, spared by the goodwill of some of Fanning's men, especially Major Elrod.

Though he often yielded to the wishes of his men, as was the case with Dougan, Fanning was not always so magnanimous. Often he found it necessary to employ much harsher methods to maintain authority over such a motley crew. One tale which was widely circulated in the years after the war gives a good example of Fanning's managerial style.

One day as Fanning rested under the shade of a tree, some of his men began to openly question his ability to command. One unnamed lieutenant in particular was very vocal in his opinions, and as the conversation continued, he became more and more agitated.

The man became so enraged that one of Fanning's more loyal followers, who was standing by the tree where the Colonel was resting, clandestinely raised his rifle to gun down the agitator. Fanning, however, motioned to his friend not to shoot the lieutenant and stealthily drew his sword. Save for the sentinel with the rifle, the rest of the camp still thought Fanning was asleep.

Finally, the lieutenant worked himself into a frenzy, grabbed a musket with bayonet attached, and charged his reclining commander. He raised his arm for a mighty blow, and just as the weapon was inches from Fanning's body, the Loyalist commander rolled out of its path and the weapon plunged into the earth.

In an instant, the colonel thrust the blade into the vitals of his attacker, who fell dead at Fanning's feet.

Cool as ice, his hand still clutching the sword protruding from the dead man's side, Fanning looked at his now silent men and remarked, "It is in this way that I punish those who disregard my authority."[19]

9

Loyalist Highwater Mark

All of the Loyalist activities in the Cape Fear Valley during the past months had not gone unnoticed by Whig authorities. Governor Burke ordered out the Whig militia of the western and central counties of the state in an effort to amass a large enough force to crush the Loyalists once and for all-in-one decisive campaign.

One group was gathering along the Pee Dee River composed of men from the extreme western counties of the state. The plan Burke was formulating called for this force to act in conjunction with a force to be raised in the central part of the state. In particular, militiamen from Caswell, Randolph, Chatham, Wake and Orange counties were directed to gather at Ramsey's Mills in the forks of the Deep and Haw rivers. There the governor was assembling an army under the command of General John Butler which would be in a position for a quick strike deep into the Loyalists' stronghold between the Pee Dee and Cape Fear rivers.[1]

A former sheriff of Orange County, John Butler had played an active role in the struggle for American independence since the earliest days of the Revolution, leading a force from Orange County down to Cross Creek during the Moore's Creek campaign in 1776. He was highly regarded by the Whigs, and led North Carolina militia during several campaigns alongside the regular Continental army. By the late summer of 1781 he could add battles at Stono Ferry, Camden, and Guilford Court House to his military résumé.

Governor Burke decided that he could better direct the operations of his campaign if he were closer to the action. So he departed the relatively safe haven of Halifax in early September and headed west to Hillsborough. So oblivious was he to danger that not only did he rent a house in Hillsborough, he also considered bringing along his wife. He arrived in town, fortunately on this occasion spouseless, by September 9, 1781.[2] Since the presence of so many of the King's supporters in the central part of the province provided Fanning with an efficient intelligence-gathering network, word of Burke's relocation to Hillsborough reached Fanning before the governor even got to town. This must have been welcome news, since he and Major Craig had discussed the possibility of capturing the chief Whig executive of North Carolina in much the same fashion as Fanning and his men bagged the Chatham County court officials back in July.[3]

We will never know exactly who concocted such a bold strike which, if properly executied, could remove most of the civilian leadership of the rebellious Whig government. Circumstances had now come together where they could put their theory to the test, especially since Burke's hubris now placed him well within Fanning's grasp at the very time the Loyalists were mobilizing for a major strike.[4]

Fanning sent out word to the people in his district to report for action against the Whigs, and his proclamation brought in nearly nine hundred and fifty militiamen. As was usually the case, many of those who reported were ill equipped, and Fanning was lucky to add four hundred and thirty-five of these recruits to his command.[5]

On September 9, 1781, Loyalist Colonel Archibald MacDugald with two hundred Highlanders from Cumberland County and Colonel Hector McNeill with seventy from Bladen rode into Fanning's camp at Cox's Mill. Fanning had already served with McNeill, but he knew little of McDugald, who had seen action as an ensign with Hamilton's Royal North Carolina Regiment at such battles as Guilford Court House.[6]

Buoyed by this accession of strength, Fanning worked out the final details of the coming raid on Hillsborough in his mind. There were several factors to consider, the most important being how many Whig troops were in Hillsborough. Also a factor was whether General Butler's forces were still at Ramsey's Mill.

A monument commemorating the Battle of Lindley's Mill.

Having worked out a plan on the information then available, Fanning shared it with Captain John Rains. His second in command enthusiastic, Fanning put the plan into motion.

At this point, it was still necessary that details of the coming campaign be kept secret, at least until more timely intelligence could be gathered. This was true even of McDugald and McNeill, as the actions of the Highlanders under McNeill at Beatti's Bridge may have led Fanning to question their resolve. Their dispositions ready, the Loyalist army—over six hundred strong—departed Cox's Mill on the morning of September 11, 1781. Sixteen miles away, when they were in the process of fording Rocky River, Fanning departed from his army and rode off to a friend's house to gain further news about the Whigs. Here he learned that Butler was still off to the southeast at Ramsey's Mill.[7]

He also learned that a much smaller force of Whigs was encamped between Fanning and Butler. This particular detachment of Whigs, consisting of twenty-five men who had been gathered from along the New Hope River to scour the country for Loyalists back in early August, offered a potentially fast-moving threat to Fanning's column. They also made a tempting target.[8]

When Fanning returned to his army, he was surprised to discover that, in his absence, McNeill and McDugald, thinking the target of their mission was Butler's army, had directed the Loyalist army onto the road leading southeast toward the forks of the Deep and Haw. Before they had gone too far astray, Fanning halted their advance and sought out the two Highland commanders.

With fresh information as to Butler's whereabouts, Fanning decided that the time had come to enlighten his fellow officers as to the group's true destination—Hillsborough. The boldness of the plan shocked the two men, but it did not deter them. They agreed to accompany Fanning on this bold enterprise.[9]

Shortly after Fanning had redirected his army onto the road for Hillsborough, he dispatched Captain Richard Edwards and a force of about twenty-five men from the Orange County Loyalist Militia to ride southeast and destroy the force of Orange County Whig Militia under Allen and Young. In addition to silencing this potential threat, Fanning may also have hoped to use the attack as a diversion to create the impression that his whole army was in southeastern Chatham County, thus holding Butler immobile.

Edwards' force made its way to Kirk's Farm by sunrise the next day, but in the process of surrounding the house were spotted by a sentinel named Couch, who gave the alarm before being killed. His compatriots were slow to react, however, and their delay gave the Loyalists time to hide in a nearby thicket.

When Captain Allen and company finally did emerge from their slumber to ascertain the cause of the alarm, they were ambushed by the Loyalists. The Whigs put up a stout defense, but were soon overpowered; "...some important lives were lost on both sides, and others mortally wounded," Carruthers noted. "Allen and Young were both severely wounded, the former recovered, but the latter died of his wounds within a few days. Captain Edwards was killed on the spot, and ten were left dead on the field. Nearly a third of the whole number engaged were either killed or wounded; and some of the latter died of their wounds within a few days."[10]

Thus ended the Battle of Kirk's Farm. The fate of the Whig survivors, whether they escaped or were captured and paroled, has not been recorded.[11] Their job finished, the Loyalist detachment now under the command of Edwards' brother, Edward (yes, his name was Edward Edwards), hastened back to the main body of Loyalists headed north for Hillsborough.

The Loyalist army pressed on into the night toward its objective. Speed was now of the essence. In the pre-dawn darkness of September 12, 1781, Fanning divided his command into three wings to cover the approaches into Hillsborough. Their movements concealed by a thick fog, the Loyalists were able to take up their positions undetected. They were ready to descend upon the town at dawn.

At seven o'clock, the Loyalists attacked. Resistance was sporadic, the surprise so complete that not even the force of Continental soldiers in town had a chance to organize resistance. Some random individuals did fire a few shots from the windows of houses, but these snipers were quickly silenced.[12]

Once in town, Fanning directed a force to head straight to Governor Burke's quarters. Barricaded inside the house, armed only with pistols and swords, the governor and his entourage put up a spirited fight. "To escape was impracticable and resistance was in vain," Burke recalled, "yet the savage manners and appearance of the men made me expect nothing but massacre, and I preferred dying sword in hand, than yielding to their barbarity."[13]

Soon, "a gentleman in the uniform of a British officer" rode up and convinced Burke that if he and his men surrendered, their lives would be spared. Burke accepted these terms, handed over his sword and capitulated. Shortly thereafter, several of the Loyalists wanted to string up their prisoner, but cooler heads prevailed. Fearing for their valuable prisoners' safety, Fanning placed them under guard of several Highlanders who harbored no ill will against Governor Burke personally.[14]

Hearing of the governor's surrender, several of the Whigs remaining in town decided it was time to make a run for it. This included several of those guarding prisoners in the jail. Among those attempting to flee the scene was Colonel Archibald Lytle, an officer in the Continental Army home on parole after being captured at Charles Town in May of 1780. Fortunately for Lytle, he was wearing his military helmet, for he was spotted making his escape by Colonel Fanning, who promptly rode him down and took a swipe at his head with a sword. The sword broke in two on the metal plate of Lytle's hat, but still managed to inflict a severe injury.[15]

The Loyalist next set about the task of capturing a group of Continental soldiers who were holed up in the town's church, located on the corner of Churton and Tryon streets. This was accomplished with little resistance, for most of the Continentals were raw recruits headed for General Greene's army in South Carolina.[16]

The first objectives met, the Loyalists went about the task of liberating the jail. There they found 30 Loyalist and British prisoners, whom they promptly released. Here they also took two "swivels" or small cannons.[17]

The entire raid on Hillsborough was finished by 9:00 a.m. Fanning summed up his accomplishments for the day: "…we lost non nor suffered no damage except one man wounded: we killed 15 of the Rebels and wounded 20. also took upward of 200 prisoners. Amongst which was the Governor, his Councel, and part of the Continental Colonels, Several Captains and Subalterns & 71 Continental soldiers out of a Church."[18]

At this point, when it would have been wise to gather up all the spoils and make haste back to friendly territory, discipline broke down and as a result the Loyalist army was unnecessarily detained at Hillsborough. Several of the men began breaking into the town's stores, and it was not long before a good supply of liquor was found. The spirits flowed freely, and soon the Tories were ranging up and down the streets of Hillsborough engaged in merrymaking.

Noon found the Loyalists still looking more like an unruly mob than an army. Fanning, however, decided that enough time had been wasted and began to restore order among his forces. The valuable prisoners were kept under the watchful eye of Captain John McLean, a Highlander who lived along Upper Little River in Cumberland County. He was one of the few present who did not drink and thus still had his wits about him. Because of his abstinence from strong drink, his comrades referred to him as "Sober John."

Fanning instructed the Scotsmen under Colonel McNeill to take the lead as the Loyalists marched out of town down the road leading back toward Woody's Ford on the Haw River. Fanning's men would follow, with the prisoners under the watchful eye of "Sober John" bringing up the rear.

9. Loyalist Highwater Mark

The Loyalist raiders camped near Mitchell Mountain in Orange County, after their raid on Hillsborough.

By the early part of the afternoon, the Loyalists had departed Hillsborough, leaving behind a number of their comrades who had become so drunk they could not make the march, or some who were enjoying the revelries so much that they refused to leave. Before the sun went down, these stragglers found themselves prisoners of the Whigs.[19]

As the Loyalists and their prisoners headed southwest out of town, the effects of the past days' exertions were evident on the men. They had been on the move constantly for nearly forty-eight hours, in which time they had covered over forty miles, partook of a largescale raid, and caroused for nearly six hours. They were in desperate need of rest.

Taking this into consideration, and perhaps not believing that his men were in a condition to attempt a night crossing of the Haw River, Fanning called a halt near Mitchell Mountain in southwestern Orange County. His force had covered eighteen miles since leaving town, and the stopping place was only a short ride from Woody's Ford. Located approximately a mile downstream from the modern town of Saxapahaw, this was once a popular crossing of the Haw, whose waters along this stretch are filled with many dangerous rapids which add to the challenge of safely wading across. This delay would prove to be costly.

Woody's Ford across the Haw River was about a mile downstream from this set of rapids at Saxapahaw, in Alamance County.

* * *

Several people who were in Hillsborough when the Loyalists descended upon the town were able to escape and spread the alarm. Among those was Col. Alexander Mebane, who took advantage of the woods and brush growing unkempt in the side streets of Hillsborough and made his way out of town. Clear of the Tory dragnet, Mebane headed on foot for his home in the Hawfields section. There he spread the news of what had happened and set about raising a force to liberate the captives, one of whom was his brother, John.[20]

Someone also managed to get word of the raid to General Butler, whose army was still in the vicinity of Ramsay's Mill. Upon hearing the news, Butler put his force in motion north, hoping to cut off the Loyalists' retreat before they could make it safely back into their settlements beyond the Deep River.

Butler was faced with a compelling question: where was Fanning headed? Clearly the Loyalists wanted to deposit their valuable prisoners with the British authorities down at Wilmington. To accomplish this, the Loyalists had three options. First, they could head west for Fanning's stronghold at Cox's Mill and from there send the prisoners with a lightly armed, swift escort the rest of the way. Second, they could make their way back into the Sandhills south of Deep River and head in a more roundabout way to Wilmington through friendly territory. Finally, the Tories could take the direct route to Wilmington via Chatham Court House, Cross Creek and Elizabethtown.

To account for all of these variables, Butler decided to make a stand at Lindley's Mill on Cane Creek, a rather large stream which in those days meandered along the Chatham/Orange border but is now in Alamance County. High ground near the ford of Cane Creek covered the route to the creek, while the strategic position placed his army at a vital road junction through which Fanning would have to pass regardless of how he intended to head to Wilmington.

Butler's only legitimate chance to liberate the prisoners was to beat Fanning to Lindley's Mill.

* * *

At the Loyalist camp near Mitchell Mountain, Col. Hector McNeill was having a restless night. Whether it was the strong drink or stress of the campaign, his sleep was now tormented by what he took to be a premonition of his own death in a coming battle. Like many of his fellow Highlanders, McNeill was superstitious and put great stock in such portents. He even shared the bad news with some of his fellow commanders sleeping nearby, including McDugald, who years later related details of this story to the Reverend Carruthers. McDugald attempted to cheer up Elder Hector by making light of the dream. His spirits were raised somewhat, but the old Scotsman, just to be safe, decided that morning to trade in his official British red coat for a hunting shirt so that he would not be so conspicuous if action did come.[21]

* * *

The Loyalists broke camp at dawn on the morning of September 13, 1781, and renewed their trek toward Fanning's stronghold at Cox's Mill. Early that morning they reached Woody's Ford, crossing the Haw River without incident. This must have been quite a relief to Fanning, for the crossing of the Haw placed his army in danger of being destroyed piecemeal while negotiating the river. The Whigs thus missed their best opportunity for capturing the Loyalist raiders and liberating the valuable prisoners. Although they were closer to more familiar haunts along the Deep River, Fanning knew there was much dangerous ground to cover between Woody's Ford and the British base at Wilmington.

Once on the west side of the Haw, the march resumed, with the Highlanders still leading the way. At approximately 9:30 a.m., Captain "Sober

John" McLean, who had personally been with the advance elements of the column instead of with his men guarding the prisoners, found Colonel Fanning and warned of a potentially disastrous oversight. Colonel McNeill had failed to put scouts out in advance of the column.

Realizing the gravity of the situation, Fanning rode forward to seek out Elder Hector and find the reason for the oversight. History is silent as to McNeill's reasons. Perhaps he was preoccupied with the visions of his coming doom. Fanning found him amongst his men on the road near the ford of Stafford's Branch,

Site of the Whig ambush of the Loyalists at Lindley's Mill. Cane Creek is visible to the right, while the plateau from where they launched the attack is on the left.

and asked the old Highlander for an explanation.[22] Before McNeill could respond, the sounds of gunfire erupted from the front of the column. The Highlanders had stumbled blindly into an ambush set by the Whigs.

General Butler had been successful in the race to the road junction at Lindley's Mill. The terrain where he placed his men was a natural site for an ambush. The road down which the Loyalists were travelling from Hillsborough was narrow and winding as it passed over rolling terrain on the north side of Cane Creek. As the road descended toward Cane Creek, it crossed Stafford's Branch and made a sharp turn to the right at the base of the hill as it intersected with another road which followed the north bank of Cane Creek. The road then headed west in the low grounds between the hill and the creek before coming to the crossing place at Thomas Lindley's Mill.[23]

As the first Highlanders crossed Stafford's Branch and rounded the bend at the base of the hill, Whigs who were concealed along the plateau open fire with murderous effect. Several of the Scotsmen fell, while those who were able found cover along the creek bank or in a declivity on the east side of Stafford's Branch.

After the initial shock, the Highlanders fought back, and made several attempts to dislodge the Whigs from the natural fortress, but none were successful. Finally, McNeill ordered his men to retreat back up the road to regroup. Major McDugald, who was standing near his commander, heard the order to withdraw and was outraged. He berated his commander for his lack of courage and chastised him for running from the scene of danger. These sharp words changed the old Scotsman's mind, and Colonel McNeill personally led a renewed charge of the positions atop the plateau.[24]

As the Highlanders rushed onward, the Whigs let loose another volley, making good McNeill's premonitions. Elder Hector fell to the ground dead, his body riddled by, as Fanning later recalled, "…8 balls through him and five through his horse."[25]

"The Colonel is dead!" someone exclaimed.

"It's a lie," yelled McDugald, knowing that the death of their trusted commander would have adverse effects on the morale of his men. He was right in his assumption, for years later Carruthers recorded that many of the Scotsmen confessed "…that had it been known at the time, they would not have fired another gun, but would have sought safety in any way they could."[26]

The Scottish commanders on the field were able to disengage their men from the fray with the Whigs on the plateau and effect an orderly retreat a short distance back up the Hillsborough Road, much as McNeill had wanted to do in the first place. A hasty conference ensued among the leaders of the Scots as to who would take command now that McNeill was dead. All agreed that his death had to be concealed until the crisis had passed, but all were equally averse to assuming command. Finally, someone nominated McDugald, who, like his comrades, was reluctant to take over for their dead leader. But the vote was unanimous in his favor, and the young major from Cumberland County was now in command of the Highlanders.[27]

Soon after the attack at Stafford's Branch began, Fanning realized the true danger to his scattered column. He quickly surmised that the assault, though initially quite deadly, was a diversion. His scouts reported that a large body of troops was in motion to strike at the prisoners at the rear of the column.

Once he had reported Colonel McNeill's negligence to Fanning, "Sober John" had quickly returned to his men and the prisoners who had been ordered to halt for a rest break. The prisoners were all sitting on the

The Spring Friends Meeting House, Alamance County, North Carolina.

ground when the first shots rang out at Stafford's Branch. They jumped to their feet, looking for their liberators, but McLean ordered them to sit down and be quiet, as he would kill anyone who tried to escape.[28]

As the roar of battle continued, McLean's men herded the prisoners into the Spring Friends Meeting House, which historian Algie Newlin points out stood at the time of the battle on the south side of the cemetery. They would be easier to keep an eye on in this building, and could be guarded by fewer men, freeing up some of McLean's troops to join the battle.[29] Meanwhile, Fanning ordered his troops, including the Scots under McDugald, to fall back to the vicinity of the church. He had correctly anticipated Butler's main intention of striking at this part of the Loyalist column in an effort to liberate the prisoners.

The details of the ensuing fight near the Spring Friends Meeting House are meager. Things must have looked bleak at this point, compelling McDugald to contemplate the drastic measures Carruthers recounted years later. "A few years ago, an old Quaker friend, who appeared to have been well informed on this subject, and whose powers, though he was then about fourscore, were unimpaired by age, told me that Col. McDugald, after he took command, came, under great excitement, and—to use his own language—'in a foam of sweat,' to the house in which the prisoners were then kept, and took an oath that if the Whigs did flank him, as they were trying to do, and drive him to extremities, he would put his prisoners all to death, before he would suffer them to be taken from him."[30] Because of his strong Whig bias, we have to take any of Carruthers' accounts of Loyalist atrocities with a proverbial grain of salt. However, given the fact that he was occasionally in direct contact with McDugald after the war, there may have been some truth to this particular episode. Fanning makes no mention of the events that transpired at the Spring Friends Meeting House or any decision to execute the prisoners in his *Narrative*.

Perhaps the Loyalist leaders remembered what had happened to their friend, Colonel Slingsby, earlier that summer at Elizabethtown when the Loyalists were overpowered by paroled Whig prisoners whom Fanning believed used concealed weapons to kill their guards in their sleep. Unlike Slingsby's prisoners, the captives from Hillsborough had yet to be paroled, so were free to take up arms at this point and attempt to liberate themselves without violating any code of honor. Regardless of how he came up with such a drastic step, McDugald shared the information about their fast-approaching execution with the prisoners. He also relayed word of what he planned to do to the Whig attackers as well. Seeing the Scotsman's sincerity, the stunned Whigs called off their attack and returned to their position on the plateau between Stafford's Branch and Lindley's Mill to contemplate their next move.[31]

The respite provided by the Whigs' withdrawal presented Fanning with time to implement a simple yet effective counterattack. Once more the Highlanders would head down the Hillsborough Road toward Lindley's Mill, only this time they would leave the road before crossing Stafford's Branch. Instead, they would strike overland for Cane Creek, and using the bank of that watercourse as cover to move into position opposite the Whigs' strong position on the southeast end of the plateau. With the Highlanders under McDugald thus engaged once again near the ford across Stafford's Branch, Fanning would take his men and strike at the rear of the Whigs' position directly across the plateau. This pincer movement would catch the Whigs between two forces and, he hoped, overwhelm them.[32]

The Loyalist counterattack was vigorous, and was very nearly a complete success. The attack caught the Whigs off guard, and a panic-stricken flight seemed imminent. As Carruthers noted, "...General Butler ordered a retreat, and commenced it himself. The men, in obedience to orders, were following his example, when Colonel Robert Mebane got before them, and by arguments and remonstrances, so far inspired them with his own heroic spirit that enough of them returned to renew the battle and keep the ground." Indeed, Mebane deserves credit for saving the Whigs from sure destruction by his bravery and coolness. "A more bold and deliberate act of courage is hardly on record than was done by Col. Robert Mebane in the hottest of the battle. In the midst of the conflict with Fanning, when the Whigs must have been nearly between two fires, as the Scotch were advancing up the hill, they got out of ammunition and Mebane walked slowly along the line, carrying his hat full of powder and telling every man to take a handful, or just what he needed. The day was warm ... and near the middle of the day, as the battle commenced about 10 o'clock, and by wiping the sweat off his face with his hands, after handling the powder, when he got thro', his face was nearly as black as the powder itself."[33]

At this climatic point in the struggle, when it looked as though the Whigs would be overwhelmed, fate intervened on their behalf. Colonel Fanning fell grievously wounded, a bullet striking him in the left arm, breaking the bone in several places and severing an artery. Fanning was hurriedly taken from his horse and led to the rear to have his wounds cared for.[34]

Command of Fanning's counterattack now devolved on Captain Rains, but with the loss of their leader, the Chatham and Randolph militia lost much of their spirit to press the fight. A lull ensued, and soon both sides disengaged from the struggle and allowed their opponent to move away—the Whigs moving up the road toward Alamance Creek and the Loyalists heading to the crossing over Cane Creek at Lindley's Mill. As the final elements of the Loyalists crossed the creek, a few Whigs fired some parting shots from the wooded hills overlooking the ford.

The victory proved a costly one for the King's forces. Over four hours, each side had more than a hundred men killed and wounded, making this the most deadly battle of the Tory War, and one of the most deadly episodes in the state's history before the carnage unleashed by the War Between the States in the 1860s. Many of the casualties were officers in their respective armies. The most critical losses of command were obviously with the Loyalists, with Colonel Elder Hector McNeill dead and Colonel Fanning nearly so.

10

The Dash to Wilmington

McDugald now found himself in command and vested with the responsibility of transporting their valuable prisoners to Major Craig at Wilmington. Common sense would tell him that Whig forces would probably try another attempt to liberate these valuable prisoners. Complicating the matter further was the fact that his strike force was now encumbered with wounded and prisoners, several of whom were without horses.

To reduce the risk of attack, McDugald chose not to take the direct route to Wilmington through Cross Creek, as his line of march would take his depleted force dangerously close to Whig territory east of the Cape Fear. Nor did he make the detour to where they started at Cox's Mill, familiar territory to Fanning and his command, but not to the Highlanders. McDugald chose to take his force south to McPhaul's Mill via Connor Dowd's, through the familiar haunts of the Sandhills beyond Deep River in what is today Moore, Lee and Hoke counties, a region whose inhabitants were clearly sympathetic to the British cause. In addition, many of the wounded could be dropped off along the way at their respective homes.

To get there, though, McDugald's column had to cross Chatham County, a region divided in its sympathies and, since the raid on Hillsborough, swarming with Whigs. Speed was of the essence, so the Loyalists quickly moved out after the battle, and were near Hickory Mountain in western Chatham County when they stopped to make camp on the night of September 13, 1781.

Next morning, between Hickory Mountain and the ford across Rocky River, a small party of Whigs interrupted the Loyalists' march. The Whigs' numbers were small, "…a dozen or twenty in number…" Carruthers wrote, and were more a nuisance than a threat. The Loyalists quickly brushed them aside and continued their march southward.[1]

As their march continued on past Bear Creek toward Dowd's Ferry on Deep River, someone decided that the trek would go much faster if the prisoners were all mounted. "Sober John" McLean rode up to the governor, dismounted and offered his horse. "I am your prisoner, sir, and must

Brown Marsh Presbyterian Church, in Bladen County, North Carolina.

expect to fare as a prisoner," Burke replied. Whether this was true humility or an attempt to impede the group's progress is uncertain, but McLean insisted and soon Governor Burke was riding along at a much brisker pace toward Deep River. Not long afterwards, "Sober John" acquired another mount and was able to ride instead of jogging along with those in his custody.[2]

Soon, the Loyalists were at the Irishman Connor Dowd's on Deep River. Dowd ran quite a mercantile operation, with a tavern, mills, stores and a tannery surrounding this crossing along the Deep River. Establishing his businesses during the 1760s, Dowd operated both gristmill and lumber cutting services, and it was probably his planing mill where the Scotsman MacFadyen was able to obtain the finished lumber used at the House in the Horseshoe. By the time hostilities broke out, he was one of the most prosperous merchants in this part of the province.

Dowd suffered dearly for his support of the British government. He was an ardent support of the King throughout the war, a fact that sometimes brought him into conflict with his Whig neighbors such as Alston, who hauled Dowd into court in Cross Creek for refusing to sign a Loyalty oath to the Whig government in April of 1778. No doubt it was the importance of the mills and other infrastructure important to people on both sides which kept many of his more virulent antagonists at bay, despite his extensive and long-term commissary efforts for the Crown. He gathered supplies for the Loyalist army under MacDonald which met disaster at the Battle of Moore's Creek in 1776. So far, no record has come forward showing that he provided supplies for the Loyalist forces destroyed at Ramseur's Mill in June of 1780. But, in the spring of 1781, as the British army marched through the area following the Battle of Guilford Courthouse, he gathered a company of fifty horsemen to join Cornwallis when that officer returned as promised from Wilmington to Hillsborough. But Dowd, like many of his Loyalist neighbors was undermined by the British high command which sent his Lordship north on his quixotic march into Virginia.

Despite being let down yet again, Dowd continued his support for the cause, placing his eldest son, Owen, in command of the company of the horsemen Connor had raised for Cornwallis. Later that summer, the elder Dowd even outfitted and supplied the forces which Fanning used for the raid on Hillsborough. Now the Loyalist army was there, but instead of being able to celebrate such a crushing victory over the Whigs, they brought sad news for Connor Dowd—Captain Owen Dowd was dead, having fallen during the Battle at Lindley's Mill.[3] Details of the younger Dowd's death have not been preserved, but his body rests in what at the time was the family cemetery near his father's mill.

The raiders stayed only long enough to replenish their supplies and deposit some of the wounded. They crossed Deep River into what was relatively safe territory,

Connor Dowd lost much due to his support of the Royal cause, including his son, Captain Owen Dowd, killed at the Battle of Lindley's Mill.

and spent the night near the home of a family named McRae, probably the home of Gilbert McRae.[4] That evening at the McRae home occurred an unusual event, preserved by Carruthers, which shows what length the Highlanders went to keep Governor Burke comfortable. The incident was related to Carruthers by Collin McRae, an eyewitness. "My father lived on Deep River. My mother's maiden name was Burke. When the Governor of that name was taken prisoner at Hillsboro,' by Fanning and his company, they stopped at our house all night on their way to Wilmington. The Governor was put into an additional apartment, at the end of the house, and there closely quartered. Our bag of meal was seized and cooked immediately; and having been previously robbed, my mother had no bed clothes, except one cotton sheet, which was carefully wrapped round my infant brother, John, by my mother's side. One of the company seized hold of one corner of this sheet and continued to jerk and shake it until the infant rolled out on the floor. By way of retaliation, my mother made some attempts before day to let her namesake, the Governor, escape, but without success."[5] Had this upset mother been successful in her clandestine efforts to help Governor Burke escape, she would have accomplished out of spite what Butler and his entire army of Whigs never managed to pull off.

Leaving McRae's, McDugald continued his march south, heading along what was known as the Connor Road across present Lee County. They took this road to the Pee Dee Road, then headed south by the Loyalist muster ground at the Dry Fork of Little Crain Creek, south through the Sandhills toward the Loyalist stronghold at McPhaul's Mill. These high, sandy hills were in those days covered with a forest of longleaf pines and were sparsely settled, most of the inhabitants being Scottish Highlanders. Most outsiders, if given an option, avoided travel through the region. Governor Burke was later to refer to this section through which they passed as "...vast pathless tracks of intermingled Sand and Swamp very thinly inhabited and which ought not to be inhabited at all."[6] Years later, as modes of transportation improved, providing access to the region, people learned that these forests were a source where tar, pitch, turpentine and lumber could be extracted and sent to market on plank roads or later railroads, providing a source of income which Governor Burke could never have imagined. Upon their arrival at McPhaul's Mill, Colonel McDugald and his tired troopers were met by Colonel Ray of the Cumberland militia who had a body of troops to escort the prisoners the rest of the way to Wilmington. Since speed was of the utmost concern, Ray picked a small body of his swiftest horsemen for the job. Accompanying the fleet band was McDugald and at least one contingent of Fanning's men from Orange County under Captain Stephen Holloway.

Meanwhile, down at Wilmington, Major Craig began to receive vague information about the capture of the Whig governor, the pursuit of General Butler and the engagement at Lindley's Mill. In an effort to lend support, he left with a detachment from his garrison and headed up the King's Highway toward Cross Creek along what he correctly guessed would be their route to Wilmington. On September 23, 1781, they met the Loyalists and their valuable prisoners at Livingston Creek. Craig claims that this junction was made "...without any previous communication with them, as I only guessed at their route from my knowledge of their usual mode of conducting themselves."[7]

This was a fortuitous meeting as far as the Loyalists were concerned, for they were being hotly pursued down the King's Highway in lower Bladen County by a body of horsemen which up until then was thought to be a body of Whig partisans under Colonel Thomas Brown. Fifty Whig horsemen appeared at Livingston Creek bridge within four hours of Ray and McDugald. Major Craig ordered out some of his cavalry supported by sixty infantrymen to disperse them. This small group of British drove the Whigs back up the road about three miles before making a discovery which halted their advance—a body of troops nearly two hundred strong had taken up a defensive position to meet the British attack.[8] The British quickly regrouped, then drove forward again. The Whig lines held briefly before they turned and retreated toward Elizabethtown. At this point, with orders not to venture off too far, the British detachment returned to rejoin Major Craig.

Soon thereafter, it became clear to Major Craig and his compatriots that the force they had engaged was not Colonel Brown's Bladen militia roving the countryside. Instead, it was General Butler and advance elements of his whole army—nearly five hundred strong—who had been in hot pursuit of the Highlanders and Governor Burke. "Indeed his march was so rapid that I could not conceive it to be him, & I must confess that error prevented our destroying his corps completely, for he as little expected to see us as I did him."[9]

Their valuable prisoners in tow, the British headed back to Wilmington. Fanning later summed up the action by pointing out, with a slight touch of ironic humor, that they, "introduced Thomas Burk then Governor and his Regiment of Rebels to Major Craig who very well accepted them and Major Craig introduced his Excellency and Regiment to the provo Master."[10]

Major Craig later wrote a glowing report to his superiors concerning the Loyalists' efforts to deliver Burke to Wilmington. "A Col. Ray, who met them at the Raft Swamp & Col. McDougal who jointly managed rather than commanded them from thence have also very high merit. The latter distinguished himself much in the action with Butler. The route they came from Hillsborough here is upwards of two hundred & thirty miles, thro' a country which it scarce possible to have an idea of without seeing it. Their difficulties from every circumstance of want of provisions, fatigue & the danger of being intercepted, were such as require great resolution to contend with."[11]

The Loyalists stayed in Wilmington about three days before departing for McPhaul's Mill. Both Ray and McDugald knew the march home would be a dangerous one. Word had reached the British garrison that General Butler and his Whig army had not returned home to the central part of the province, but instead were lurking about Brown Marsh in Bladen County waiting to intercept the Loyalists on their way home. Though Butler left no account of the action nor any details about the planning behind this particular operation, we can assume that he was hoping to ambush McDugald, Ray and the other Loyalist raiders as they were strung out along a causeway/bridge that crossed through the boggy cypress swamp of Brown Marsh. Butler's little army had been augmented by elements of the local Whig militia units from Bladen and Duplin counties. In light of this information, Craig dispatched Major Daniel Manson and a hundred and eighty British Regulars of the Royal North Carolina Regiment from Wilmington to accompany the Loyalist militia as far as Brown Marsh. Though he had spent several years in South Carolina working as a shipbuilder before the war broke out, Manson was a native of Scotland and a good choice to coordinate the activities with his fellow Scots. McDugald or Ray would have suspected that the Whigs were likely camped at Baldwin's Old Field, a bit of high ground on the edge of Brown Marsh often used as a gathering point for the local Whig militia to drill. The Whigs could just as easily have been using the higher ground near where the Presbyterian congregation met a few miles north of the bridge. Scouts soon ascertained Butler's exact location (somewhere in the vicinity of modern Clarkton) and reported back to the British. Based on this fresh intelligence, Manson decided to attack the unsuspecting Whigs before they discovered that the Loyalists had been reinforced.

The British rode through the night across a region of swamps and forests which required expert guides. When near Butler's encampment, Manson divided his army into three separate wings: the British regulars from the Royal North Carolina Regiment, the Highlanders with the Anson County Loyalist Militia and Fanning's Loyalist militia contingent from Randolph and Chatham counties under Captain Holloway. Each was to have a guide thoroughly familiar with the terrain to lead the respective unit into position for an attack upon the camp.

The guides on this occasion did not prove to be up to the task, and soon the Loyalists were lost, flailing about through the nearly impenetrable

10. The Dash to Wilmington

Strong evidence supports the Red Hill community in northern Columbus County to be the site where the Loyalists routed the Whigs during the Battle of Brown Marsh.

undergrowth of Brown Marsh. Despite this major setback, Manson and Holloway were able to extricate their men from the swamp and bring them into position for the attack. The Highlanders, however, were conspicuously absent. The time spent groping about in the swamp alerted Butler's men to the presence of the British, and the Whigs hastily began taking up a defensive position awaiting the enemy's arrival. Undeterred by the loss of the element of surprise and the absence of a critical part of his strike force, Major Manson ordered an attack in the predawn blackness, and soon thereafter the Loyalist forces commenced their assault.[12]

Consternation reigned in the Whig camp. From various "traditionary accounts" Carruthers was able to piece together what happened next. "This was quite a spirited affair but was soon over. General Butler ordered a retreat after the first fire, under a mistaken apprehension that the enemy had artillery, of which he was destitute. Colonel Robert Mebane and Colonel Thomas Owen, however, attempted to keep up some semblance of defense and managed to persuade a few of their comrades to make a stand. The two colonels made quite a manly resistance for a while, but were overpowered."[13] This desperate and heroic stand by Mebane and Owen likely averted the total annihilation of Butler's army, especially the part made up of the militia units from the central part of the state, for whom the surroundings of the swampy lowlands of southeastern North Carolina were quite alien to their more familiar woods in the Piedmont.

We are fortunate that in lieu of any official Whig report of this battle, one participant—Captain James Shipman of the Bladen Militia—penned an account of the fighting here at Brown Marsh as part of his pension application before the Bladen County Court of Pleas & Quarter Sessions meeting at Elizabethtown on February 4, 1833. Shipman recalled, "General Butler, after marching his forces to Baldwin's Old Field on the Brown Marsh, was there attacked by the British and Tories under Major Manson. The backcountry men fled immediately. The Bladen Militia under Col. Owens, & the Sampson Militia under Capt. [David] Dodd, stood their ground until their ammunition was expended. A man by the name of Sigourrer, a brave soldier belonging to the Bladen Militia was killed; a lad by the name of Stephens belonging to his (Shipman's) Company, was also killed by his side. One or two of Capt. Dodd's Company was also killed & wounded. The Back Country Militia lost a great many of their horses."[14]

In less than an hour, the Battle of Brown Marsh was over. The British had routed the Whigs and were now in possession of their camp, while what was left of the Whigs were beating a hasty retreat north, General Butler leading the way. The victory had cost the Loyalists two killed and five wounded. The two dead were members of Fanning's command, and included their leader, Captain Holloway.

Since there are no official Whig accounts of their defeat, only an approximation of the total casualties can be made. Major Manson reported to Craig that "The Rebels were completely dispers'd, leaving twenty dead & five & twenty prisoners. They had also a number of wounded who in the darkness of the night got off. We took between 30 & 40 horses but the militia the next day got upwards of a hundred more who were running loose in the woods."[15] Manson's mention of the large number of horses captured in his official report to Major Craig penned shortly after the fight jibes with the Whig Shipman's account penned over five decades later in which Capt. Shipman recalls, "The Back Country militia lost a great many of their horses."[16]

Next day, the King's supporters went their separate ways—the Loyalists returned to McPhaul's Mill while Major Manson and the British regulars returned to Wilmington. Their victory in the night battle fought in Brown Marsh had been a great one—Butler lost nearly a third of his men. The outcome could have been even more catastrophic for the Whigs had the Highlanders been in position. Some might suggest that Ray's Anson County militia were not just groping about in the predawn darkness lost in the well-nigh impenetrable swamp, but like McNeill at Beatti's Bridge, they had kinsmen on the Whig side that they were reluctant to see killed. To be fair, night battles were rarely fought during the eighteenth century, and coordinating troop movements was difficult under the best of conditions. To gain the element of surprise, the King's forces at Brown Marsh were both blind and, in one sense deaf, as they could not rely on the shouted orders, drums or whistles upon which they were accustomed to maneuver. Thus, Manson's strike force won their stunning victory under the most trying of circumstances.

* * *

As McDugald and his band were making their dash for Wilmington, Fanning was in bad shape, hidden in the woods and guarded by three men. He lost a great deal of blood from the wound in his arm, and this left him weak and immobile.[17] To make matters worse, a Whig patrol under Captain William O'Neal, the same O'Neal who had refused Fanning's offer to fight a battle at Cox's Mill back in August, had been dispatched by General Butler three days after the Battle of Lindley's Mill to search for the wounded Fanning. O'Neal and his men scoured the countryside, but were unsuccessful in their search.[18]

On September 17, Fanning and his companions were joined by seventeen men who had split from McDugald at Connor Dowd's and returned to see to their commander's safety. They carefully moved their wounded leader from his hiding place along Cane Creek to a safer locale on Big Brush Creek, not far from the Loyalists' stronghold at Cox's Mill. There Fanning went through the long process of rest and recuperation. There were no transfusions in those days, so the body had to replace the lost blood on its own, which was a slow process.[19]

The wounding of Fanning was a tragic blow to the Loyalists' cause during their finest hour. His loss meant the Loyalists were deprived of their most daring, cunning and resourceful leader during one of the most critical times of the Tory War. Fanning's absence over the next few weeks would be keenly felt, and would prove to be a far more lethal blow to the Loyalists than the loss of Governor Burke was to the Whigs.

11

The Fall of Wilmington

As Fanning lay in bed recuperating from the wound he had received at Lindley's Mill, events well beyond his control were coming together to undo his hard-earned victories. To the north in Virginia, Cornwallis had been outmaneuvered and was penned down at Yorktown, but to the south and west lay the more immediate threat. A large host had gathered whose goal was to crush the Tories and drive Major Craig and the British garrison from Wilmington. This was the second prong of Governor Burke's planned offensive whereby he hoped to utilize the large militia force in western Carolina to drive through the Loyalist strongholds between the Cape Fear and Pee Dee Rivers from the west, in conjunction with Butler's strike from the east. From there they would head on to Wilmington and take on Major Craig.

To command this force from the west, Burke chose General Griffith Rutherford, a man who had worked fanatically to further the Revolutionary cause. In the legislature, he was the author of such legislation as the Confiscation Act, and on the battlefields in the western part of the Carolinas he was ever active, and is perhaps best known for his role in the expedition which effectively crushed the Cherokee. His activities were stymied upon being captured at the Battle of Camden when Gates' army was crushed in August of 1780. From there he was taken first to Charles Town, then put on a prison ship and sent to St. Augustine, where he remained until exchanged in the summer of 1781.

An experience as a prisoner of war mellows some individuals, but not men like Griffith Rutherford. His stay aboard the British prison ship added fire to his hatred of the enemies of the Revolution. In August, Rutherford received word to embody the Whig militia of the western part of North Carolina. He in turn sent out a call to the various militia commanders to rendezvous at "the plantation of a Mr. Robinson" on Little River in Montgomery County on September 15, 1781.[1]

When the appointed day came, a large force gathered along Little River—nine hundred and fifty infantry and two hundred cavalry. Most of them were raw recruits in need of training. To accomplish this, Rutherford spent two weeks teaching his army the rudiments of military skills. He was fortunate to have many veterans of his previous campaigns like William Graham and Joseph Graham on hand.

On October 1, 1781, General Rutherford and his army headed east out of the Uwharries, toward the Sandhills and Cross Creek. "After crossing Drowning Creek a few miles, the army turned right, aiming to keep between the heads of the waters which run into Waccamaw on the right and Rockfish and Cape Fear on the left," Graham later recalled.[2]

Meanwhile, the Loyalists were attempting to regroup follow-

The grave of Colonel Archibald McDugald, beside Cameron's Hill Presbyterian Church in Harnett County, North Carolina. Exiled after the war, McDugald returned home disillusioned from Nova Scotia. His Moore County neighbors turned a blind eye to the former Loyalist officer living in their midst.

ing their exertions to capture Governor Burke, the Battle of Lindley's Mill and the ensuing dash to Wilmington. Several of the commands had dispersed and their men returned to their homes to rest. They also had to contend with the problem of operating under new leadership—"Elder" Hector McNeill being dead and Colonel Fanning still suffering from his wounds, bedridden at his hideout on Brush Creek nearly four weeks following the battle.

Colonel McDugald commanded temporarily, long enough to see the valuable prisoners safely transported to Wilmington and deposited with Major Craig. But in an effort to keep the morale of the Scots high, another Hector McNeill was given command. Their reasoning was that many of the Scots would not know that he was not the same person as their trusted leader, the other Hector McNeill, and it was hoped this would conceal the death from them. McDugald, however, continued to act as the defacto leader of the Scots.

On October 15, 1781, the combined Loyalist forces in the vicinity of McPhaul's Mill were resting in a camp along Raft Swamp. Estimates place their strength at between three hundred and six hundred men. Rutherford, encamped at Monroe's Bridge on Drowning Creek, received word of this encampment and sent Major Graham forward with the dragoons to overtake them, while the main body of Rutherford's army followed behind. Rutherford had been joined by the remnants of Butler's army, which gave him a force of nearly 1,500 men.

Scouts quickly brought word of this advance back to the Tory encampment, and the leaders present—Elrod, Ray and McNeill—decided that the best thing to do was to fall back and not take on such a large force unless absolutely necessary or if a strategic advantage too good to be passed up presented itself. McDugald, who had been away visiting a friend who lived nearby, returned and agreed with their assessment and plan of action.[3]

The Loyalists found a strategic advantage at a place near the modern town of Red Springs on the Lowery Road overlooking where a causeway emerged from Little Raft Swamp, but before their full dispositions could be made they were surprised by Major Graham and the dragoons. "The enemy broke and fled as fast as they could"; wrote Graham, "but the stout horses and expert riders of the west soon overtook them; and when they came in contact with the sand-hill ponies, went through, trod down, and turned over horses and riders. After their first fire, the enemy thought of no further resistance, but endeavored to make their escape, and aimed for a branch of Raft Swamp in their front, over which there was a causeway two hundred yards wide. Our troops entered the causeway with them, using sabre against all they could reach. As soon as it was felt, the Tories would throw themselves off each side into the ditch, quitting their horses and making off in the swamp; the dragoons near the front fired their pistols at them in their retreat. By the time the Whigs got half way through, the causeway was crowded with dismounted ponies for twenty steps before them, so that it was impossible to pass. Two or three stout men dismounted, and commenced pushing them over into the ditch, out of the way. When it was a little cleared, the dragoons rushed over; the front troop, now scattered, pursued the Tories in all directions."[4]

This sudden advance sent most of the Loyalists into a flight for safety back up the Lowery Road toward the causeway across Raft Swamp. Some (about thirty-five or so) tried to hold the line that had been hastily established on a rise of ground, but were overrun by Major Graham's horsemen, who shot several individuals in the act of surrendering. As the Loyalists headed up the road, their escape was delayed by the narrow causeway across Raft Swamp. Such a tight packed group of fugitives made easy targets for the pursuing Whigs. Fortunately for the Loyalists, their leaders realized it as well, and organized a rear-guard to buy time for their troops. A desperate hand-to-hand fight ensued, and most of the Loyalists managed to escape to the east side of Raft Swamp.[5]

Graham continues his account of the battle. "They gave a general fire, and their guns being empty, was the signal for the dragoons to charge them at full speed. They fled, and in half a mile entered a causeway which leads across the main Raft Swamp. Our front entered it with them, and here again the same scene was acted as at the last causeway. As soon as one of our men would reach forward and strike a Tory with the point of the sabre, the rider would tumble into the ditch and make off through the mud, leaving his horse in the way; the pistols in front were fired at them as before. The causeway was long, and some breaches in it increased the difficulty of reaching them. The mounted infantry, with Colonel Owen, was ordered to dismount and come forward; but our cavalry and Tory ponies swarming in the broken causeway, so impeded their advance that it was getting too dark to see to shoot by the time they reached the front. As the enemy were much scattered and completely beaten, it was thought inexpedient to pursue the victory farther. The men were collected by the sound of the trumpet, at the west side of the swamp, and marched back to where General Rutherford had encamped, near McFall's Mill, where they arrived about 10 o'clock at night."[6]

Amidst this chaos and panic there were several incidents of Loyalist bravery. "It was at this stage of the fight, so relates Ex-Sheriff Red MacMillan of Hoke County, that little David Bethune (ancestor of Hon. Lauchlin Bethune), leaned against a pine out of harm's way and began playing on his bagpipe 'The Campbells Are Coming,'" wrote Governor Angus McLean. "This encouraged the Tories so much that they extricated themselves from the surging crowd of Whigs and succeeded in assembling across the swamp in an old field near where the little piper had begun his tune."[7]

Here the Loyalists obtained a brief respite, and used the time to take stock of the situation. Tired, they had managed to extract themselves from possible annihilation in Raft Swamp, but soon General Rutherford would be along with the main body of troops. The best thing to do was to disperse, let Rutherford and his men raid and pass on, then reassemble on another—safer—day in the future. It was a tried-and-true tactic which, as stated earlier, was particularly effective against armies composed primarily of militia troops called up for short periods of time.

Thus ended the Battle of Raft Swamp. Estimates of respective losses vary considerably. This would turn out to be the last battle or skirmish fought between the Whigs and Tories in the Lumber River region, leading some to place more importance on the fight than is actually due. Some have even gone so far as to hypothesize that this was a crushing defeat which broke the power of the Loyalists in North Carolina. As will be seen, this was hardly the case, and other events developing in Virginia were far more important to the war than this running skirmish across Raft Swamp.

Major Craig commented on how the Highlanders would deal with the current invasion. "I believe him [Rutherford] to have about 1000 or 1200. They are on the other side the N.W. & their only view is to subdue the tories & distress them they will, but as they are admirably expert at swamping, they will catch but very few I hope."[8]

Rutherford spared no efforts in his attempt to ferret the Highlanders out of their lair along Raft Swamp. "Early next morning," Graham wrote, "General Rutherford had the field officers convened at his quarters, and explained his views to them; that an attempt must be made to rout the Tories out of their swamps and hiding places; otherwise they would be as troublesome to us, as General Marion had been to the British in the like situation, and that we should try driving the Raft Swamp on that day." So the Whig army fanned out across the Raft Swamp and marched from one end of it to the other. The only thing they spooked out of the brush, though, was a herd of cows. The Loyalists had long since departed.[9]

From Raft Swamp Rutherford marched his men to Brown Marsh, where they camped near the scene of Butler's embarrassing defeat. There he rested and reviewed his troops, hoping, no doubt, to demonstrate to the populace that despite the drubbing the Whigs had taken earlier at this spot, they were still a force to be reckoned with. Even acting Governor Martin came down to the encampment to make a speech and confer with Rutherford. The psychological effect of having the highest-ranking member of the Whig government in North Carolina making an appearance so deep in Loyalist country was worth the risks. Fanning's absence from the field since Lindley's Mill in September no doubt weighed heavily in the decision to put their chief executive in such a risky situation.

After spending several days at Brown Marsh, Rutherford divided his army, sending Colonel Robert Smith with about three hundred mounted men down the west side of the river along the road to Wilmington. The General took the remainder of the men and crossed the Cape Fear at Waddell's Ferry, near the mouth of Brown's Creek south of Elizabethtown, crossed South River and proceeded down the Negro Head Road to attack the British at Wilmington from the north.[10] A siege ensued, which witnessed several minor engagements, but no decisive action.

11. The Fall of Wilmington

* * *

Fanning was laid low for twenty-four days by the wounds he had received at Lindley's Mill. In the first week of October 1781, he reports finally being "able to set up" and soon thereafter sent four of his most trusted followers—captains Hooker, Rains, Knight and Lindley, off to the British garrison at Wilmington for much needed supplies.

While they were gone on their errand, the enterprising Fanning assembled a hundred and forty followers and set out on a raid in which he seized a large quantity of leather meant for the Continental Army in South Carolina. The Loyalists used what they could, then destroyed the rest.

The exertions of this minor expedition left the Loyalist leader exhausted, as he was still much weakened from his wounds, but there was little opportunity to rest on this occasion. Less than an hour after he and his band returned to their hideout on Brush Creek, frightened scouts reported back to camp with the unbelievable tale that no fewer than six hundred Whigs were bearing down on their position. Fanning discounted this estimate, and events later proved that he was correct, as only a hundred and seventy were actually present. But the news, coupled with the current state of their leader's health, led many of the Loyalists to flee before the action began.[11] With his remaining men Fanning formed two opposite facing lines and led the hour-long contest despite the fact that he was so weak he could not even mount his horse unassisted. The first onslaught of the Whigs was repulsed after an hour's worth of fighting which saw three Loyalists killed and three wounded. The Whigs lost one dead and "several wounded."

After retreating a mile, the Whigs regrouped and prepared for another attack. Realizing that this probably meant the Whigs had been reinforced, Fanning ordered his men, already outnumbered and low on ammunition, to stealthily withdraw and break up into small parties before the attack commenced.[12]

The Loyalists moved about in small parties in the wilds of the Uwharries until the middle of October when the four aforementioned captains returned from Wilmington with medical supplies and "5000 Cartridges." These men also brought Fanning a couple of interesting letters. One from Major Craig contained congratulatory remarks for Fanning and his men, "for their Gallantry and good behavior." It also contained the news that Fanning's second in command and good friend, John Rains, had been promoted to the rank of major. Rains was a loyal and faithful comrade to Fanning, joining him early in his operations in North Carolina. He even cared for his wounded friend and leader in the Rains home in western Chatham County along Brush Creek.[13]

The most curious piece of correspondence which Fanning received came from Edmund Fanning, notorious for the part he played in the War of the Regulation in North Carolina and his support of Governor Tryon. Edmund was apparently trying to associate himself with David as the latter's fame grew thanks to the capture of Governor Burke. But the hollowness of claims at familiarity were made plain by Edmund's reference to the Loyalist partisan's father, dead since 1754.[14]

As soon as the siege at Wilmington began, Craig sent a number of dispatches to Colonel Fanning but was doubtful that any made it through. On October 22, 1781, he wrote in a report to Balfour, "Fanning who for spirit & activity is the best among them is recovering & has collected again about three hundred men. I have sent to him to take the opportunity of Rutherford being down here to lay waste the counties from whence his men come which will dissipate his Army in a moment. I am only afraid of his not getting my messages as our communication is exceedingly difficult, however I trust a good deal in his good sense which tho' plain is not deficient in point of thought."[15]

Thus Fanning remained active in central North Carolina, hoping to draw off Rutherford or a portion of his force from Wilmington. Fanning mainly disrupted the Whigs' lines of communications, raided their supplies and picked off random patrols. In early November, the Loyalists intercepted a dispatch sent from Virginia to General Greene in South Carolina. The letter bore ominous news for the King's forces—Cornwallis had surrendered his army at Yorktown.

* * *

Down at Wilmington, the momentous news arrived in Rutherford's camp overlooking the approach to the bridge over the Northeast Cape Fear on November 17, 1781. Colonel Light Horse Harry Lee, riding south out of Virginia, brought the news that Cornwallis had given up at Yorktown on October 19. Excitement and celebration erupted in the Whig lines, and a "feu de joie" was fired from all the rifles in Rutherford's little army.

That very day, more news arrived. Major Craig and the British garrison were evacuating Wilmington. This last bit of news brought the celebrations to a premature halt, and Rutherford ordered his forces across the Northeast Cape Fear. They met no resistance, and encamped that night within four miles of town. The next morning before Rutherford could move up to attack, the British were aboard ships and headed for the mouth of the Cape Fear and the Atlantic. Thus did Major Craig's well-orchestrated operations in North Carolina come to a close.

General Rutherford's men entered Wilmington close on the heels of the British, and acted very little the part of liberators. As the historian Samuel Ashe noted, "But the distresses of the people of Wilmington were not quite over. They had grave complaints to make of the spoilation of their property at the hands of Rutherford's militia, who appear to have regarded that the town had been captured and was subject to plunder. The depredations were inexcusable."[16]

12

Abandoned in North Carolina

Though most of Rutherford's men from western Carolina absconded with whatever they could get from the inhabitants of Wilmington, the most popular item to take home was salt, an important and scarce commodity on the frontier during the Revolutionary War. Loaded down with their pilfered goods and a bag or so of salt, the Whigs headed home, not en masse, but in random bodies. The route home for many of these victorious Whigs led them right into the clutches of Colonel Fanning and his Loyalist partisans who during the final two weeks of November 1781 kept busy capturing these men. Fanning noted, "for the space of 14 or 15 days I fell in with and took more or less of them every day...."[1]

One of the most exciting of these captures was a party under the command of Captain Thomas Kennedy of Burke County who was headed home with "a number of horses and a quantity of household furniture." After a running fight, Kennedy and eight men were captured, along with the group's plunder. Kennedy must have been quite apprehensive of having fallen into the clutches of the notorious Fanning, for he soon told the Loyalists that his comrade, Captain John Lopp of Rowan County, was not far behind at the head of sixty men. He further agreed that, in exchange for the lives of his men, neither he nor his men would interfere if Fanning decided to ambush Lopp's party. Fanning agreed, locked Kennedy and ten captives in a nearby house, placed two men to guard them, then headed off to set up his ambush.

With two men left to guard Kennedy, Fanning was left with thirteen men to take on about sixty, but he proceeded with his ambush despite the disparity in numbers. Fanning recounted the incident. "I mounted my men and placed them in Concealment along the Road and on their coming up I ordered them to fire and then for to charge, which we did three times through them—they immediately dispersed through the woods and it being nearly dark we could not tell what Injury they had suffered."[2] As promised, Kennedy kept his men quiet and under control as agreed. So well did he live up to his end of the bargain that Colonel Fanning paroled them all.

12. Abandoned in North Carolina

Balfour Cemetery, off the end of the runway at Asheboro Regional Airport near Asheboro, North Carolina.

Just as the successful activities of the previous spring had drawn large numbers of Whig troops into the area, the successful attacks against Rutherford's troops also had severe repercussions. By December 10, 1781, Colonel Elijah Isaacs, a virulent Whig from Burke County who, like Rutherford, had been captured at Camden and sent off to prison at St. Augustine, came into the Deep River settlement at the head of three hundred men. He made his headquarters at Fanning's base at Cox's Mill, and from there, "Ravaged the whole settlement and distroyed a number of houses belonging to the friends of Government."[3]

One of Fanning's supporters who had the misfortune of being taken prisoner by Isaacs' men was David Jackson of Guilford County, a man who had been an outspoken Loyalist early in the war. He served as a captain under Colonel Pyle, was captured after Moore's Creek and later escaped from the Halifax Gaol with Pyle and a few other men. Once back in the Deep River country, Jackson spent the summer of 1776 trying to rally resistance to the Whigs. Several acts of violence were perpetrated against the Whigs in the region, and Jackson was a prime suspect. Shortly after a bounty of £100 was placed on his head in November of 1776, he was captured by Thomas Jenkins and carted off to Halifax. Jackson's life was spared, and he returned to his home and remained at peace. There is no mention of his activities before Isaacs descended upon the neighborhood. He was apparently hanged because of his activities earlier in the war.[4]

Fanning did not try to give battle to the much larger force. Instead, he shifted his operations to the south and southeast out of harm's way. The loss of his supply base at Wilmington greatly hindered his ability to assemble and equip a large enough force to deal with Isaacs, so he operated with small bands by raiding the homes of the Whig leadership and their outposts on the outside of Isaacs' grasps.

One of these raids took place at the home of Captain John Cox. Fanning hit this farm when no one was home, so he and his men did a thorough job of destroying the place. Their work of destruction finished, the Loyalists went on to the home of Cox's father, Robert, who lived in the forks of Big Juniper Creek and McLendon's Creek, just west of the present town of Carthage. John Cox, Robert Lowe and William Jackson were at the elder Cox's house and heard the Loyalists approaching. They escaped before anyone knew they were there. Finding no one home, Fanning put the place to the torch.

Curiosity got the better of the three Whig fugitives, and they soon returned to witness the destruction from what they hoped was a secret vantage point. They were discovered by a Loyalist scout, who reported their presence to Fanning. The Colonel ordered his men to seize them. The Whigs split up and fled with the Loyalists in hot pursuit. John Cox got away, but his friends were not so lucky. Jackson was killed by Fanning near Juniper Creek. Lowe was wounded by Captain Stephen Walker and brought back to the ruins of Robert Cox's farm. Lowe had been a member of Fanning's band before deserting to the Whigs. He was recognized by his former commander who immediately ordered that he be executed. When the first volley from the executioners' rifles failed to kill him, Fanning pulled his pistol and personally ended Lowe's life.[5]

Fanning next heard that Captain Charles Golson was nearby plundering Loyalist property and quickly set off in pursuit. Unable to bring them to a fight, he did manage to pick up one of Golson's men, who was promptly executed. Unsatisfied, Fanning decided to pay a visit to Golson's home. With two companions he found and burned Golson's farm. He also found an unnamed person who had meted out harsh treatment to Loyalist prisoners. "I fell in with a man who had been very anxious for to have some of my men Executed. I sent word for him to moderate and he should have nothing to fear, but if he persevered I would certainly Kill him; this he took no notice of, but persisted for several months, and in observing me that day he attempted to escape from me, but I Shot him."[6]

Soon after Isaacs' departure, Fanning returned to his old haunts

12. Abandoned in North Carolina

accompanied by only three companions. With these men he rode over into Chatham County to pay a visit to John Thompson, "a Rebel majestrate," who was in possession of a horse owned by one of Fanning's men. Thompson wisely gave up the beast without a struggle, but he also gave the Loyalists something potentially far more useful—news of the possibility of a truce. Fanning had come to realize that his cause was in jeopardy soon after Major Craig evacuated Wilmington. He even advised neutrality to many of his friends when Isaacs was ravaging the Deep River valley. Several of his fellow Loyalist commanders, including Archibald McDugald and "One Eyed" Hector McNeill, had lost heart and sought asylum in a "truce ground" established in South Carolina by Major Micajah Gainey and General Francis Marion. But much to his credit, Fanning did not abandon his followers in central North Carolina while there was still hope.

News of the Whigs' willingness to strike a deal gave Fanning an opportunity to achieve peace without abandoning his friends. So after consulting briefly with the three men accompanying him, he decided to offer his terms for peace to the Whig authorities. His demands included the following conditions. "1st that every friend of Government shall be allowed to return to their Respective homes unmolested—2nd that they shall be under no Restriction of doing or causing to be done anything prejuditial to the interest of his majesties Government. 3rd that they shall not be under any obligation to act in any public station or even to take up arms or be compelled to do any thing injurious to his Majestys good Government. 4th that they shall not pay or Cause to be paid any taxes or money levied by your laws during the continuance of the present War to support your army their Industry."[7]

Several of his Whig antagonists were supportive of Fanning's demands, including Captain Matthew Ramsey, who passed the word on to General Butler. But there were several who did not covet peace, so the Loyalists were forced to be constantly on their guard against treachery.

One of the Loyalists killed during the time these negotiations were taking place was Captain William Lindley, who had quit the Loyalist army, apparently with the consent of Fanning, and headed west to the young settlements beyond the Blue Ridge. For reasons unknown, three of his former comrades who had changed allegiances tracked him into the wilderness and brutally murdered him with swords. Fanning soon got word of the foul deed. Two of the offenders, William White and John Magaherty, were apprehended and summarily executed—hanged from the same limb of a tree. The third member of the murderous trio managed to escape.[8] It is interesting that during these lawless times with the Loyalists being under such tremendous pressure from Whig raiders, Fanning and his followers made sure White and Magaherty were punished, even though Lindley was no longer a member of the team.

Fanning had a tough time keeping up with Whig treachery. For example, on January 11, 1782, knowing that Fanning was to meet with the Whigs at Balaam Thompson's on the Deep River near the Wilcox Iron Works under a flag of truce, Captain Golson and Captain Robert Scoby were lying in wait with a party of men to ambush the Loyalists at the meeting. A disaster was averted, however, with a warning from Thompson, but the damage was done. Had Fanning been left unmolested and signed the parole offered, he and his men would have remained at peace in an area "twenty miles East and West fifteen North and South" of Harmon Cox's Mill on the east side of Deep River.[9]

Fanning appears to have still harbored hopes of peace, as for the next month he did not pursue his antagonists with his characteristic vigor. On the night of February 11, 1782, he came across a party of Whigs under Golson and Hinds which he promptly attacked. Next morning he concluded a truce with these men and set about compiling another list of terms for peace to be presented to General Butler, which he submitted February 26, 1782. There were now nine items on the list, and the truce was to last for six months to a year.

On March 5, 1782, Butler sent word back that he did not feel that it was in his power to agree to such far-reaching conditions but would forward them on to Governor Burke, now back on the job in Halifax following a controversial escape from Charles Town. Butler also asked that a temporary truce be enacted until an answer from Burke could be sent. But before this letter made it to Fanning, another act of treachery on the part of the Whigs cast the Deep River country into a renewed period of terror and bloodshed, this one particularly fierce and personal.

Most of the Whig commanders in central North Carolina were glad to have a respite from the long years of struggle and were eager to end the war. But there were some who, for personal reasons, wished to continue the struggle. Most virulent among these was Colonel Andrew Balfour, Fanning's old nemesis, who, upon hearing of a potential truce with the Loyalists, sent word that there was "no resting place for a Toryes foot Upon the Earth."[10]

Words were not Balfour's sole forte. He set out with twenty-seven men to ride into Fanning's temporary truce ground to exterminate the Loyalist leader and his band. Balfour nearly accomplished his task, for he came upon Fanning and six of his comrades in a house, "where we were fiddling and dancing." Fanning spied the group coming up to the house and was able to escape with his comrades up the road, where they fought off the Whigs' attack until nightfall.[11]

Faced with such belligerence, Fanning was left with no alternative but to resume hostilities. He immediately sent word for his men to assemble. Twenty-five answered the call. This gathering was quite a spectacle, for the men were all attired in a uniform Fanning had designed. This was, incidentally, the first recorded mention of Fanning's men wearing a specific uniform. Fanning described the outfit. "Linen frocks died Black, With Red Cuffs[do] Ellbows and shoulders cape also, and Belted with Scarlet, which was a total Disguise to the Rebels which the red was all fringed with Large white fringe."[12]

On March 10, 1782, Fanning set out on a raid against the Whigs of Randolph County, "in order to give them a small scorge."[13] Their first target was Colonel Balfour, whose plantation stood near the site of the present location of the Asheboro Municipal Airport. The Loyalists arrived at Balfour's, "where we came upon him, he endeavored to make his Escape, but we soon prevented him, having Fired at him and wounded him, the first ball he Received was through one of his Arms, and Ranged through his body, and the other through his neck, which put an end to his committing any more ill Deeds."[14]

In his account, Fanning neglects to mention the presence of Balfour's daughter and sister. Both apparently made a heroic effort to save the life of Balfour, but were unsuccessful, being removed from him by force when they attempted to shield him from harm. Carruthers preserved a letter written by Margaret Balfour, the Colonel's sister, written six months after her ordeal, in which she recounted her remembrance of Fanning's visit. "On the 10th of March, about twenty-five armed Ruffians came to the house with the intention to kill my brother. Tibby and I endeavoured to prevent them; but it was all in vain. The wretches cut and bruised us both a great deal, and dragged us from the dear man then before our eyes. The worthless, base, horrible Fanning shot a bullet into his head, which soon put a period to the life of the best of men, and the most affectionate and dutiful husband, father, son and brother. The sight was so shocking, that it is impossible for tongue to express any thing like our feelings, but the barbarians, not in the least touched with our anguish, drove us out of the house, and took everything that they could carry off except the negroes who happened to be all from home at the time. It being Sunday, never were creatures in more distress."[15]

His most belligerent adversary silenced, Fanning and his men continued on to the house of other Whig leaders in the vicinity. From Balfour's they proceeded to William Millikan's, "who lived on Back Creek, about two miles south of Johnsonville or the old cross roads." Millikan was not home, so the Loyalists destroyed his house and belongings before moving on.[16] "On leaving Milliken's," continued Carruthers, "they compelled his son Benjamin and a young man by the name of Joshua Lowe to go along and pilot them to the house of Col. John Collins where he met with disappointment; for Collins was not at home, but they burned his house."[17]

Fanning's activities during the remainder of the day on March 10, 1782, included a visit to Colonel John Collier's house, which Carruthers placed, "about three miles from Bell's Mill, and in a south-west direction." Collier, as was stated earlier, was especially disliked by the Loyalists for his unsavory ways of acquiring property.[18]

The Loyalists sent the two unwilling pilots ahead to ascertain if Collier was home. They were hailed by a sentinel, Benjamin Fincher, who was promptly shot in the chest. The bullets were not lethal, and Fincher survived to tell the tale. Collier was alerted by the shots, and following the old ruse of yelling to fictitious men, he made his escape on a horse kept close at hand for just such a situation. He did not get off unscathed, however. "he made his Escape having Recd 3 Balls through his shirt, but I took care to Distroy the whole of his plantation."[19]

Late that night and in the wee hours of the morning, Fanning's command moved on to Captain John Bryant's place, "who lived about half a mile from New Market." When Fanning and his men knocked at the door and identified themselves, Bryant at first did not believe them. After telling them to hold on until he could get his pants on, Carruthers recorded, "they damned him and his breeches, too."[20] Fanning magnanimously offered to parole Bryant if he surrendered. Bryant defiantly yelled from inside the house, "Damn you and your parole too. I have had one, and I will never take another."[21]

Fanning wrote, "I Immediately ordered the house to be Set on fire, which was instantly done, and as soon as he see the flames of the fire encreasing he called Out to me and desired me to spare his house for his wife and Children's sake and he would walk out that his house and property should be saved for his wife and children. which he came out, and when he came out he Said here Damn you, here I am, with that he received two Balls, the one through his head and the other through his Body—he came out with his Gun *cocked* and sword at the same time."[22]

Carruthers preserved an unusual anecdote of Fanning's visit to Bryant's. "Fanning then threatened death to any one who should give the alarm before daylight; but, according to his custom, as he had killed the man he was after, he destroyed no property and did no further damage. As he probably felt a little wearied after so many labors, he lay down in the cradle, and after rocking himself there very comfortably for some time, while the rest were sauntering about, they all gathered up and went off in quest of other victims."[23]

He and his men did not have long to rest, for as soon as the sun was

12. Abandoned in North Carolina 123

up they were off for the Randolph Court House where they hoped to bag several prominent Whigs gathering for a scheduled election. Forewarned, the Whig officials wisely did not attend the meeting at the courthouse, and Fanning's plans were not realized.[24]

From the courthouse the raiders went to Major Thomas Dougan's plantation on Deep River. Dougan not being home, the Loyalists destroyed all of his property before departing.[25]

Soon after leaving Dougan's, the Loyalists came across a man later identified by Archibald Murphey as Daniel Clifton. Fanning recognized him merely as "a Commissary from Salisbury who had some of my men prisoners and almost perished them and wanted to hang Some of them." Fanning put Clifton's fate into the hands of his former victims, and the Whig was shortly thereafter hanged.[26]

With all of this activity and the death of so many prominent leaders, it was only a short time before the Whigs retaliated. A body of three hundred horsemen descended upon the area, but the weather being damp and rainy neither side's firearms would function properly. Outnumbered better than ten to one, Fanning and his men disappeared into the woods without attempting an ambush.[27]

Fanning's "scorge" had worked. The Loyalists had wiped out several of the most virulent and overzealous Whigs in the region. In addition, by early April the Whigs were once again ready to negotiate, or at least they pretended to be. Several Whig commanders in the field closest to the region controlled by Fanning wrote letters stating that they were desirous of ending the violence and bloodshed. A temporary truce soon followed.[28]

A Major Williams brought word that Burke was ready to discuss terms once again and would do everything in his power to get it by the Assembly. Fanning stood by the terms he had presented earlier, and promised to remain inactive until he should hear back from the governor.

Ten days later Williams returned with bad news. Burke had not been successful in convincing the Assembly to ratify the truce. The vote was reportedly close; "a Col. who came from over the mountains, and was one of the Assembly," arrived and protested vigorously. He was most upset about the restrictions on Continental soldiers and the free intercourse between Fanning's territory and the British base at Charles Town. Strike those provisions, Williams said, and the Whigs would agree to the terms.

Just when it seemed as though he was on the verge of obtaining an honorable end to the conflict, Fanning grew obstinate. Quite likely, he sensed treachery: "my answer was that I would forfeit my life before I would withdraw any one of the Articles that I presented. as I still wish to hold the same Connection with the British as formerly. I likewise told him that I understood that they had picked out 24 of their best horses and men from Virginia in order to pursue me; and my Answer was to Mr. Williams that they might do their best and be Damned as I was fully determined to still Support my Integrity, and to exert myself in the Behalf of the King and Country more *sincere* then I ever did. with this Mr. Williams Departed."[29]

Surviving records indicate that the latest round of negotiations with Fanning were not being conducted in good faith and were from the start a clever ruse concocted by Governor Burke to assure the safety of the Assembly when they met at Hillsboro in April of 1782. None could know better than Governor Burke the danger posed by Fanning to an official meeting in Hillsboro. The most compelling evidence supporting this conclusion is perhaps the wording of the letters which passed between Burke and the fleet footed Butler. On receiving Fanning's terms in early March, Butler forwarded them with a note stating, "I take Fanning's to be a very ridiculous piece tho I doubt not that he is in Earnest...."[30]

Burke received the letter March 2, 1782, and immediately replied, "Yours of the 6th Instant reached me Just now. The Inclosures are indeed of little moment, and I suppose before this you have many reasons besides what can be drawn from them to Conclude that a force ought Immediately to be advance against Fanning and his party."[31]

Burke had good reason to resort to such subterfuge as feigned peace negotiations. On March 16, 1782, he appointed Major Thomas Hogg to command an expedition into the Deep River country to subdue the Loyalists and keep Fanning occupied. Hogg was an experienced leader, but when the troops he gathered in Franklin County were ready to march, a dispute arose between Hogg and a Major Crofton, the militia's normal leader, over who was to be in command.[32] Thus, the expedition did not materialize, and for a while it seemed as though Hillsboro would be once again a vulnerable target. Burke did order Butler to send two hundred well-armed men to Hillsboro on March 23, 1782. He especially noted, "I also request that you will provide Patrols of good horse to be employed to watch the roads leading from Haw River."[33]

Burke still needed to be sure that Fanning did not disrupt the session. Thus he sent Williams off on a bogus mission to discuss terms with Fanning which he was not in the least inclined to grant. There is no evidence that Fanning's proposals were even discussed at the Assembly, let alone mulled over for three days.[34]

13

The End in the Carolinas

"I concluded within myself that it was Better for me to try and settle myself being weary of the disagreeable mode of Living I had Bourne with for some Considerable time." Thus wrote Colonel Fanning of his decision in April of 1782 to try to set his life on a new course. For nearly seven years, all he had known was the chaos and turmoil of internecine war. Fighting, bloodshed, incarcerations, murder and pillage were all common occurrences since he had been a teenager. There is little wonder that the twenty-six-year-old veteran should crave peace and tranquility.

One of the first things he did to accomplish his new goal was to take a wife. Fanning chose for a bride Sarah Carr, the sixteen-year-old sister of one of his most trusted subalterns, Captain William Carr. The girl's father, Joseph Carr, who lived in Randolph County near the Deep River, encouraged the relationship. There are no details of the courtship. But as subsequent events played out, Fanning's choice in a bride was a wise one, for she stuck by him through some of the most trying episodes yet awaiting the couple in the future in East Florida and New Brunswick, burying her husband four decades later in Nova Scotia, far away from the Uwharrie Mountains of her nativity.[1]

Upon hearing the news of the engagement, Captain Carr and Captain William Hooker decided to make a triple ceremony of the event. But the episode ended in tragedy. "They both left me to make themselves—and the Supposed wives Ready. and the Day before we was to be coupled, the Rebels before mentioned with those Good horses came upon them and Capt. Hookers his horse being tied so fast he could not get him loose until they catched him and murdered him on the spot." Saddened by the loss of their friend, Carr and Fanning still went through with their respective weddings. Afterwards, they "Kept two Days merriment."[2]

Shortly after the conclusion of this brief honeymoon, Fanning went into hiding, and spread the rumor about that he had departed for Charles Town. The Whigs suspected a ruse, and sent a couple of messages into the Loyalists' camp addressed to Colonel Fanning with General Alexander

Faith Rock, along the Deep River in Randolph County.

Leslie's name forged at the end. Upon recognizing that these documents were false, Fanning immediately wrote a reply to the Whigs who sent them. He did have the foresight to sign Major Rains' name to the letter.

"Sir I am very sorry to think that there is so many Damned foolish Rebels in the world to think Col: Fanning should even be Deceived by such Damned infernal writings as I have received from you, Col: Fanning is gone to Charles town and is not Return here until he comes with forses Sufficient to Defend this part of the Country, and I would have you to disband and be gone Immediately for if ever I hear of any of your people coming with any thing of the sort I will come and Kill him myself."[3]

In his typical fashion, Fanning was not willing to depart for Charles Town without having a farewell party with his men. "'I concluded to have a frolic with my old friends before we parted,' he wrote, and in an effort to obtain some alcoholic beverages, on May 2nd, 1782, he set out in pursuit of a wagon he had learned the day before was heading for market on the Pee Dee in South Carolina."[4]

The wagon was overtaken eleven miles away. Walking next to the wagon was John Latham, who lived on Little River in southern Randolph County. Fanning had no quarrel with Latham, but was merely in search of provisions. When he enquired about the wagon's contents, Latham told him, "Some flaxseed, beeswax, etc." When asked if he had any food, Latham replied in the affirmative but told Fanning he hoped the Loyalists wouldn't take it from him as there was little to eat along the way.

Heedless of the man's request, Fanning bound onto the wagon to search for provisions. As he flung back the tarp, he was surprised to find not only food but a person—Andrew Hunter. Hunter was accompanying his neighbor to market, and as soon as they saw the Loyalist raiders approaching, he hid under the tarp. Seems that Hunter was a Whig and had violated his parole sometime in the past, and knew what would happen to him if he were captured by Fanning.

Now, his worse dreams had come true, for not only had he been discovered, Fanning immediately recognized him. "Ah! You infernal rascal—I have you now," Carruthers records Fanning saying. "Come out here, and be saying your prayers as fast as you can; for you have very few minutes to live."[5] Of more immediate concern to Fanning's men were the provisions, and they prevailed upon their leader to postpone the execution until after lunch. A rope was flung down at Hunter's feet, and he was told that he had fifteen minutes to live.

As the Loyalists feasted, Hunter stood nearby, frantically eyeing every avenue of escape. He cast a glance at the weapons stacked nearby, but his plan to seize a weapon was thwarted when Fanning told his men, "Stand by your guns, or that rascal will get one and kill some of us before we know what we are about."[6]

Abner Smally finished his meal before his comrades, and walked over to converse with the condemned man, whom he apparently already knew. Hunter asked if he could perhaps change Fanning's mind, but Smally replied that such was virtually impossible. As they continued talking, they walked a few feet away from the dining Loyalists and closer to their horses, haphazardly tethered to some bushes.

Seeing this as perhaps his last opportunity to escape, Hunter bound on the nearest horse, which just happened to be Fanning's favorite mare, Red Doe, or Bay Doe as she is sometimes known. At first, the horse stood still as orders were shouted to kill Hunter. A shot was fired. The bullet missed its target, and the horse bolted.

Fanning warned his men to shoot high and not wound the valuable beast. As he galloped off, Hunter lying close to the horse, more shots were fired. Captain Carr finally hit the target but it was too late. Hunter had escaped on Fanning's favorite horse, carrying away the pistols he had received from Major Craig and all his important papers.[7]

Fanning was unable to track the fugitive and, after only a short chase, returned and ordered Latham to guide the Loyalists to Hunter's house. Fanning seized Hunter's wife, three slaves and eight horses before returning to his lair along Deep River. He sent Latham to tell Hunter that he would exchange all of this booty for Red Doe and all his papers. A few days later, Hunter sent Fanning a reply, stating that the horse had been sent west to bring back medical help, but would be returned as soon as possible. He also asked Fanning to release his wife since he was wounded and needed her to look after him.

Fanning realized that this was merely an effort to stall for time, and that he would probably never see Red Doe again. Realizing that it was well-nigh impossible to retrieve his valuable horse with so little time, Fanning released all of Hunter's horses except one. He did compensate himself, however, by keeping an unspecified number of Hunter's slaves.[8]

Captured slaves in tow, Fanning and his young bride made their way south in early May 1782 to the Pee Dee River in northern South Carolina. Here the Loyalist Major Micajah Gainey and Whig General Francis Marion had established a neutral zone where Loyalists could find safety and escape retribution from the Whigs. Several Loyalists from North Carolina had found refuge there, including Colonel Archibald McDugald.

Fanning, however, had been excluded by name from the truce. Still, he was allowed by his fellow Loyalists to enter, and many of his comrades welcomed him openly. The Fannings found refuge here with Major Gainey for a month.[9]

The arrival of such a prominent person did not go unnoticed by General Marion. Little went on in northeastern South Carolina without the Swamp Fox finding out. On June 9, 1782, Marion warned Colonel Peter Horry to be on the lookout for trouble from the Loyalist leader. "Col. Fanning, with thirty men, came a few days ago in the truce, and is thought will endeavor to make his way to Charles Town; but it is not unlikely he may make some attempt on your post, as his number is increased since he came. You will, therefore, guard against any sudden attack, by keeping a lookout at Wragg's and Black River Ferries."[10]

Three days later, Marion wrote Horry with more news of Fanning and the happenings inside the truce grounds. "Mr. Fanning is very busy in recruiting men. On Friday next Ganey is to have a meeting of his people, to see who are to go to town, and who stay. I only wait until then, when I shall march over the river and overawe those who may be wavering, or will not give up or go to town."[11]

The results of this reported meeting of Loyalists is unknown, but shortly after Marion penned the above letter Fanning was headed for Charles Town. Leaving his wife and belongings in the care of Major Gainey, Fanning and a guide he hired to show him the way to Charles Town for "20 Guineas" headed out on June 15, 1782.

That afternoon, as they were riding along the road, they were joined by a body of horsemen under Colonel George Baylor, commander of the First Continental Dragoons. Fanning told these men that he and his companion were "Some of the Rebel party then on our way to General Marion's Quarter." The dragoons believed the story, and the two Loyalists rode along with the Continentals.

That evening, as the sun was going down, Fanning and his guide made their camp in the woods near their new friends. After bidding the Continentals good evening, the Loyalists retired, but arose in the night and escaped under cover of darkness. Whether Baylor and his men ever learned the true identity of their famous guest is not known.[12]

By the 17th, the Loyalists arrived in Charles Town. Once safely inside the British lines, Fanning sent a flag of truce back to General Marion asking for safe passage for his wife. He was surprised when Mrs. Fanning appeared in Charles Town two days later. Her speedy arrival was explained by the fact that shortly after Colonel Fanning had departed, Gainey had asked Marion for safe passage for her.[13]

The matter of granting safe conduct to Charles Town for Mrs. Fanning created quite a stir among Marion's men. His officers vehemently advised against granting the request. Marion, however, did not share their vindictiveness. He is reported to have told them, "Let but his wife and property reach the British lines, and Fanning will follow. Force them to remain, and we only keep a serpent in our bosom."[14]

This was both a wise and noble gesture by the Swamp Fox, but his directive was not fully obeyed. Someone relieved Mrs. Fanning of her property. Colonel Fanning reports that the Whigs "would not let her have any of our property or even a Negro to wait on her."[15]

Whether or not this episode led to hard feelings on the part of Fanning toward Marion is unknown, but soon after this incident, word spread that Fanning was bent on taking Marion. The rumor made it all the way to the ears of General Greene, who wrote in a letter to General Marion on July 9, 1782, a warning. "It is said that Fanning is determined to have you, dead or alive, therefore, take care of yourself."[16]

Despite the surrender of Cornwallis at Yorktown in October of 1781, the British doggedly held on to the port city of Charles Town. General Alexander Leslie, who had been appointed to replace Cornwallis shortly after the latter was captured, had been forced to consolidate the British holdings to the environs of the city, and thus had lost all the hard-fought gains attained in the fierce fighting of 1780–81. Most activity on the part of the British was mainly confined to raids and foraging expeditions.[17] Shortly after the Fannings made their way to the city, bad news arrived. General Leslie received official word on August 7, 1782, that he would have to evacuate British forces from Charles Town.[18]

On September 5, 1782, Fanning set out on what would prove to be his last foray into central North Carolina. This time, his objectives were of a purely personal nature. Fanning was out to visit Andrew Hunter and retrieve his valuable horse, Red Doe.

His exit from Charles Town did not go unnoticed by the Whigs. In a letter dated September 9, 1782, Thomas Farr sent a warning to General Greene telling of the famed Loyalist's movements. "That Colo. Fanning had long been soliciting Gen. Leslie for a Command to come out into the Country offering for a handsome reward to carry the Head to Gen. Leslie of yourself, Gen. Marion or any other person he might require, and that he, Fanning had actually come out of Town last Thursday or Friday with only a Negro to endeavour to accomplish some vile Purpose. Would it not be proper that Gen. Marion should have a hint of this?"[19]

In the five months since his daring escape, Andrew Hunter had recovered from his wounds well enough to resume his activities along Little River. But with the return of his wife by Fanning, Hunter had grown quite attached to Red Doe, and refused an offer to trade five slaves for the horse.

For nearly two weeks, Fanning ranged through the Deep and Pee Dee country in a vain quest to regain his mare. He made a brief visit to his old base at Cox's Mill on Deep River, where he found nailed to a wall a paper containing a proclamation from Governor Martin offering terms of pardon to all Loyalists who wished to surrender. Fanning tore the paper from the wall, folded it up and carried it away as a souvenir.[20]

By the 22nd, Fanning decided it was time to leave for Charles Town, lest he be once again left behind by a British evacuation. En route, Fanning learned that the man he had been diligently seeking in North Carolina was actually hiding in South Carolina, quite possibly in the Mars Bluff section of Florence County, along with Red Doe. As Fanning came into the neighborhood where Hunter and the horse were hiding, he sent a friend ahead to a farmhouse to ascertain Hunter's whereabouts. Fanning's friend was recognized as being a companion of the Loyalist's, and the inhabitant gave directions which led in the opposite direction from where Hunter lay. As soon as the Loyalists departed, Hunter's friend sent word that Fanning was in the neighborhood.

A partisan of Fanning's caliber was not long duped by such a stratagem, and he quickly realized that his less experienced companion had been fooled. They turned about and galloped through the forest to a house a half-mile away, outrunning the man sent to sound the alarm. On seeing the horsemen approach, the person sent to sound the alarm jumped from his horse and took off running across an open field. He turned upon his pursuers, pointed his pistols and pulled the triggers, but nothing happened. "With this," Fanning noted, "I ordered one of my men to fire at

13. The End in the Carolinas

him, who shot him through the body, and dispatched his presence from this world."[21]

Two more men were waiting in the house, but they offered to neither flee nor fight. Instead, they informed Fanning that word of his arrival in their neighborhood had reached them half an hour before, and that Hunter had fled with the mare to safety. Furthermore, several ambushes had been set to cover their friend's flight.

Thus ended Fanning's efforts to recapture his valuable mare, but some of his men who were staying behind in central North Carolina kept an eye out for the elusive Hunter, and one day came across him on the west side of the river near Cox's Mill. A chase ensued, with a desperate Hunter trying frantically to elude his pursuers. Though he was mounted on a swift horse, his escape route over the Buffalo Ford was blocked by Fanning's men. Hunter turned north, but after a while he was cut off by another of Fanning's men. Desperate, Hunter turned his beast into the woods in an effort to cross Deep River. When he emerged from the woods, he found that he was at the top of a steep, rocky cliff which descended sharply to the boisterous waters of the Deep. His pursuers were closing in, so Hunter made a bold decision.

In a remarkable display of horsemanship, Hunter rode Red Doe down the rock, and at the ledge jutting out over the river, horse and rider plunged into Deep River. They somehow negotiated the turbulent, rock-strewn waters, and emerged safely on the north side. His Loyalist pursuers, meanwhile, drew up at the top of the cliff. Declining to imitate Hunter, they fired a few shots at him as he dashed off to safety in the woods across the river.[22] Ever after, the rock outcropping down which Hunter made his ride to safety has been known as Faith Rock.

Years later, versions of the tale of this episode and Hunter's escape in South Carolina would become confused in the recounting of the deeds by Hunter's neighbors around Mars Bluff, and several fanciful stories of an escape across the Pee Dee similar to the dash through the Deep sprung up. There is even an apocryphal tale of a challenge for a duel at Charles Town arising from the incidents along the Pee Dee.[23]

In that late September evening back in 1782, David Fanning realized that the prudent thing to do was continue on toward Charles Town and give up on recovering his valuable steed. So he, his two men, a slave and two black children who had inexplicably come into his possession headed back to the city. They arrived by September 28, 1782, and found that "…the shipping was ready for me to embark for St. Augustine."[24]

14

Exile in Search of a Home

When Colonel Fanning boarded the transport ship *New Blessing* at Charles Town with his wife Sarah on November 6, 1782, he must have realized that, for all intents and purposes, the war was over. Whether he felt relief, regret, or any combination of the two has not been recorded, but one thing is certain—if Fanning thought that the move was to bring an end to his tribulations, he was sadly mistaken, as life in East Florida proved to be filled with almost as many dangers and disappointments as he had experienced in the war-torn Carolinas.

The loss of the thirteen colonies was a major disruption to the British Atlantic-based empire. In addition to the effects it had on trade and commerce, thousands of people were adversely affected at a personal level, as many were uprooted from their homes and forced to look elsewhere for another place to settle. Adding to the burden was the fact that most families were forced to resettle in communities where they had few familial connections such as the ones enjoyed by many of the colonists that had been nurtured in their respective provinces over a generation or more.

The evacuation of the Loyalists from the rebellious colonies at the end of the war put a strain on the British government to safely and securely evacuate the provinces and set up places for the Loyalists to settle. In theory, the Loyalists could go anywhere in the British Empire, but the practical matter of transportation and supply limited their options. Historian William Nelson notes, "Several thousand Tories, mostly from the Southern states, went to the West Indies. There was even a plan, which Lord Sydney discouraged, for a Loyalist colony in Australia. By far the greater number of refugees, however, settled eventually in what remained of British North America, most of them in Nova Scotia and what became New Brunswick."[1] These places were quite foreign and offered little to appeal to the displaced people, especially those from the southern colonies.

Members of this great Loyalist diaspora were fortunate to have such a variety of locales in which to resettle and get their lives started anew, but most had very little time to make a detailed and thorough examination of all but a few places. When discussing what became of the Loyalists from North Carolina after the war, historian Robert DeMond notes, "Some Tories ... went to Florida and to the British West Indies before finally settling in Nova Scotia. In fact, some appear to have visited nearly all these places before finally finding a resting place."[2] Fanning was one of those North Carolina Loyalists who ended up in Canada only after trying to start his life anew in a place with a much more salubrious climate.

Many Loyalists in the southern colonies chose East Florida as the most desirable place to resettle. The close proximity to their former homes as well as the relatively warm climate in East Florida were important factors in luring Loyalists from the Carolinas and Georgia. However, East Florida had the added benefit of being a place where those who owned them could legally bring their slaves. Governor Patrick Tonyn actively recruited Loyalists to resettle in East Florida, and several thousand took him up on his offer.[3] Being able to bring their enslaved workers to a place such as East Florida would have been especially desirable to people who came from such a labor-intensive agrarian way of life who would have needed help in clearing land and planting crops for survival, not just for economic gain.

The Loyalists' trip down the coast from Charles Town to St. Augustine was one fraught with danger. The channel leading into St. Augustine was shallow, and required an expert pilot to safely negotiate, especially in periods of bad weather. Loyalist refugee Elizabeth Lichtenstein Johnston sailed upon a ship that was part of a flotilla of Loyalists that traveled to St. Augustine a month after Fanning, and found the trip to be one beset with challenges. Johnston noted, "We arrived there safely, with many more Loyalists, though we saw many vessels lying stranded along the shore that had been wrecked on the sand bar. Fortunately, however, no lives were lost, though much of the poor Loyalists' property was destroyed. We got over with only once thumping on the bar."[4] Although Fanning did not mention the wrecks which strewed the shoreline along Anastasia Island, he did recall that the *New Blessing* waited eight days for the proper conditions of weather and tide to cooperate so they could safely pass into port.[5]

The *New Blessing* landed on November 25, 1782, at St. Augustine, the seat of government for British East Florida. The town, guarded by the guns of the Castillo de San Marcos, was old even in those days, having been founded in 1565 by the Spaniards. Spain lost the city, along with the rest of Florida, to the British at the end of the French and Indian War in 1763. While the rest of her American colonies south of Nova Scotia had fallen into rebellion, East and West Florida remained loyal to Great Britain, and served as a base for attacks into the Southern colonies. Now, at war's end, it was a refuge for displaced Loyalists mainly from the provinces along the

Looking north from the lighthouse on Anastasia Island toward St. Augustine, Florida.

southeastern seaboard of North America. Between July of 1782 and June of 1783, 7,500 refugees swelled East Florida's population to over 17,000.[6] Many of the Loyalists arrived with few supplies and had to rely on the British government for sustenance until they could plant and harvest their crops. Historian Charles Loch Mowat notes, "Government rations were continued until the end of September, 1783, or even later, and the population was encouraged to raise crops during the summer."[7] Most of the Loyalist refugees concentrated on planting staples they could consume as soon as possible. Whether Fanning had time to investigate the opportunities of expanding into more lucrative agricultural commodities such as indigo or sugarcane is unknown.

The Matanzas River, a wide body of water separating Anastasia Island from St. Augustine and the mainland, was the first locale in Florida to catch Fanning's eye as a potential site for a new home, and after only three days at St. Augustine, he and his young wife, along with a few enslaved people he brought out of South Carolina, headed down the Matanzas with a view to settle. But they did not tarry long upon the banks of the Matanzas. Unfortunately, Fanning did not say why. Nor did he say exactly how they traveled, though more than likely they availed themselves of a small watercraft. The German traveler Johann David Schoepf, who visited East Florida during the waning days of British control, observed that many people utilized the sandy beach when traveling south of St. Augustine. Schoepf notes, "The inhabitants foot it along the beach to Matanzas, Musquetoes, Cape Canaveral, wherever they please, in all commodiousness; there is difficulty only at inlets and small streams where there is no means of being set over (a plantation, say, or a fisherman's cabin) and the passenger cannot swim."⁸ Thus, there were many options open to the Fannings as they moved on from St. Augustine and the Matanzas.

The Fannings headed further south and took up land along the Halifax River in what is now Volusia County. Since there are no extant records giving the actual location of Fanning's new home, the best clue to its location is his claim that it was "about fifty-five miles from St. Augustine,"⁹ which places Fanning's farm on land that is today very close to downtown Daytona Beach. Fanning's farm was near the King's Road, an important road which connected New Smyrna with St. Augustine. Historian Pleasant Gold describes this part of what is now Volusia County. "There were lateral roads built to the plantations that lay along its route. These plantations lined the Halifax River, and the hummock land that lies west of the ridge that parallels the bank of the stream was almost a continuation of sugar fields, with sugar mills on the higher ground, ruins of which can be seen in some places to the present day."¹⁰

Fanning's work on his new homestead was interrupted in late February of 1783 by Major Andrew Deveaux, an exiled South Carolina Loyalist in East Florida who was organizing an expedition to attack the Spaniards in the Bahamas and was looking for volunteers. Deveaux gained a reputation as a skilled fighter in his home state of South Carolina, and had little trouble gathering soldiers among the Loyalist refugees for his latest adventure.¹¹

Eager to once again engage in military maneuvers, Colonel Fanning set about raising a complement of thirty men, all of whom signed a document called "Articles of Agreement between Major Deavoce and the Volunteers, for an expedition immediately against New Providence." Arrangements were made with Deveaux to leave St. Augustine and swing by Halifax River to pick up Fanning and his group on or around March 15, 1783, but he never showed up. Instead, Deveaux sailed straight from St. Augustine to the Bahamas, leaving Fanning and his men eagerly waiting to join the action.¹²

The main reason the convoy did not head south to pick up Fanning's part of the expedition was due to the weather, as a storm struck the ships shortly after they left port. Expedition member David Wheeler, who was with the group all the way from the beginning at St. Augustine, writes, "I sailed in company with the *Perseverance,* a private ship of war, together with Colonel Deveaux, whose fleet we had taken under our protection. On the passage we parted with the convoy in a gale of wind, but fortunately, fell in with them again, the island of Abacos then in sight; we anchored there, and detached the smaller vessels to the other adjacent islands, in order to recruit and know the strength of the enemy."¹³

While Fanning and his men waited, Deveaux and his force of about seventy Loyalists from St. Augustine, escorted by the British warships *Perseverance* and *Whitby Warrior*, arrived in the Bahamas on April 6, where they more than doubled the size of their raiding party with volunteers from the British colonists residing in the area. With approximately two hundred and fifty men, they crossed over to New Providence where they arrived April 13. British Loyalist forces captured the fort guarding the east side of the entrance to Nassau with little trouble. The South Carolinian manned his newly captured fort with a contingent of manikins made from straw specially constructed as a ruse to trick the Spaniards into believing there were more troops on hand than was the case. The stratagem, plus a "well directed shot at the Governor's house,"[14] worked. Spanish governor Claraco y Saaz and his force of about seven hundred regular Spanish troops, surrendered to Deveaux and his motley assortment of Loyalist refugees on April 18, 1783.

These military maneuvers came too late in the war to have any major lasting impact on future events in North America. Even at the local level, there was little long-term benefit from the raid, as efforts were already underway among peace negotiators in Europe to work out an exchange of the Bahamas for Florida. Thus, the Bahamas would have reverted to British control regardless of Deveaux and his Loyalist strike force. When the Treaty of Paris was signed in 1783 it not only ended the Revolution, the Spaniards ceded control of the Bahamas to Great Britain while regaining control of East and West Florida from the British. The loss of East Florida, which seemed to be entering a period of expansion and prosperity, came as a shock to many of the refugees. Mowat notes, "The crowded life of the still expanding province was cut short. On receiving the news, Tonyn published a proclamation on April 21st, 1783, announcing the cession of the province and requesting the inhabitants to lose no time in settling their affairs."[15] Thus, the Loyalists had little time to celebrate their success in the Bahamas.

Before word of these treaties reached those near the Halifax River in East Florida, a series of events transpired which nearly terminated Fanning's life. A mysterious illness took hold of the enslaved workers on his farm, killing six. Fanning himself fell ill and contracted the illness, but the symptoms did not show up until he was away from home on business at St. Augustine. He describes his situation. "Some time after I went to St. Augustine I was taken sick and lay at the point of death for three weeks."[16] Once again, his rock-hard constitution pulled him through. Soon, Fanning was well enough to return to his home to recuperate, though the malady did leave him worn down.

Despite his weakened condition, Fanning went to the fields to get the crops in the ground, and there he had another close brush with death. The weakened Loyalist made a tempting target for an attack and was nearly done in by one of the enslaved workers he brought with him from the Carolinas. Still being weak from his illness, Fanning needed to take a break from his labors in the hot Florida sun, and found a patch of grass in the shade of some trees. Just as he was dozing off, the enslaved worker seized Fanning's loaded rifle, and tried shooting him through the head at close range. The shot missed but came close enough to split the Loyalist's hat. Fanning got to his feet, and tried to subdue his attacker, who clubbed him over the head with the empty weapon. Fanning tried to escape but, after traveling about sixty paces, tripped in some vines near the edge of the field. Seeing him on the ground, his antagonist closed the distance, delivering several blows with the rifle barrel across the Loyalist's feet, leaving them a bruised and bloodied mess. Winded from the unexpected resistance, Fanning's attacker took a moment to catch his breath, at which point Fanning was able to get hold of the gun barrel and attempt to wrest it away. The Loyalist held onto the weapon, even though his assailant was biting him vigorously in an attempt to make him let go. His attacker was not successful, so he let go of the gun barrel and grabbed a hoe that was lying on the ground nearby. Fanning notes, "At last he run for his hoe and made one stroke at me and broke one of the bones of my left arm. But I took the opportunity of giving him a stroke on his temple with which I brought him down. I then mended my blows until he appeared to be dead."[17] Hearing the commotion, Fanning's wife and a neighbor eventually arrived on the scene, too late to participate in the fighting. Fanning's antagonist came to and made his way home but died the next day from the effects of the fight.

Soon after this brush with death, ominous rumors began circulating in East Florida claiming that a peace agreement had been reached, and that both Floridas would be evacuated by the British. Accustomed to hearing misinformation and chicanery from his Whig adversaries during the war, Colonel Fanning did not at first believe these rumors. But one day he was looking through a newspaper and saw a copy of a speech by King George III which gave confirmation to the validity of the rumors. Official word of the loss of the Floridas was given by Governor Tonyn in a proclamation on April 21, 1783.[18]

The Spanish agreed to let the British have until March 19, 1785, to vacate the province, with the deadline being extended by Governor Vicente Manuel de Cespedes y Velasco, the newly appointed governor of Florida Oriental, to July of 1785. For many of the Loyalist inhabitants this was not adequate time to settle their affairs before departing the province and heading elsewhere within the British Empire. There was much unrest throughout the province due to the decision to return East Florida to Spain. The unrest even reached down into Fanning's own neighborhood, where a sergeant led eight men in a mutiny at the Mosquito blockhouse. Siebert notes, "They were soon captured by a party of refugees serving in the militia. This party was rewarded by British General McArthur, who gave them fifty guineas, this sum being doubled by the garrison at St. Augustine."[19] There is no indication of whether Fanning became caught up in the turmoil or joined in any sort of organized resistance. Joining such a group would have been unwise due to his needing to stay on the good side of British authorities in order to settle his Loyalist claims. We do know that he traveled about armed, thanks to the nearly fatal encounter with his enslaved person in the spring of 1783 mentioned earlier. The weapon may have been a necessity as a defense against all manner of threats, including disaffected Loyalists.

Fanning spent the remainder of 1783 attempting to get his own affairs in order. During November, at the instigation of several fellow Loyalist officers, he entered a claim for the losses he sustained during the long war in America. These were reckoned at £1,625.10. This was the first of several attempts to regain these lost sums. Several prominent Loyalists from the Carolinas who were present in East Florida signed Fanning's claim, including Lt. Colonel John Hamilton, Captains John Leggett and Daniel McNeill of the Royal North Carolina Regiment, and Captains Alexander Campbell, George Dawkins and Moses Whitley of the Royal South Carolina Regiment.[20] In a claim later filed in Canada in January of 1787, Fanning points out that his original claim filed in East Florida was not successful. "Says that he made out his claim in Novr. 1783 at St. Augustine & gave it with a power of attry to Coll. John Hamilton to act for him; to Coll. Hutchins who sailed for England, soon after but by letter from Coll. Hamilton he is informed that it did not arrive on time."[21] Thus, Fanning found it necessary to submit his claim again three years later at St. John, New Brunswick.

Several of Fanning's friends and neighbors in East Florida urged him to take advantage of the shipping provided by the British government to leave the province and accompany them to Nova Scotia, where many of the refugees were expecting to be given compensation for their losses and grants of land for establishing new homes. Fanning claims there was not enough time to settle his personal business in East Florida before most of his friends departed for Canada. He may also have been looking at other options, including the rich agricultural lands near the Mississippi River in West Florida.

One option not open to Fanning was to return to North Carolina. Faced with the challenge of restoring peace and stability to their state following a brutal civil war, the Whig government in the spring of 1783 passed the "Act of Pardon and Oblivion." This measure would hopefully restore order by forgiving many of their Loyalist adversaries for their actions during the late war. "That all manner of treasons, misprision of treason, felony or misdemeanor, committed or done since the fourth day of July, seventeen hundred and seventy six, by any person or persons whatsoever, be pardoned, released, and put into total oblivion." But not all of the Loyalists benefited from this magnanimous gesture. Those exempted from the act included any who had accepted commissions in the British army, those named specifically in any of the Confiscation Acts passed during the war, and those who had left with the British and not yet returned. In addition, Loyalists, "guilty of deliberate and willful murder, robbery, rape or house burning," were excluded. Finally, there were three individuals named by the Whigs who were specifically exempt from receiving their mercy— Peter Mallett, Samuel Andrews and David Fanning.[22]

Why exactly these three men were singled out was not mentioned in the act. Mallett, a Wilmington merchant who had served the Whig cause since the early days of the Revolution, drew the ire of some of the more radical elements of the Whig leadership because of a dispute over supplies that ended up in British hands as well as having stood watch in Wilmington during the British occupation in 1781, but he had his banishment removed in short order.[23] Andrews had been a Loyalist from the earliest days of the conflict, eventually rising to the rank of major after having distinguished himself during the capture of Governor Burke and the subsequent dash to Wilmington following the Battle of Lindley's Mill in September of 1781. Chronicler of Loyalists Lorenzo Sabine says of Andrews, "Obnoxious to the Whigs by his course during the war, he was one of the three whom they refused to pardon, in the act of oblivion."[24] Andrews went to East Florida in 1782, and eventually ended up in Shelburne County, Nova Scotia, where he received a grant for two hundred and fifty acres of land along the Tusket River in 1788.[25]

Being exempted from the pardon was the price Fanning paid for being the province's most successful Loyalist partisan fighter. Unable to best him in the field, his vengeful former antagonists linked his name with some very serious crimes. Fanning notes, "Many people are fools enough to think, because our three names are particularly put in this Act, that we are all guilty of the crimes set forth, but I defy the world to charge me with rape, or anything more than I have set forth in this Journal."[26]

Colonel Fanning visited St. Augustine for the last time on March 10, 1784, just as word arrived that the province would indeed be abandoned. Many of the East Florida refugees held out hope that they would not be forced from their newfound homes. But powerful forces in Europe decided otherwise. Mowat notes, "It was not, apparently, until sometime in the spring of 1784 that the uncertainty was ended, when Tonyn received a dispatch of December 4th, 1783, containing definitive orders for evacuation of the province."[27] Fanning arrived petition in hand from the inhabitants of the settlement at Mosquito Inlet for Governor Tonyn, asking that a schooner be sent south to pick up some of the poorer residents who were having a difficult time coming up with funds to pay for their passage out of the province. The governor was sympathetic but maintained there was no material support or shipping which he could provide to these people.[28]

Disappointed and disillusioned, Fanning returned from his visit with the governor on March 13, 1784, and made a public address to his neighbors who yet remained.

> "My good and worthy friends: I am now going to make some remarks as to your disagreeable situation. The distresses to which the unfortunate loyalists in America are now reduced are too poignant not to command the pity and commiseration of every friend to human nature. The man that is steeled against such a forcible impression is a monster that should be drove from the circle of cultivated society. In most situations, when calamities and misfortunes press upon our minds, hope buoys us up and keeps us from sinking into the ocean of despondency and despair, but the unfortunate loyalists have no hopes to cheer up their spirits; even this last refuge of the afflicted is denied us of enjoying peace and happiness which our forefathers and ourselves were born under. During a seven years' war we have been induced to brave every danger and difficulty in support of the Government under which we were born, in hopes that we and our children would reap the fruits of our labour in peace and serenity. Instead of that reasonable expectation, we find ourselves at the conclusion of a war sacrificed to the indignation of our enemies, expelled our native country, and thrown on the wide world friendless and unsupported. It is needless to repeat the many promises of support and protection held out to the public by the King and those acting under his authority. These promises have been violated in every instance, and the national faith which we had been accustomed to look upon as sacred, basely bartered for an inglorious peace, even to this province which the loyalists from the other colonies have fled to for shelter, now denied us. The Spaniards are in a short time to take possession of this province, and whilst we are together we had better draw up a decent petition to have protection and throw ourselves on their mercy. If they deny us we will have few to condemn us, for what cruel and relenting necessity may compel us to adopt. Innumerable are the difficulties at present to encounter. Stripped of our property, drove from our homes, excluded from the company and care of our dearest connections, robbed of the blessing of a free and mild government, betrayed and deserted by our friends, what is it can repay us for our misery, dragging out a wretched life of obscurity and want? Heaven only that smooths the rugged paths of life can reconcile us to our misfortunes. Also, my hopes of ever receiving anything from Government for losses or services are vanished, as I cannot support any other opinion than whenever Great Britain sees it her interest to withdraw her force and protection from us, let us go where we will, we never can say we are safe from such difficulties as we have

14. Exile in Search of a Home   141

been induced to brave since the commencement of the late war, and for the same reason I shall in a few days get out in open boats to West Florida to settle myself at or near Fort Notches on the Mississippi River."[29]

There is no mention in Fanning's journal or later correspondence of exactly why he chose to head to West Florida at this point in time. The area had been a haven for Loyalists from the Carolinas and Georgia during the American Revolution, so it would have been a place where many inhabitants were sympathetic to Loyalist refugees. But the province, like East Florida, reverted to Spain after the war. Perhaps Fanning was enticed by reports of the valuable farmland that existed near Natchez. Historian Clinton Howard notes, "The early reports from Pensacola and even Mobile were not encouraging to dreams of quick tropical wealth. It was only the discovery of the rich farming land near Natchez which began a boom which had its effects upon the country, even in spite of the retrocession to Spain in 1783."[30] A chance to obtain some of the rich and fertile bottomlands for a new farm and pursue peaceful agricultural pursuits must have appealed to the war-weary Loyalist.

A week after his return from St. Augustine, Colonel Fanning, who evidence indicates had never been on the ocean prior to the evacuation of Charles Town in November of 1782, set out on March 20, 1784, at the head of a flotilla of seven open sailboats on a voyage around the coast of Florida to the mouth of the Mississippi and three hundred and sixty miles upriver to Natchez, in what is now the state of Mississippi. The total distance for such a journey is over twelve hundred miles and is a voyage which would test even a skilled sailing crew of the modern era equipped with the most advanced navigational equipment. There was not even a lighthouse along the way in those days marking the numerous reefs and shoals, adding to the danger of an extremely perilous voyage.

Fanning's flotilla set sail from Mosquito Inlet, hugging the coast along the way, never out of sight of land. They passed Cape Canaveral and stuck together as far south as the vicinity of Jupiter Inlet. Fanning's boat sailed in advance of the rest of the expedition in order to scout ahead as well as to go ashore periodically to hunt for wild game. Aboard his open sailboat was Fanning, his pregnant wife, an 18-year-old whose name was not recorded, and two enslaved persons. They made their way as far down the coast as a place identified in his journal as "Scibirsken" or Key Biscayne, before halting. Here they waited and kept a watchful eye on the sea for the arrival of the other boats, but after twelve days their companions had not shown up. Fanning decided that the missing members of his flotilla must have passed in the night, so they set sail and continued onward, hoping to catch up.[31]

This telescope was handed down among Fanning's descendants in Nova Scotia for several generations until it was donated to the Canadian War Museum in the 1980s. Exactly when Fanning first obtained this telescope is unknown, but his trip around Florida would have been an ideal time to use such an instrument (Image telescope CWM 1985315-001-verso, courtesy of the Canadian War Museum, Ottawa, Ontario).

The open sailboat island-hopped down the Florida Keys, eventually making it to Key West. Ignorant of Florida geography, Fanning did not realize that the Keys veer away from the mainland and extend well into the Gulf of Mexico. With a small open craft such as his, it would have been wise to pass through the Keys and cut across Florida Bay early, avoiding an extended open water crossing. But Fanning's boat pressed down the Florida Keys and away from the mainland. Fortunately, it avoided any mishaps as it passed along the Florida Reef, a coral reef system that stretches south along the outer edge of the Florida Keys for more than a hundred and seventy miles from Fowey Rocks southwest to the Marquesas Keys. Fanning would have started dealing with the treacherous reefs and currents almost immediately after leaving Key Biscayne.

A few miles off Key West, Fanning learned valuable information from the crew of a schooner, but not without some difficulty. The schooner's crew was Spanish, and they were as ignorant of the English language as Fanning was Spanish. Luckily, however, there were some Creek Indians with the Spaniards, and thanks to his years as an Indian trader when he had availed himself of the opportunity to learn to speak their tongue, they were able to converse. Once the Creeks understood where Fanning was

14. Exile in Search of a Home

headed, they informed him of the danger of trying to reach Mississippi in a small open sailboat. Fanning writes, "They had some Creek Indians on board, and then, bound for Havana; the Spaniards I could not understand, but they understood the Creek language and my speaking to the Indians and informing of the Indians that I was going to Mississippi, he told me that my boat was too small, and it would be impossible for me to make the main land, as it was three days' sail before I could make land." The Loyalists also learned that six families of refugees from St. Augustine had perished on a sea voyage similar to the one Fanning was undertaking. There was no way of being certain, but these unfortunate souls were possibly the Loyalists that he had pulled away from at Jupiter Inlet and waited for in vain at Key Biscayne.[32]

The Spaniards informed Fanning of his true location—on the edge of the Gulf of Mexico. It was suicidal in their opinion to try to sail north from there directly to the Florida mainland. They should instead make the crossing to the mainland via the shallower and more protected waters of what is today known as Florida Bay, a thousand-square-mile body of water dotted with mangrove islands and sandy keys where people could take refuge from bad weather. This was sage advice, as the distance directly across open waters of the Gulf of Mexico from Key West to Cape Sable is roughly sixty-five miles.

Maps drawn during the period, including William Gerard de Brahm's *Chart of the South End of East Florida and Martiers* published in 1771 show this particular body of water as Richmond Bay, with the section from Cape Sable east being known as Grant's Lake. Fanning unfortunately does not elaborate upon the various species of wildlife he saw in this area where today people from all over the world travel to see the wonders of this unique ecosystem, but the sight must have been quite impressive. Perhaps he saw one of the large red birds described by de Brahm, who writes, "None of the islands is inhabited by any of the human species, but constantly visited by the English from New Providence, and Spaniards from Cuba, for the sake of wrecks, madeira wood, tortoise, shrimps, fish and birds: of the latter a variety exists on the islands and about Cape Sable, amongst which is peculiarly a large red bird, which measures six feet from toe to its bill's end (which is crooked, and has its maxillary motion on its upper part, as on that of a parrot), and is called flamingo; besides small deers, bears, racoons, and squirrels."[33] The Fannings had little time for nature study as they pushed along on their dangerous journey.

Armed with this intelligence given him by the Spaniards, Fanning proceeded to the island of Key West, where his party landed and made plans to ride out a storm which was brewing. They were accompanied by the Spanish schooner, and soon joined by another Spanish vessel. The two groups got along rather well, the Spaniards sharing stories of the horrors and tortures which the Native Americans of South Florida meted out to those unwary travelers who fell into their hands. This testimony compelled Fanning's 18-year-old companion to ask for permission to leave the expedition and sail with the Spaniards, to which Fanning acquiesced. Fanning notes, "I had one white lad of eighteen years of age, and by the different accounts we had of the Spaniards he got scared. I told him not to lose his life on my account." The Spaniards also reiterated the advice given earlier—it was unwise to sail in an open boat from Key West to the mainland. They did provide an alternate course, however: Backtrack up the Keys and cross Florida Bay at a narrower spot. The route they suggested for this crossing would be a much more manageable thirty-five miles to the Florida mainland.[34]

The weather relented after fifteen days. The Spaniards were the first to depart, but not before stealing a good deal of the group's clothes and bedding. Fanning's crew now consisted of himself, his pregnant wife, and the two teenage enslaved laborers. Armed with the sailing advice of their late cohabiters of Key West, they backtracked up the Keys to a location which Fanning calls "Key Bockes." This is the island known as Vaca Key, where today stands the city of Marathon.[35]

They sailed north across Florida Bay from Vaca Key, heading first for an island called Sandy Key which the Spaniards said they would encounter lying a little beyond the halfway point of the voyage. Fanning reports that the group was out of sight of land for eight hours. They continued north from Sandy Key, making landfall on May 20, 1784, at Cabo de Arena or Cape Sable, the southernmost point on the Florida peninsula. Located west of Flamingo in what is now Everglades National Park, the safe anchorage provided by the cape was a popular spot for people to stop while passing through the remote area, especially those who were fishing or hunting turtles in the shallow waters of Florida Bay and the Gulf of Mexico. Naturalist John James Audubon, who visited this locale half a century after Fanning, found a freshwater well on shore near Cape Sable. Audubon notes, "Having filled our cask from a fine well, long since dug in the sand of Cape Sable, either by Seminole Indians or pirates, no matter which, we left Sandy Isle about full tide, and proceeded homewards, giving a call here and there at different keys, with the view of procuring rare birds, and also their nests and eggs."[36] Fanning makes no mention of how his party procured fresh water, so whether the well mentioned by Audubon was dug after the Fannings' stay at Cape Sable is uncertain.

Fanning ran across another schooner in the waters near Cape Sable, this one from New Providence and captained by an Italian named Baptist. Among other things, they heard more warnings about the hostility of

14. Exile in Search of a Home

Looking south across Florida Bay from Cape Sable in Everglades National Park. This is where the Fannings ended their ill-fated voyage around Florida.

the Native Americans along the southwest coast of Florida. Realizing the inadvisability of continuing the voyage by sea in their small boat the rest of the way to the Mississippi River, Fanning decided the wisest course of action was to ask Baptist for passage back to New Providence. Here began a series of haggling and arguing which nearly turned fatal. Baptist's price began at two hundred Spanish dollars, but soon fell to a hundred and fifty. Fanning felt this an exorbitant sum, and refused to pay, at which point he returned to his camp at Cape Sable. Three days later, the schooner reappeared, and Fanning once more refused to pay the sum.

Next morning, one of Fanning's servants headed up the beach to gather some chickens they had put ashore to forage earlier, while the Colonel headed out to do a bit of hunting. While he was gone, the crew from the schooner abducted the girl and took her back to their boat, then took her from there and concealed her in the woods. Fanning spied the whole transaction and confronted the abductors. This was a bit foolhardy, as the colonel had only one round in his rifle. The sailors did not put up a fight, but merely told him to take up the matter with Baptist. He saw Baptist approaching up the beach, gun cocked and laying across his left arm. The two men negotiated over the release of the girl, which would involve the payment of a hundred and fifty Spanish dollars for passage to New Providence.

Fanning agreed, and soon had the family's belongings loaded on board, but it was necessary for the group to stay on land a few days longer. The schooner had to head up to Ponce de Leon Bay on the northwest end of the island making up Cape Sable to finish gathering turtles but promised they would soon return. Those familiar with the conditions in the Florida Everglades in early summer can understand what a miserable time Fanning's party must have endured camping at Cape Sable, regardless of the trials with the unscrupulous Baptist. Intense heat and swarms of mosquitoes combine to make this locale one of the most unpleasant places in North America during the summer.

Baptist returned on June 15, but as soon as the Fannings were aboard, they discovered his terms had changed. He now wanted Fanning to sign for two hundred pieces of eight. Fanning refused, so Baptist ordered the family's belongings off the ship. Colonel Fanning began preparing to disembark, at which point Mrs. Fanning raised her concerns and strongly encouraged her husband to sign the paper, as there was no telling what misfortunes awaited them if they returned to Cape Sable and resumed their journey for West Florida. Upon hearing his wife's admonitions, Fanning agreed to sign, but only for the aforementioned one hundred and fifty Spanish dollars. This was fine with Baptist, and soon the schooner was headed back for New Providence, albeit in a roundabout way.

The ship headed across Florida Bay for what was apparently the turtlers' base at Upper Matecumbe Key near the present location of Islamorada, where they spent nearly a month anchored. On June 30, Baptist and Fanning quarreled once more, this time over Fanning's pronouncement to have Baptist hanged when they got to New Providence. Fanning notes, "On the 30 of June, as we were laying at New Madamcumba after our having several words, he told me that he understood by my negroes that I intended to have him hung after my arrival at New Providence if he had turned my wife on shore, and in case she had died that I should do my endeavors to hang him in Providence, and told me if it had not been for killing my wife he would be damned if he did not drown me overboard long ago, only on account of my wife."[37]

Relief came to the Fannings nearly two weeks later when three ships from the Bahamas arrived at Upper Matecumbe Key, commanded by captains Samuel Clutsam, William Bunch and William Smith, respectively. These men expressed outrage at the treatment Fanning's party received at the hands of Baptist and offered to assist them in any way possible. They obtained passage from Captain Clutsam to New Providence for the sum of fifty Spanish dollars, Captain Bunch proclaiming that the contract with Baptist was void as it was contrary to the laws established to help distressed voyagers.

After a pleasant voyage, they arrived in Nassau September 3, 1784. Clutsam and Fanning got along so well that he only charged him thirty Spanish dollars for the trip. Soon after their arrival in port, Clutsam

14. Exile in Search of a Home

discovered that his passenger was the famed Carolina Loyalist, and proceeded to knock an extra ten dollars off the price for a fellow Loyalist. Fanning had kind words for these three men who had come to his aid in a moment of need. "During the course of my being on board of Capt. Clutsam he found me in every necessary and made no charge for any provisions or anything I received of him. His humanity was so great, that if ever in my power to render any service to him or any of those gentlemen, nothing shall ever be wanting on my part to do them service."[38] There is no evidence indicating whether Fanning in later years was able to return the Bahamians' hospitality. Fanning did engage in building ships in Nova Scotia during the first decade of the nineteenth century, including the schooner *Ferebee and Phoebe*. Some of the vessels were built to make voyages to the West Indies, but there is no record stating whether Fanning himself ever made the trip.[39]

Fanning's stay in the Bahamas was brief and he unfortunately gives no details as to why he chose not to settle there on a permanent basis. Historian Carole Waterson Troxler maintains that many of the Loyalist refugees were not confident they could survive and prosper in the Bahamas Islands because the amount of fertile land available to new arrivals was very limited. Troxler notes, "With a climate which promised to facilitate a plantation economy, the Bahamas seemed to be a place where slave-owning refugees could rebuild their lives. Even so, the Bahamas were not regarded with anything like enthusiasm. Men who knew its soil considered it unsuited to serious agriculture."[40] Fertile land was extremely important to most of the Loyalist refugees, most of whom lived an agricultural based existence.

Concerns about the ability of the soils to sustain long-term agricultural production proved justified. Less than half a century after the Loyalists established their new farms in the Bahamas, the soils became exhausted. Historian A. Talbot Bethel notes, "Although the Colony was prosperous for a number of years owing to the great stimulus given it by the new immigrants, the prosperity was not destined to be permanent. The soil, which at best was thin, was exhausted of its strength by the middle of the first decade of the nineteenth century. Its value decreased, and with it passed away a great part of the value of the slaves that had been employed upon it."[41] Such thin soils would have been problematic and had little appeal to people accustomed to an almost endless supply of fertile land such as was available in the southern provinces of North America.

The Fannings remained on New Providence for less than a month. After a short respite, they made the decision to head north to Nova Scotia where Colonel Fanning joined many of his former associates who went there straight from East Florida. They took passage twenty days after their arrival in the Bahamas aboard a ship commanded by Captain Jacob Bell, bound for Canada. Like many Loyalist refugees, Fanning was a reluctant settler in Nova Scotia, settling there not by choice but by necessity. Historian Neil MacKinnon observes, "They had come to Nova Scotia because they had little other choice. It was the most accessible land in which to resettle."[42] Thus, the aversion to the place was not unique to Fanning, but was one he shared with many other Loyalists, especially those from the Carolinas who ended up in the province.

Colonel Fanning and his family experienced many hardships after the war, as did many of their fellow refugees caught up in the Loyalist diaspora that came about with the upheaval resulting from the American Revolution.[43] Among the many factors making his story unique and important are his trials and tribulations which nearly cost David and Sarah Fanning their lives, especially on their ill-fated voyage around the Florida peninsula. Fanning's experiences in East Florida provide valuable insights into the vicissitudes endured by the Loyalists from all walks of life who were uprooted from their homes and farms not once but twice because of their decision to remain loyal to King and country.

15

Triumph and Tragedy in New Brunswick

Fanning no doubt would have remained on his newly acquired farm south of St. Augustine on the banks of the Halifax River, but with the return of East Florida to Spanish control, remaining was not possible for British subjects unless one took an oath to the Spanish king and converted to Catholicism. After a brief respite in the Bahama Islands, Fanning made the decision to head north. Like many of his fellow exiles driven from their homes in warmer climes, Fanning came to the Canadian Maritimes by necessity and not by choice, and in this inhospitable place he and his family endured many hardships during his time here in the province, especially in those early years. But unlike most of the Loyalist refugees who settled in this harsh part of the world, Fanning managed to persevere and eventually prospered in his newfound home. Fanning first settled in that part of Nova Scotia which became New Brunswick, where he lived a successful life until he was banished from the province for a crime he adamantly maintained he did not commit.

Along the southeastern coast of Canada, the Bay of Fundy stretches northeast from the Gulf of Maine. The Bay of Fundy is a unique body of water, as it is the scene of the highest tides in the world. At some places along the bay, tides exceeding fifty feet are not uncommon. These dangerous waters are full of sea life, and for generations hardy souls living along its shores have challenged the fogs and currents to make a living from the sea.

The shores of the Bay of Fundy are hilly to mountainous, and the physical resemblance to the north of Britain makes it easy to understand why it was called Nova Scotia. The northwestern shore of the bay is particularly rugged, with high-forested mountains and rock-strewn beaches. This region can be brutally cold, especially those parts a few miles inland from the moderating effects of the water.

On the northwestern shore, the Saint John River flows down out of the hills into the Bay of Fundy. This is a large river whose headwaters are four hundred and fifty miles away in the Appalachian Mountains of Maine, and the river is carrying quite a load of water when it enters the bay. But despite its size, the river is no match for the 28½-feet tides. As the tide rises, the waters of the river slowly stop flowing downstream, and eventually water begins to head back up the river, creating a cataract known as the Reversing Falls. To this day it is quite a tourist attraction, as well as hazard to navigation.

The French had been the first Europeans to try to carve out a home from this rugged wilderness. The town of Annapolis Royal, across the Bay of Fundy on the Annapolis Basin, is the second oldest inhabited city in North America, having been founded by the French in 1605. But the French lost this part of the world in 1710, and many of the French settlers left Acadia, most being forced out by the British, though some fled into the interior and settled in remote areas along the Saint John River and its tributaries. By the time the American Revolution began, the region was sparsely populated, and many portions of the land were still as much a wilderness as it was when the Native Americans had the place all to themselves.

Thousands of Loyalists, including Fanning and his pregnant wife, arrived in the remote northwestern region of Nova Scotia, swelling the population to the point where it became necessary by the end of 1784 to sever the western half of the province to create New Brunswick. The small villages along the mouth of the Saint John saw the most dramatic growth, and in the same year as New Brunswick was created the two towns were merged to form Saint John, Canada's first incorporated city.[1]

Despite their rugged scenic beauty, Nova Scotia and New Brunswick were not the first choice as the place to start over for most members of the Loyalist diaspora. Climatic differences between their former homes and the region of storms and frequent fog helped shape their opinions, as did perceptions of the inhospitableness of the land where blackflies and mosquitoes are prolific. The climate of Atlantic Canada is strongly influenced by the effects of the warm waters of the Gulf Stream interacting with the cold waters of the Labrador Current. Climatologists Robert Rohli and Anthony Vega explain, "Farther north, the Gulf Stream curves eastward away from the continent, and the cold Labrador current replaces the departing Gulf Stream, at times reaching as far south as Maryland. This cold current often chills the warmer air overlying it, resulting in frequent coastal fogs in the Atlantic Provinces of New Brunswick, Nova Scotia, Prince Edward Island, and Newfoundland and in northern New England. This cold water may either stabilize the local atmosphere, trapping the fog near the surface, or produce storminess along the margins between the air over the cold water and the warmer air adjacent to it."[2]

15. Triumph and Tragedy in New Brunswick 151

Word of the harsh climatic conditions awaiting settlers in Nova Scotia persisted long after the arrival of the Loyalists, and became engrained in people's perceptions of what the place was like. Promoters later had to go to great lengths to dispel some of the negative connotations potential settlers had of the viability of Nova Scotia as a place to settle. Martin notes, "The temperature of Nova Scotia is milder and the heat less intense in summer than is the case in Quebec. The air is highly salubrious, 80 years being a frequent age in the full use of bodily and mental faculties, many settlers pass 100 with ease and comfort. There are no diseases generated in the colony, which is also free from intermittent and other fevers." Martin continues his glowing account by making several interesting observations on the agricultural productions of the province. "In order to correct the prevailing idea in England that Nova Scotia is a region of snow and fog, I may state that the orchards of the province are equal to those in any part of America, plums, pears, quinces, and cherries are found in all gardens and most excellent quality cider of superior quality forms an article of export, and peaches and grapes ripen in ordinary seasons without artificial aid."[3] There was not much he could say, however, about the biting insects.

Like many of his fellow refugees, Fanning was a reluctant settler in Nova Scotia, settling there not by choice but by necessity. There was an aversion to the place shared with many other Loyalists from the Carolinas who ended up in the province. When discussing what became of the Loyalists from North Carolina after the war, historian Robert DeMond notes, "Some Tories, as we have mentioned, went to Florida and to the British West Indies before finally settling in Nova Scotia. In fact, some appear to have visited nearly all these places before finally finding a resting place."[4]

Historian Carole Troxler states that Atlantic Canada was a place that held little appeal to Loyalists from North Carolina. Troxler notes, "Except for a handful of militiamen who chose to go there in the evacuation of Charles Town, North Carolina, loyalists approached Nova Scotia with great reluctance. Even the Scots, who might have identified with its name, were unenthusiastic. The loss of East Florida, with its warm climate and proximity to their homes, made Nova Scotia seem colder, more remote and less pleasant than it really was."[5]

This hesitancy to move to Nova Scotia was not unique to refugees from the Carolinas and Georgia, as other refugees saw little appeal to settling in what they perceived to be a harsh environment. However, there were few options available for the Loyalists to resettle on such short notice within reasonable distance to the British colonies in North America. Historian Neil MacKinnon observes, "They had come to Nova Scotia because they had little other choice. It was the most accessible land in which to resettle. Canada was a distant interior wilderness inhabited by people of a

Fanning's Rocks, on the west bank of the St. John River, Grand Bay, New Brunswick.

different faith and language. Some had gone to the West Indies, but most considered it an alien land of excessive heat and yellow fever. For different reasons Britain was also an alien land."[6]

Fanning never tells exactly why he left the Bahamas and headed north, but one can reasonably conclude that it had more to do with his unfinished efforts to settle his claims for losses with the British government than with a desire to settle in Nova Scotia. He arrived on September 23, 1784, at the Loyalist settlement at the mouth of the St. John River in that part of Nova Scotia soon afterward carved away and designated as the province of New Brunswick. He remained there only briefly before heading to Halifax to get an audience with Nova Scotia Governor John Parr, but was unsuccessful.[7]

Fanning spent many years trying to settle his claims for losses during the war but, like many of the Loyalists, was only partially successful. Disappointment at the amount of compensation received was a common refrain among the Loyalists. When discussing the bad treatment many of the Loyalists received at the hands of the claims commissioners, historian Donald Barr Chidsey notes, "Some of the doughtiest fighters among the Loyalists were scamped. Colonel David Fanning, the South Carolina hero, a Tory leader who had been sensationally successful in the field, did not do so well with the compensation commissioners as he had against the Patriots. He put in a claim for £1,635 and got £60."[8]

15. Triumph and Tragedy in New Brunswick

Fanning returned to the St. John River by November of 1784, there to endure his first winter in New Brunswick. The settlement was being built to house the refugees in as orderly a fashion as possible, but many found conditions to be very Spartan. The British government did not have much time to plan the settlement. Historian William Raymond notes, "A vast impetus was given to the development of the country north of the Bay of Fundy by the coming of the Loyalists. In the course of a few months, it passed from the condition of a comparatively unknown region with a mere handful of English speaking people to that of an independent province with an enterprising class of inhabitants—poor in purse, indeed; but rich in experience, determination, energy, education, intellect and other qualities essential to the building up of a country." Elaborating on the harsh conditions, Raymond observed, "Frequently had these poor settlers to go from fifty to one hundred miles through wild woods or on the ice to procure precarious supply for their famishing families. The privations and sufferings endured in some instances almost exceeds belief."[9]

Peter Fisher preserved several valuable observations that testify to the harsh conditions experienced by the Loyalists in New Brunswick during the first years after the Loyalists arrived. Fisher notes, "Frequently in the piercing cold of winter a part of the family had to remain up during the night to keep fire in their huts to prevent the other part from freezing. Some very destitute families made use of boards to supply the want of bedding; father or some of the elder children remaining up by turns and warming suitable pieces of boards which they applied alternately to the smaller children to keep them warm; with many similar expedients."[10]

Fanning acquired a more permanent place to live for his growing family when he purchased two hundred acres from Job Dill and Thomas Dale in Connay Township on Grand Bay in King's County. This was the first in a long series of land transactions in New Brunswick. Most of his holdings were along Grand Bay and Long Reach. It has even been suggested that he owned a place in Fredericton, the fledgling capital of the province, and at Kingston, the county seat of King's County.[11]

Writing in 1890, the historian Howe described the Fannings' first home in New Brunswick. "The lot of land No. Ten that Colonel Fanning purchased in Connay township is about a quarter of a mile below Brandy Point, and almost directly opposite 'Land's End,' the lowest point of land on the eastern side of the St. John River above Grand Bay. From shore to shore the river at that point is about a mile wide. On that lot he settled and the site of the log house he built during the summer of 1785, can still be easily traced and is but a few yards from the bank of the river and is marked by a large birch tree that is growing on the mound. The large rocks or boulders on the shore of the river, that mark the front of the lot are to this day known as 'Fanning's rocks.'"[12]

His home at Long Reach was where Fanning compiled his account of his wartime experiences into what he termed his "Narrative." He dated the introductory remarks, "King's County, Long Reach, New Brunswick June 24th 1790." The original manuscript version as well as any copies made and distributed in New Brunswick have long since been lost. A notation on the manuscript Jonas Howe later transcribed shows that it was dictated to his daughter, Feribee, so this particular copy must have been penned many years later, as Colonel Fanning's daughter would have been less than six years old when Fanning first compiled his experiences.[13]

Fanning's reasons for compiling an account of his adventures in the war went beyond mere literary ambition. The most practical reason was to substantiate his service claims in his ongoing efforts to get retribution from the British government. Another motive would have been political aspirations. Fanning was considering running for a spot in the Provincial Assembly in 1790, so publishing the accounts of his exploits was a good way to enhance his reputation and win votes. We know that his "Narrative" in some form was published and available for public consumption, as his political enemies would later refer to it as a "foolish publication."[14]

Fanning was elected to the Provincial Assembly of New Brunswick in 1791, and served in that post until 1801. Fanning was an adequate and dependable legislator, as evidenced by the fact that he was in 1793 named chairman of the Committee of the Whole House. Besides working on such legislation as a bill for registering livestock identification marks, Fanning introduced a bill on January 27, 1798, calling for "the registering of Marriages, Births, and Deaths." He also sat on a committee to study laws that had expired. But Fanning's legislative accomplishments are overshadowed by the fact that he has the dubious distinction of being the first member of the New Brunswick Assembly to be removed for a felony conviction.[15]

Colonel Fanning obtained a 200-acre tract of land in April of 1795 with a working gristmill where wheat and other cereals were ground, up the river opposite Spoon Island near Hampstead in Queen's County. This plus the adjacent 289 acres he had previously purchased in 1788 gave him 489 contiguous acres. His motivation for moving to this new estate seems to have been worrisome neighbors. In a letter to Ward Chipman he confided, "I wish not to let anyone settle near me again."[16] If Fanning thought this move up the St. John would bring him peace and tranquility he was sadly mistaken. The five years spent at this farm in Queens County were filled with strife and turmoil.

Howe preserved a story of one encounter Colonel Fanning had with

15. Triumph and Tragedy in New Brunswick

Fanning's Brook, near Hampstead, New Brunswick, is where Fanning operated his gristmill.

a man named Kitchen on a cold winter's day near Fanning's mill. "Among the residents of Hampstead at that early period was a well-known miller, a man of large size and great strength, named Kitchen, with whom few of the early Loyalist settlers were disposed to quarrel. With this man Colonel Fanning had a misunderstanding, and from him received a challenge to settle the matter with their fists. The colonel being a much smaller man hesitated on account of the great difference between them in size and height. The hesitation caused Kitchen to taunt him with the name of coward, at which the impetuous Southerner accepted the challenge, but claimed the choice of place which was granted, and as it was the winter season, choose the frozen surface of the river. On that day a slight fall of snow had taken place and after the two men had repaired to the place selected and began the combat, the wisdom of the colonel's choice became apparent, and on the slippery surface of the frozen river, the huge and powerful Kitchen proved to be no match for the wiry and athletic Southerner—and 'beat himself' as the old residents asserted, 'by his own falls.'"[17] Fanning was thus still limber enough to engage in physical combat despite the brutally cold weather on the slippery ice of the St. John River.

Fanning's encounters with several members of the local leadership became quite intense. This was especially true of one Justice of the Peace in particular, John Golding. By October 1799, the situation had deteriorated to the point where Fanning felt compelled to leave New Brunswick. "I was fully convinced that the Inhabitants of that province was Determined to take my life," he wrote Governor Guy Carleton.[18]

He wrote a letter to Jonathan Odell on October 3, 1799, outlining his concerns and future plans. "Having found it absolutely necessary for the security of my life and property to remove from this Province to some other parts of the Kings Dominion, and having left landed property in the state of Virginia, worth about £4000, and as I acted as Colonel of the Loyalists in the state of North Carolina, my property was not legally Confiscated and I wish to try to recover it again. I beg the favor of you, Sir, to ask his Excellency, Governor Carleton, if [he] will be good enough to give me, under the seal of this province that I am a British subject, and that I have desire to go into the state of Virginia, to obtain my lands there; to recover my Debts and other property there; when I first advertised all in this Country for sale I had no thought that I could have sold all my lands off so soon; but I have applicants for all my lands, and if I can obtain a Certificate from his Excellency I wish to leave the province by the 10th of November next, if I can get my Business arranged, by that time, I shall go to New Providence, or Upper Canada, it is unDetermined as yet. I thank you Sir to let me know as soon as possable whether I can get such a Certificate & protection or not, and what the Charges will be, and I will send you the money. Or whether my presents at Head Quarters is necessary on the occasion or not."[19]

Fanning advertised his lands for sale, and shortly thereafter received word from Carleton advising against leaving New Brunswick. Fanning wrote, "...your Excellency used every argument, in your power, to prosuade me that I was mistaken of the evil Desires of the people of that province which after a long Consideration, I thought I might Perhaps over Come some of those Difficulties; if I could keep some of those wicked and malicious people out of office."[20]

Fanning sent a letter to Odell on January 4, 1800, complaining of the appointment of several individuals to positions as Justices of the Peace, specifically Seth Bryan "at the head of Washeademoyke," John Golding, John Calwell and Ebenezer Seely. He wrote of the latter three, "...neither of them are able to read the Law or scarcely write his name."[21] He included samples of Golding's writings to illustrate the man's precarious grasp of the English language, and distributed samples throughout the community to enlighten his neighbors as to their Justice's ignorance. Fanning would later realize that making the man's ignorance public was a mistake. "I must now inform your Excellency that this letter and golding's writing was the Downfall of me for I showed his nonsensical writing to a great number of his friends & relations, and others, in the province, in order to see if I could not get him to lay Down his Commission, as I thought he was a

Disgrace to it. Upon this Golding took every advantage he Could to Ruin me, and all that he or any of his friends Could do to hurt my Character was daily their study, and he and Thomas Hanford was the Only ones that Caused the girl to sware as she Did against me."[22]

The girl referred to was Sarah London, who came down the St. John River with her brother on a boat loaded with grain headed for Fanning's mill on Sunday, July 27, 1800. The boat pulled ashore briefly at the landing at Fanning's house so Sarah could disembark and go visit Sarah and Feribee Fanning. Her brother continued a short distance down to the mill landing, within view of the house. London, described as "a quick-tempered girl and bold in her manners," proceeded to Fanning's house. The actions that day at the Fanning home became embroiled in much controversy and political intrigue, so much so that one can conclude that the only people who will ever know what truly happened are Fanning and London. From later testimony, it appears that some sort of sexual encounter was suggested, whether by the girl, Fanning or mutual consent is unknown. Regardless of what transpired, Fanning was accused of attempted rape, which London later changed to rape, of which Fanning was tried and convicted at Gagetown by what he considered to be a hostile jury made up mainly of his political enemies. The evidence suggests that the whole episode was carefully orchestrated by Golding, who coached London about what to say at the trial. There is little surprise that on October 2, 1800, the jury at Gagetown returned with a guilty verdict and next day sentenced Fanning to pay for the crime with his life.[23]

Fanning's lawyers—Thomas Wetmore and Charles Peters—wrote a lengthy petition to Governor Carleton asking that their client be pardoned. The main reason given was the lack of evidence against their client, as well as the girl's changing story.[24] Other petitions soon followed, including one from Sarah Fanning dated October 9, 1800, in which she mentioned Sarah London's contradictory statements and lack of evidence. Mrs. Fanning ended her petition with an appeal to Carleton's mercy because the execution would not only be a "manifest injustice" but would also "leave your Petitioner and Children totally destitute of a means of support."[25] Looking back at the correspondence which survives, we can reason that it was the prospect of leaving Mrs. Fanning and her young children destitute which helped save her husband's life, more so than any secret Masonic cabal or other such plots.

Governor Carleton was convinced that Fanning had been wrongly sentenced to death by the local court, and on October 30, 1800, he issued a pardon. Fanning did not lose his life on the gallows at Gagetown. However, the pardon was not all good news, as Carleton exiled Fanning from New Brunswick forever. Carleton's pardon directed, "...the said David

Fanning do leave our said Province of New Brunswick on or before the fifteenth day of November next and be not again found within the same hereby remitting to the said David Fanning all Forfeiture by him suffered in consequence of the conviction and Judgement aforesaid."[26]

This left Fanning with virtually no time to settle his business affairs. He was released from jail on October 23, 1800, and on his way home he was waylaid by two of Golding's sons; "...and the villain was still not satisfied," he wrote of Golding, "and after I was liberated he issued the following kind of a warrant as he call'd it and sent his sons after me, with the Constable with a sword and gun who used violence with their hands and many threats with their sword, and gun, and tore my Coat, to get me back to go before their father, until the Constable told them that he did not think that his warrant would Justify Such Conduct."[27]

Fanning dictated a letter on October 31, 1800, to Constable Robert Boyle for delivery to Lt. Governor Carleton which outlined the turmoil and strife that had befallen him. Fanning wrote:

"Enumerable has been the Difficulties that I have Incountered; I took up arms in an early day of my life, and During a seven years war I was induced to brave every Danger and Difficulty in the support of the government under which I and my forefathers was born; in hopes that I and my Children would reep the fruites of my labour in peace and security; but instead of that reasonable Expectation I am very sorry to add, that at the Conclusion of an unsuccessful war, I was sacrificed to the Imbartation of my Enimies; Stripped of my property; Drove from home; Excluded from the Company and Cause of my Dearest Connections; Expold my native Country; and thrown on the wide world friendless and unsupported; and now even New Brunswick the last place of refuge to where the afflected had fled to for shelter, is denighed me and those very persons that I Defended the lives, Liberties, and properties, are now thirsting for my Blood, and makes those faithful and intrepid services a principal grounds of their Calumnies against me. The Foxes have holes and The birds of the air have nests, But the son of man hath no resting place where on to lay his head; should your Excellency Denigh this my last petition, &ca. &ca. &ca.

"Heaven only which smoothe's the Rugged pathes of life Can Reconcile me to misfortune, which Cruel and relenting necessity must Compell me to addopt, a redress for a grievance of so Deep a Dye. &ca. &ca. And as the purrogative power is fully invested in your Excellency without any advice of your Council, I hope upon a mature Deliberation that your Excellency will grant me a License for some Certain time to come to that province, and settle all my business, and upon Receiving such license at your request, I will enter into Bond, and security, that I will not mollest any one in their person or property only to seek my own in a legal way."[28]

Fanning and his family left New Brunswick before the November 15, 1800, deadline, and headed across the Bay of Fundy to the shores of Nova Scotia.

16

A Home in Nova Scotia

On a clear day, if one looks out from St. John across the Bay of Fundy, a series of hills is discernible along the horizon. This landmass is the northwest coast of Nova Scotia, and it was toward these hills that Colonel Fanning fled with his family to begin life anew after his calamitous experiences in New Brunswick. Why, one might ask, would a person settle so close to the place from whence he had been exiled? There were two main reasons for this. First was simply the fact that Lt. Governor Carleton's pardon imposed scant time for Fanning to conclude his business affairs before departing the province. By moving only as far away as was absolutely necessary, Fanning was still in close enough contact with his former associates and neighbors to conclude as much unfinished business as possible such as selling off his extensive landholdings.

The other important reason for not traveling too far away was the fact that Fanning knew he was innocent and believed he would be exonerated whenever cooler heads finally prevailed. In this belief he was sadly mistaken. He would spend a good portion of his remaining days in vain attempts to prove his innocence, or at the very least be granted permission to return to settle his affairs. How tantalizing it must have been for him in his later years when he stood on the shore of Nova Scotia and looked northwest across the Bay of Fundy to see the hills of New Brunswick looming on the horizon.

As October of 1800 drew to a close, the family headed east across the Bay of Fundy and sailed through the Digby Gut into the Annapolis Basin, a broad expanse of water which is separated from the larger Bay of Fundy by a low range of hills known as the North Mountains. These mountains are breached by a half-mile gap—the Digby Gut—which allows passage to the open waters of the Bay from the sheltered waters of the basin. One writer has likened the scenic beauty of the Annapolis Basin to that of the Bay of Naples in Italy.[1]

Evidence indicates that the Fannings first made their home in Nova Scotia on land on the western shore of the Annapolis Basin near the Digby

Gut hard by Beamon's Mountain. Whether they lived in a house already standing or if Fanning and his sons hastily constructed a log cabin is unknown, but there was little time for construction before the onset of winter.

Nearby was the town of Digby, founded in 1783 by a group of exiled Loyalists who named their town in honor of Admiral Robert Digby. The town was a small but thriving community, which boasted of a fine harbor, an Anglican church and an active Masonic Lodge.[2] The initial wave of settlers did not really like the place, and most left after the British government ceased issuing rations, as the land proved very harsh to till with the agricultural implements of the day, especially when compared to the fertile soil many had left behind in the Carolinas. Few of Digby's original exiles could see the potential of the place, since they were for the most part farmers and not fishermen. Until he could get his legal affairs settled, Fanning did not have the luxury of being able to seek greener pastures elsewhere, and learned to adapt to the place.

Understandably, the folks around Digby were not keen on the idea of having such a person of Fanning's reputation settling in their midst. After all, he was personally banned from entering not one but two provinces—North Carolina and New Brunswick. Fanning noted some of the Nova Scotians' concerns with his presence amongst them in a letter dated December 8, 1800, to Munson Jarvis. "The inhabitants of this town was very much against my landing at first. They seem much better Reconciled now and friendly." He went on to describe some of the trials facing him and how he hoped to make a living in his new home. "If I should stay here the next season I shall want salt to cure fish with. I am told that the Inhabitants of this town make large sums by those little herring. they smoke them and sends them to york and Elsewhere. I should be glad if you could supply me with salt. I understand that the fishery begins abought the first of June. it will take 40 Dollars to supply my stock with hay this winter, as I have to give 12 &14 Dollars per Tun, freight included."[3] There is no evidence Fanning ever engaged in pelagic fishing activities along the Grand Banks, but he instead concentrated his efforts on the local inshore waters.

An outcast in a new community with few friends presents a prime target for the local hucksters, and Fanning was in Nova Scotia only a short time before he made the acquaintance of several unscrupulous individuals. Soon, as in New Brunswick, Fanning became embroiled in legal troubles.

Fanning's major business enterprise in Nova Scotia was not the herring fisheries but was instead shipbuilding. Unclear is the total number of vessels fitted out, or just how he got started in such an endeavor. This was strange business for a backwoods trader, partisan commander and miller.

16. A Home in Nova Scotia 161

A view of Digby Gut. Fanning's home would have been on the left side of this photograph.

Perhaps his ill-fated voyage around Florida fostered a love for the sea. More than likely the astute Fanning was taking advantage of an opportunity to engage in something more lucrative than fishing.

The only ship which Fanning owned for which we know a name was the schooner *Ferebee and Phoebe*. Historian Isaiah Wilson mentions this as being a ship owned by Fanning, but gives few details about the vessel such as size or dates she was in operation. The vessel was placed in the West India trade. Wilson notes, "In January, 1794, Messrs. Isaac Bonnell and Elisha Budd , formed themselves into a co-partnership under style and firm of 'Bonnell & Budd.' For prosecuting an extensive business in shipping and commerce. In conjunction with Ambrose Haight and John Stewart, Deputy Sheriff, they purchased one-fourth of the schooner *Ferebee and Phoebe*, of Col. David Fanning. The owners placed her on the West India route. Finding the vessel unsuitable for the service, Captain Adam Walker and William Franklin Bonnell, senior, son of the first partner, were added to the firm, which was then designated Bonnell, Budd & Co.'"[4] Whether Fanning ever personally accompanied the ship on one of her early trips to the Caribbean is unknown.

Fanning's first mention of his shipbuilding endeavors came in a letter written to Munson Jarvis dated December 12, 1801, in which he lays out his plans to build a ship with Talmon Squires. Fanning listed a number of supplies needed and asked for Jarvis to extend credit to buy the items.[5] Between March 22 and November 26, 1802, he and Squires built a ship whose purpose was to travel between Canada and the West Indies. There is no evidence this vessel ever traded across the Atlantic directly with Great Britain. He noted that they "...took great pains to make her the best vessel that ever was built in either of the two provinces." For reasons unclear, Squires hit hard financial times and was unable to keep up with his share of the bills. "My partner was not able to pay sixpence in the pound, altho half owner," noted Fanning. Eventually, Squires was forced to sell his share of the vessel, and this was when Fanning's troubles in Annapolis County began.[6]

"He sold his half to the worst Rogues that I ever came across, they all joined to get my half," wrote Fanning. To accomplish this, his new partners and their accomplices brought thirteen suits against him over an eighteen-month period. The records of the proceedings are unfortunately lost.[7]

However, the wily old Loyalist was not intimidated by this battery of lawyers. "I stood my own very well in all but the last Suit, and Kept one quarter of the said vessel and half of a sloop I bought of 60 Tons." These suits cost him a total of £1,350. In the final suit, however, Fanning naively agreed to enter into arbitration before a panel of judges, whose ruling he found very disappointing. "Four of those pretended arbitrators would not even see my accounts or hear my evidences, and awarded me to pay the others £12.14.6." Fanning's temper flared when he heard their verdict. He told the court that he did not intend to pay. For this, he was confined to the gaol at Annapolis Royal, there to consider his actions.[8]

These unrelenting lawsuits left Fanning and his family in dire straits by the early spring of 1806. Living for a short period in Annapolis Royal, county seat and hub of activity on the opposite end of the Annapolis Basin from Digby, he confessed to Odell, "I declare to you Sir upon my honor that me nor my family never new what it was to be condemned to as poor a fair as at the present, altho my Credit is as good as any man's in the County, yet I am Determined to git out of all their clutches between now and december next, if it should please god to spare me so long."[9]

Fanning had debts to members of the legal profession in two provinces, as Odell was working on yet another attempt to gain Fanning entry into New Brunswick. As early as 1804, Fanning had lamented to Munson Jarvis, "I never wish to wrong any man if I can help it, but how can I pay my just debts if all I have and Can get is always taken from me Rongfully, by Law, and Law Suits."[10]

The Fannings did not tarry long in Annapolis Royal but soon returned to their farm at Digby. Fanning gave Odell his low opinion of the people who had tried to bilk him at Annapolis Royal, comparing them to the folks who made his life so miserable in New Brunswick,

16. A Home in Nova Scotia

noting "They are bad in that province to sweare false but they are ten fold as bad here."[11]

By the winter of 1808, following all of his legal troubles in both New Brunswick and Nova Scotia, Fanning was ready to move elsewhere to begin life anew. In a letter to Odell dated February 9, 1808, he wrote, "I cannot live under the troubled Manner that I do long, and if I cannot git no redress I must leave this kingdom. But my present mind is to move my family to Niagara and leave them there and go to England and seek for redress first. and as I do now, and ever have, and ever shall declair myself Innocent to the Last Word, that I may speak at my Death....

"I do declair that I would not live in that province for to have the whole of it, but the loss of my riputation and property and to ly under the stigma of not being at Liberty to go anywhere I please in the king's dominions is what hurts me as well as other things."[12]

With this desire to leave pressing him, Fanning must have sat down and penned a letter to the recently appointed governor-in-chief of British North America who was grabbing so many headlines in the newspapers of the day, Sir James Henry Craig. Fanning recognized the name as that of his old friend Major Craig, the commander of the British garrison at Wilmington with whom he had worked so well back in 1781. In a letter to Captain Whitlock written February 15, 1808, he expresses his determination to leave Nova Scotia. "I am Determined to go to see governor Craig the next fall after going to Virginia to try for my property."[13]

Major Craig had moved up through the ranks in the quarter century since the two had last seen each other. He won renown for capturing Cape Town from the Dutch in 1795, and was knighted in 1797 for his services in what is now called South Africa. Craig, in bad health, arrived in Quebec to take over his new duties in September of 1807, and the newspapers of Canada were full of accounts of his convening the parliament in January 1808 amidst much pomp and circumstance. But his tenure as governor would be marked with much strife and turmoil thanks to a power struggle between French Canadians and British settlers, as well as mounting tensions between Great Britain and the United States.[14]

In the midst of taking over his new post, Craig took time on April 15, 1808, to reply to Fanning's note. "How your letter came to be so long on its way I cannot tell but tho' dated the 21st November it only reach'd me by the Halifax mail which arrived here the end of last month & I lose no time in not only informing you that it is your old commander & acquaintance who is now Governor of these parts, but in assuring you also that he entertains the same regardences now of your Services that he always did. I have never I assure you lost an opportunity of doing you Justice, but unfortunately I was not in England at the time of the transaction to which you allude, when merit of your assertions was, I really apprehend, given to another.

"I shall very readily do what I can to serve you in your object of obtaining an establishment in this Province. I have nothing to do with Civil Government of Upper Canada unless I go to that Province, but I will write to Governor Genl. & enquire what grant I can obtain for you there. In this Province we have Townships settled by American Loyalists & if you chose to take up a grant among them I can give you one and will endeavour to find you out a better situation. Let me know your ultimate wishes & in the mean time I will write Gov. Genl. to know what he can do for you in Upper Canada."[15]

This letter must have been encouraging to Fanning, for over the next year he redoubled his efforts to conclude his business affairs in New Brunswick and move away from Nova Scotia. He wrote Captain Whitlock on November 7, 1808, "I wish to have the Business finally settled immediately as my friend governor Craig has sent for me to come to him...."[16]

Fanning was also intent on wrapping up affairs in Virginia, and declared on a few occasions his intentions to return there to attempt to sell some property he had inherited from his grandfather through his father. There is no evidence known at present showing whether he ever made the trip.

Despite Fanning's early enthusiasm, by 1809 he seems to have cooled to the idea of moving to Upper Canada. Perhaps the accounts carried in the papers of turmoil and near anarchy between the French Canadians and the British discouraged him. None could know better than he the terror of civil war.

Tragedy struck the Fannings in Digby in 1810. David William, their youngest son, died suddenly of what was chronicled in the family Bible as "nervous fever." The loss deeply affected his parents. The grief-stricken father carved his son's tombstone personally, and on it is written the following inscription:

> In Memory of
> David William, son of
> David & Sarah
> Fanning
> Who died, July 15, 1810
> Aged 16 years, & 11 months
> & 11 days & 11 hours and
> 37 minutes

The boy was buried July 17, 1810, in the graveyard beside the Holy Trinity Anglican Church.[17]

16. A Home in Nova Scotia

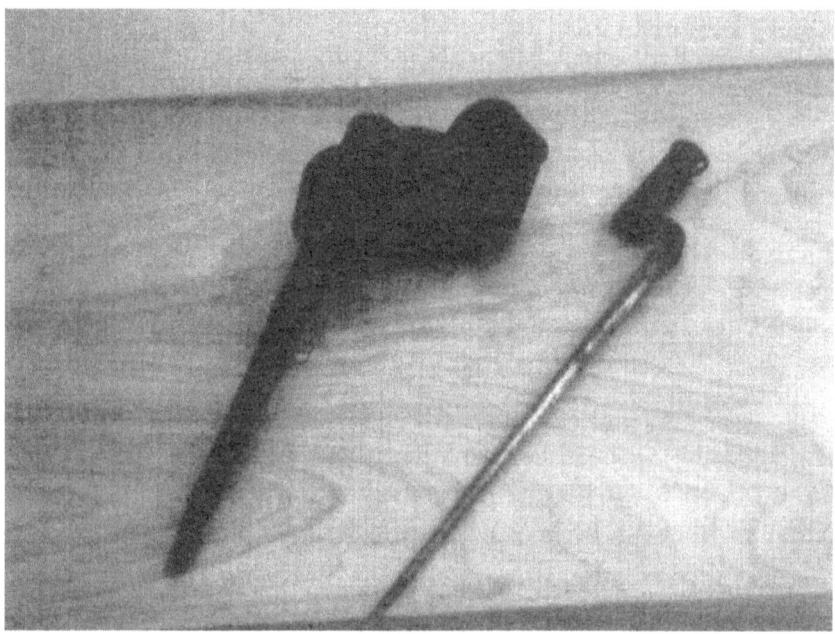

This bayonet was handed down through descendants of Colonel Fanning until Arnold Trask donated it to the Admiral Digby Museum, Digby, Nova Scotia, in the 1990s.

On June 19, 1812, war erupted once again between Great Britain and the former colonies along the Atlantic. The United States, her merchant shipping harassed by the ships of the powers of Europe, was dragged into the war on the side of France. Ever after, the war has been referred to as the War of 1812, though it dragged on till 1815. Most of the invasion routes into Canada were along the Great Lakes, but several small predatory raids affected the Maritime Provinces. American privateers lurked off the coast in hopes of capturing prizes and disrupting the seaborne commerce between Canada and the rest of the British Empire.

On more than one occasion, one of these privateers landed near Digby, and it was because of reports of the response to this threat that we have the last known account of Colonel Fanning's military activities. The Nova Scotian historian Wilson chronicles the events. "The *Halifax Journal* under date June 30, 1812, says:—'Privateers are swarming around our coast and in the Bay of Fundy; hardly a day passes but we hear of captures made by them.'" Wilson then relates the landing near Digby. "On Friday, July 31, 1812, word reached town that a Privateer had anchored between Broad Cove and Roger's Point. A detachment of Militia under *Colonels* Hatfield and Fanning marched thither, attacked the unwelcome visitor, fired over fifty shots into her, receiving some in return, and obliged the intruder to leave our shore."[18] Judge Savary states that the ship returned a few days afterwards. Following a "sharp skirmish" the ship's captain and prize master were captured and whisked away to Annapolis as prisoners of war.[19]

Wilson recounts another incident involving the militia in which Fanning may have been involved. "At one time a rumour became current that the Americans were about raiding Sissibou. The Militia officers quickly summoned their Company for practice, and that night stationed a Guard at Shook's Point. Before morning the sentries heard a crackling in the bushes. Fearing the enemy were upon them, they fired a volley in direction of the noise. Imagine their surprise and chagrin when they discovered they had shot and killed Deacon Shook's cow! For this valiant service some of the Company received a pension for life."[20]

With this, we hear the last of the military exploits of Colonel David Fanning. He left no known accounts of his activities in the War of 1812. Compared to his exploits thirty years earlier, his latest martial service must have seemed quite tame.

We know little of what transpired in Fanning's life in the years following the War of 1812. His surviving correspondence with individuals in New Brunswick was concerned less with an attempt to be allowed to return and more with getting those squatting on his land—namely John Guiggy and an individual surnamed "Mayes"—to pay. He also wanted Munson Jarvis, who had been entrusted with authority to liquidate Fanning's holdings, to pay him what was due.

On January 18, 1814, he wrote Jarvis, "I suppose this letter will meet you at the general Assembly, But come to hand where it may I hope you will instantly answer it, as those Hamiltons wishes to know wheather they can or cannot git the place. I am very much surprised that you have let Mays have that place so long as I am now informed he has sold some of the stones of the mills and Done great Damage otherwise....

"Its now near 14 years since I left that province and all that money was to have been paid in 5 years. I hope that if you have got the payment from Mays and you have all the Land I sold John Guiggy and a good Deal of the Interest from him so that you can now pay me the Sum Due me and give up my Bonds to you and Mr. Whitlock."[21] In letters dated April 10, 1816, and March 5, 1820, Fanning threatened to sue Jarvis to gain the money owed him. There is no evidence that he ever gained satisfaction in the matter.[22]

During his final years, Fanning made such an impression on his kinsman and neighbors that lore about him to this day survives among the people of Digby. This folklore is important, if not for the historical facts of the stories told but at least for the glimpse of how the people about him perceived the aging Loyalist. "Most folks said the Colonel was a grouchy old man, set in his way," remarked one of his descendants, Arnold Trask, who lived on the Lighthouse Road not far from where Fanning's home once stood.[23]

The most persistent of these tales relate to exploits of Colonel Fanning's excellent marksmanship. For example, the Rev. Allen Massie Hill once recorded a story which told of the time Fanning had an ongoing complaint with one of his neighbors over their chickens milling about on his property. "His training in war," wrote the Reverend Hill, "was not entirely forgotten, for he would shoot without mercy all the neighbor's hens that trespassed on his territory. Such a good shot was he, that he was known to fire at hens when surrounded by children."[24]

But Fanning's own fowl were not immune to attack from predators hunting in the skies above. Once, an eagle came by the Fanning homestead to take advantage of the easy pickings which the old Loyalist's flock presented. Although the Colonel was advanced in years, his eye was still keen enough to spy the predator sitting on the limb of a tree not far from the house. "You better get the hell out of here or I'll split your head with a ball," he told the eagle. The eagle, though, sat defiantly staring back at the Colonel, heedless of warnings and ignorant of past reputation. Fanning pulled out one of his pistols, took careful aim at the eagle, and fired, sending the ball right through the bird's head.[25]

In the early part of 1822, Fanning received word that individuals from North Carolina were interested in obtaining his *Narrative*. Archibald Murphey, father of the internal improvements movement in the state, was compiling material for a history of the Tory War. Through the help of his good friend, the former congressman Archibald McBryde of Moore County, Fanning's whereabouts were ascertained. A letter was dispatched from McBryde to the old Loyalist through Rev. Roger Veits of the Holy Trinity Anglican Church in Digby. The clergyman passed along the message to Fanning, and on May 15, 1822, Fanning wrote the following reply to Rev. Veits:

> "The letters you sent me appears to be a request of some gentleman in North Carolina, or elsewhere to get holt of my Journal, or narrative of my servis, During the time of the American Rebellion. I am under the necessity of saying that I would not Let any man have it on any pretence whatsoever, Unless I was well informed of the use that was to be made of it. You can say to the Gentleman that I now have a narrative of the Transactions of that war, Both of North and South Carolinas; and if any gentleman wishes to know from me of any particular transaction, or the Date, by pointing it out to me, I may give the information of it, if it Don't operate against my Coming back to look after my property. You may say, that my Journal contains more than one Quire of Fools Cap paper Closely wrote, and it would take a good pens man a month

to write it over, fit to send to the world abroad. I was offered, by Charles Cook in England fifty pounds sterling for my Journal to have it published, and I Refused him. Colonel McDougal Desired me not to Insert in it, any thing of his Servessas; as he intended going back to North Carolina to Live, and he knows that I have a Narrative of all the Transactions. If he should want any thing of the kind from me, he should write to me himself. If any person wishes to prove any thing false, respecting the conduct of the Torys, let him point what it is, and I will endeavour to give him the truth."[26]

Some interesting things can be gleaned from this note. First, it would seem that, contrary to what has been popularly believed, Fanning had not been in contact with his old comrade Colonel McDugald for nearly thirty years. McDugald had returned to North Carolina prior to February 1795 when he witnessed the will of Daniel Buie in Moore County. A year later, McDugald married Rebecca, the daughter of Daniel Buie.[27]

McDugald left North Carolina at the end of the war. As his property in Cumberland County was confiscated because he held a commission in the regular British Army, he was therefore banned by the Act of Pardon & Oblivion from returning. He went to St. Augustine in 1783, then to Nova Scotia in 1784. Unsuccessful in getting adequate compensation for his services, McDugald went to London where he lived from 1787 to 1790. He was finally able to obtain a mere £30 per annum and an extra £30 to pay for passage back to Nova Scotia.[28] Thus McDugald returned to North Carolina sometime between 1790 and 1795. He settled in Moore County, not far from his old home near Cameron's Hill, and was residing on his farm along Little Crane's Creek in the 1820s when McBryde was attempting to contact Fanning.

The only opportunity Fanning and McDugald had to discuss the contents of the *Narrative* was during the early 1790s before the latter traveled to London. At that time, when some form of Fanning's *Narrative* was circulating about his constituents in New Brunswick, McDugald must have learned of its existence and asked for Fanning to censor certain portions lest his return to North Carolina be jeopardized. It is very unfortunate that none of these early copies of Fanning's *Narrative* has yet to come to light, as the manuscript could be checked against those which survive to see if they have any further details of McDugald's services to the Royal cause which Fanning deleted later at the request of his old comrade. Perhaps the most enlightening detail gleaned from this correspondence relating to his *Narrative* is the postscript in which Fanning makes mention of his bad health. One of the most overlooked aspects of the military adventures of men like Fanning and his ilk was the wear and tear on the body, and the long-term effects of the strain on overall physical well-being. On this occasion, it was a bad ankle and knee.

16. A Home in Nova Scotia

Jonas Howe noted that, during Fanning's waning years, he was afflicted with bad health. "But the latter years of his life were years of trouble—for a long time he had suffered from dropsy and that fatal disease finally terminated his eventful life...."[29] Thus, coupled with the wearing down of the body most experience during the geriatric years, Fanning's old injuries must have been even more troublesome for him to endure than most of his contemporaries lived through. It is a testimony to his physical toughness that he survived as long as he did, especially when one takes into account the long history of abuse to his body from an early age, but he paid a penalty in his later years by having to endure severe pain as a constant companion.

The old ledger-book of Colonel Fanning's now in possession of the Admiral Digby Museum in Digby provides a glimpse into the last few years of his life. He remained combative in nature, quarrelling on one occasion with "James Titus & others" for landing a schooner on his "Lot No. 10" to dry a load of codfish in the fall of 1821. He hints at a quarrel with yet another member of the legal profession, Elkanah Morton, in his will.

But the feisty old Loyalist's body steadily deteriorated as time passed. On November 23, 1824, he leased his farm to Joseph Durland. This must have been the point when David Fanning, unable to perform the physical labor needed to live by himself, moved in with his son, Ross, who lived on a nearby farm.[30] By March 10, 1825, Fanning sensed that the end was near, as he wrote in his last will and testament

Fanning's tombstone.

Trinity Anglican Church, Digby, Nova Scotia.

that he was "ill in body but of sound and disposing mind and memory...." Even at this late hour, he did not give up thoughts of recovering his property in both the United States and New Brunswick, and reminded his heirs of the value of the property if it could be recovered.[31]

Four days later, on March 14, 1825, David Fanning passed away at the home of his son, Ross. He was buried on March 16, 1825, beside his youngest son in the graveyard at Holy Trinity Anglican Church in Digby.[32]

Ross Fanning was efficient at taking care of the details of his father's business. A notation in the Fanning ledger states that by March 18, 1825, "the Land up St. John River amt. sold for was £100." This deal was clearly in the works before the death of the Colonel. Also of note is another entry for the same date. "Paid for a grave stone for Col. David Fanning 4..2..3."[33]

The gravestone which Ross had commissioned for his father contains an oft quoted inscription which several writers have cleverly used to point out the irony in the old Loyalist's life. The tombstone contains the following verse:

> Humane, affable, gentle and kind.
> A plain, honest, open moral mind;
> He liv'd to die, in God he put his trust,
> To rise triumphant with the just.

16. A Home in Nova Scotia

Sarah passed away in 1833, and her remains joined those of her husband and son in the graveyard beside the stately old church where they rested undisturbed until 1878.

Perhaps the true irony of Fanning's end lies not in his gravestone, but with his grave itself, for by a strange twist of fate, the most notorious Loyalist of the Carolinas lies buried underneath a church, well away from his tombstone which has been twice removed from its original place.

In the late 1870s, the members of Trinity decided it was time to replace their old church with a larger building. But when those responsible for erecting the new structure began work, they were faced with a dilemma—what to do with the number of old graves, including those of the Fannings, which stood in their way. They came upon a simple solution—the structure was built as planned, and the stones were moved a short distance beyond the church. Thus several of the old occupants of the graveyard were left interred under the new building and their headstones erected just outside the church.

"As a boy, I remember standing here and hearing stories about the Colonel being buried underneath this church," remarked Trask as he stood where the old headstones were placed on the northeast corner of the church. Oddly enough, there are no stones on the site now. "A few years ago, in one of those government 'make-work' projects, a group of kids was given the job of taking down the old stones to clean them," continued Trask. "Problem was, they didn't write down where they had gotten them from. So when they brought them back they just lined them up along the fence on the back of the church grounds."[34]

Arnold Trask (right), at the tombstone of his Loyalist ancestor, Colonel David Fanning, beside Trinity Anglican Church, in Digby, Nova Scotia.

Along the back fence of Holy Trinity Anglican Church's grounds stand some of the oldest tombstones of the graveyard, arranged in neat rows conveniently and uniformly spaced to allow the free passage of lawn-mowers. In the middle of this assemblage of granite markers stands the humble monument to the man who lived through some of the most tumultuous times of the British Empire, and who left his mark on the history of three nations.

Appendix A:
Sarah Fanning Petition, 1800

The following is a transcript of Sarah Fanning's petition to Lt. Governor Thomas Carleton, asking that he spare her husband's life and commute the sentence of death handed down at Gagetown, New Brunswick, on October 3rd, 1800. The original document is housed in the Provincial Archives of New Brunswick.

Petition of Sarah Fanning
October 9th, 1800

That a Petition for Pardon being now as she is informed before Your Excellency the Petitioner humbly entreats Your Excellency to permit her in this awful moment to state a fact, which although it could not have been given in Evidence upon the trial, may in the present state of the case assist to convince Your Excellency that her Husband is not guilty.

The day of after the charge or complaint was filed by the Prosecutor Sarah London to Justice Golding, the Petitioner, impelled by a sense of her own injury, as the report presented, went to the House of the said Sarah London's Father where in the first place she met the said Father who answered the Petitioner that his Daughter had not and did not charge the Petitioner's Husband with the injury she has since sworn to have received. The Petitioner immediately after saw the Mother and Daughter together both of whom made the same Declaration and assurances to the Petitioner. Of the Truth of these Facts, the Petitioner appeals to Heaven in the most solemn manner, confident in her own mind of the innocence of her Husband, the Petitioner implores Your Excellency to have Mercy upon her and her innocent Children and stay the execution of the Law, since to suffer it to proceed would work a manifest injustice against him only but would leave Your Petitioner and Children totally destitute of the means of support.

9 Octr. 1800   Sarah Fanning

Appendix B:
House in the Horseshoe
Battle Damage

When the fighting at the House in the Horseshoe was over on July 29, 1781, there was extensive damage throughout the structure. Even though it escaped being burned by either the burning cart full of hay or an incendiary's torch thanks to Temperance Alston's deal with Col. Fanning, the house was riddled with bullet holes. The defenders must have breathed a collective sigh of relief that Major Craig did not give Fanning a small cannon after their meeting in Wilmington. It is a testament to the Scotsman MacFadyen's craftsmanship that the house even survived.

We do not know the full extent of the battle damage, but it must have been extensive if not quite catastrophic, with people shooting at the house with muskets, rifles and buckshot for three hours. It would have been several days after the battle ended before the Alstons were able to put everything back in some semblance of order, just to make it habitable. Tradition maintains that the Alstons family lived in the cabin the family originally occupied when they came to the area, which stood on a bluff overlooking the Deep River upstream near where the river begins the horseshoe bend from which the house takes its name.

One of the most frequently asked questions concerning the house is why didn't the Alstons repair the holes? Alston lost his encounter with Fanning's Loyalists, so the bullet holes were not trophies of a great victory, but reminders of an embarrassing defeat. In addition, people back in those days were much more practical than today, the house being part of a functioning farm, and not yet of historical import. Trees grew in abundance in that part of North Carolina during the eighteenth century, so there would have been no shortage of lumber with which to effect repairs.

One can speculate that Mrs. Alston may have been behind the idea of keeping some of the bullet holes in place, serving as a reminder to her husband that he should perhaps try not to antagonize people, and that it was a blessing he had not been hanged by the Tory raiders for what he had done to Kenneth Black and Thomas Taylor. But, as future events played out, Alston was never able to reign in his murderous tendencies, not just against the King's friends, but his fellow Revolutionaries as well, such as political rival Dr. George Glascock.

Alston paid the ultimate price for his violent temper, not at the hand of a former Loyalist, but one of Glascock's kinsmen, who tracked him down to Georgia where Alston was killed in his log cabin on the banks of the Oconee River in 1791.

The Alston family sold the House in the Horseshoe to Thomas Perkins, who lived there almost a decade before selling it to Governor Benjamin Williams, who used the property as a place to get away from the stress of politics by experimenting with various agricultural projects. By this time, the bullet holes had become conversation pieces, and mementoes of the battle that took place back in the summer of 1781.

Several years ago, along with former Site Manager Guy Smith and Bill Thompson of the House in the Horseshoe State Historic Site, I examined many of the holes, noticing they were not uniform in nature, serving as evidence of the motley assortment of weapons the Loyalist militias carried during the fight. Later, in 2011, with the help of Site Assistants Roy Timbs and Alex Cameron, along with site volunteer Joe Luck, we counted and measured all of the holes that are still present in the Alston House in the early twenty-first century. Below are the details from our survey of the various signs of the damage left over from the battle.

There were a dozen holes from the battle on the east side of the house, while the west side had nine. Some contained evidence of being made by a rifled shot, while others were smooth, fired from the unrifled barrel of a musket. There is even evidence of buckshot fired from a shotgun.

Below are measurements of the respective holes:

East Side of House
1"; 1¼"; 1¾"; 2" buck & ball hole, with two ¼" holes; 1"; 1¼"; ½" rifle; ³⁄₁₆" rifle; ¾"; ¾"; ½" rifle; ¾"

West Side of House
½" rifle; ½" rifle; ½" rifle; ½" rifle; ¾"; ¾"; 1" rifle; 1¾" rifle; 1¾" rifle

Appendix C:
Places Named for
Colonel David Fanning
in Canada

There are several landmarks in Canada bearing testimony to the fact that David Fanning passed through the Canadian Maritimes. The majority of these are in New Brunswick, since it was here that he first settled with his fellow refugees and subsequently became part of the history and lore for that region. Many of the physical features had not yet been named, since the Fannings were among the group of Loyalists first allotted lands in that region.

Along the western shores of the Saint John River, where it enters Grand Bay and a short distance below Brandy Point, a series of large boulders along the shore were once designated as Fanning's Rocks, and were a prominent landmark to travelers passing along this stretch of the river. This was the site where Fanning and his family first settled after leaving St. John. Today the site has been encompassed by a subdivision.

Further up the St. John River in Queen's County near Hampstead, are other physical features named for Fanning. The most prominent is a peak known as Fanning Mountain, elevation 183m/600' located at 45° 36' N, 66° 8' W. A short distance to the northeast is Fanning's Lake near the head of Fanning's Brook. These are all located near where Fanning operated his gristmill toward the close of the eighteenth century.

Across the Bay of Fundy, there are only two known physical features named for Fanning. Most of the creeks and streams already carried names by the time the Fannings arrived in Nova Scotia in the early 1800s. There is one pond named for him in this province—Lake Fanning, located at 44° 1' N, 65° 54' W, near the community of Carleton.

There is one other place, but this one is under the waters of the Digby Gut. Fannen [sic] Ledge, extends offshore adjacent to where Fanning's homestead at Digby stood, near to where his dock was located. This dock was a source of trouble for Fanning and his neighbors, many of whom drew the old Loyalist's ire by landing large catches of fish upon his dock without first asking permission.

Chapter Notes

Abbreviations used: NBM—New Brunswick Museum, St. John, New Brunswick; PANB—Provincial Archives of New Brunswick, Fredericton, New Brunswick; PANS—Public Archives of Nova Scotia, Halifax, Nova Scotia; PRO—British Public Records Office, London.

Chapter 1

1. Carruthers, Eli, *The Old North State in 1776*, 1854, 1856, reprinted by the Guilford County Genealogical Society, 1985, p. 73.

2. Savary, Alfred W., *Colonel David Fanning's Narrative*, reprinted from the *Canadian Magazine*, 1908, p. 6.

3. Howe, Jonas, "Colonel David Fanning: The Career of a Carolina Loyalist of the American Revolution: A Paper Read Before the New Brunswick Historical Society May 27th, 1890." Unpublished article housed in the Manuscript Collection, New Brunswick Museum, St. John, New Brunswick.

4. Fanning recorded his date of birth in the Fanning Family Bible, now held in the possession of the Canadian War Museum. Place of birth and information regarding his father is from Colonel Fanning's will, filed in the courthouse at Annapolis Royal, Nova Scotia, microfilm copy housed in the Admiral Digby Museum, Digby, Nova Scotia.

5. "Johnston County Court Minutes," microfilm on file at the North Carolina Department of Archives and History, Raleigh, North Carolina.

6. *Ibid.*

7. Ross, Elizabeth, "William and Needham Bryan," *Heritage of Johnston County, North Carolina*, Hunter Publishing, 1985, p. 162.

8. *Ibid.*, p. 163.

9. Carruthers, p. 34.

10. Johnson, Todd, "David Fanning: Revolutionary War Soldier," *Smithfield Herald*, July 27, 1993.

11. Powell, William, ed., *The Correspondence of William Tryon, Volume II, 1768–1818*, N.C. Department of Archives and History, pp. 678–686.

12. Carruthers, p. 34.

13. *Ibid.*

14. Hartzell, Milton, *Diseases of the Skin; Their Pathology and Treatment*, Philadelphia, J.P. Lippincott, 1917, p. 123. Erasmus Wilson recorded these interesting observations about tetter and scald-head in *A Dictionary of Medicine*, edited by Richard Quain, M.D., published in New York in 1885. "SCALD-HEAD (Saxon *scall*, a Separation or Discontinuity of the Surface).—A popular term, commonly used as the negation of ring-worm; all diseases of the scalp, in the belief of the people, being either ring-worm or scald-head. The term finds a more suitable application to that for of folliculitis of the scalp which is denominated by *kerion*. Kerion begins with circumscribed tumefaction of the scalp and profuse exudation from the hair-follicles, and terminates by elimination of the hair and baldness; the latter being generally temporary but sometimes permanent."

"Tetter—tetter is an old Saxon word,

equivalent to the French *dartre.* Tetter is defined to be 'a tickling and itching scab,' and may be taken to signify a chronic inflammation of the skin, attended with desquamation and itching. In this sense the term is popularly applied to patches of chronic eczema, and especially to those of psoriasis; but it is altogether too indefinite in its meaning for scientific use."

15. Savary, p. 5.
16. Howe, p. 15.
17. Carruthers, p. 34.
18. Marryat, Thomas, *Therapeutics; or the Art of Healing.* Bristol: W. Sheppard, 1805, p. 219.
19. Butler, Lindley, "Introduction," *The Narrative of Colonel David Fanning,* Briarpatch, 1981, p. 2.
20. Cann, Marvin, *Old Ninety Six in the South Carolina Backcountry 1700-1781,* Eastern National Park & Monument Association, 1996, p. 3; A good description of the old trail, which the author refers to as the Keowee Trail, can be found in John Logan's *History of the Upper Country of South Carolina,* Charleston: S.G. Courtney & Co., 1859, I, pp. 321-325.
21. Cann, p. 5.
22. *Ibid.,* p. 5-6.
23. Bass, Robert, *Ninety Six: The Struggle for the South Carolina Backcountry,* Sandlapper Publishing Co., 1978, p. 6.

Chapter 2

1. Carruthers, p. 34.
2. "Fletchall to President of the Council of Safety, 24 July 1775," in Robert Gibbes, *Documentary History of the American Revolution,* Appleton and Company, 1855, I, p. 123. Book hereinafter cited as "Gibbes."
3. Fanning, David, *The Narrative of Colonel David Fanning,* Lindley Butler, editor, Briarpatch, 1981, pp. 19-20.
4. Fort Charlotte is now under the waters of Clark Hill Reservoir.
5. "Papers of the First Council of Safety of the Revolutionary War Party in South Carolina," *South Carolina Genealogical Magazine* I, January 1900, pp. 40-47.
6. Fanning, p. 20.
7. "William Tennant to Henry Laurens, 20 August 1775," Gibbes, I, p. 145.
8. *Ibid.,* pp. 156-157.
9. *Ibid.,* pp. 171-173.

10. *Ibid.,* pp. 180-182.
11. "Treaty of Ninety Six September 16, 1775," Gibbes, I, p. 184-186.
12. Drayton, John, *Memoirs of the American Revolution,* Charleston, A.E. Miller, 1821, I, p. 418.
13. "Mose Cotter Deposition, 3 November 1775," quoted in William Moultrie, *Memoirs of the American Revolution,* David Longworth, 1802, I, pp. 97-100.
14. Jones, E. Alfred, "The Journal of Alexander Chesney," *Ohio State University Bulletin,* October 30, 1921, volume 26 no. 4, pp. 102-104, hereinafter cited as "Chesney." Fraser, Alexander, *United Empire Loyalists, Second Report of the Bureau of Archives for the Province of Ontario,* Toronto, 1905, reprinted by the Genealogical Publishing Company, 1994. Part I, pp. 190-194.
15. Andrew Williamson to Edward Wilkerson, November 6, 1775; Gibbes, I, pp. 209-210.
16. Fanning, p. 22.
17. Fraser, II, pp. 799-801.
18. Gibbes, I, p. 221.
19. Drayton, II, pp. 117-118.
20. *Ibid.,* p. 119.
21. "Williamson to Drayton," November 25, 1775; Gibbes, I, p. 218.
22. Gibbes, I, pp. 214-215.
23. *Ibid.,* p. 219.

Chapter 3

1. "Col. Thomson to Mr. Laurens," November 28, 1775; Gibbes, I, 222-223.
2. Fanning, p. 23.
3. Drayton, II, p. 119.
4. "Col. Richardson to Hon. H. Laurens," January 2, 1776; Gibbes, I, 246-247.
5. *Ibid.*
6. *Ibid.*
7. Fanning, p. 23.
8. *Ibid.*
9. *Ibid.,* pp. 23-24.
10. *Ibid.,* p. 24.
11. "A. Williamson Letter," July 22, 1776; Gibbes, II, pp. 26-27.
12. Drayton, II, p. 342.
13. Drayton, II, p. 342; "Rev. James Creswell to W.H. Drayton," July 27, 1776; Gibbes, II, pp. 30-31; Fanning, p. 24.
14. Drayton, II, pp. 342-343.
15. Fanning, pp. 24-25.
16. *Ibid.,* p. 25.

Chapter 4

1. Seibert, Wilbur Henry, *Loyalists in East Florida, 1774 to 1785*, Florida State Historical Society, 1929, II, pp. 363-364.
2. Fanning, p. pp. 25.
3. Fraser, 191.
4. Fanning, p.25.
5. Cashion, Edward, *The King's Ranger: Thomas Brown and the American Revolution on the Southern Frontier*, University of Georgia Press, 1989, p. 75.
6. Prisoners Sent to Charles town by Col. Richardson, 2 January 1776, Gibbes, I, 250.
7. Fanning, p. 25.
8. Cashin, p. 74.
9. *Ibid.*, p. 75.
10. Fanning, p. 26.
11. *Ibid.*
12. Draper, Lyman C., *Kings Mountain and Its Heroes*, 1881, reprinted Genealogical Publishing Company, 1967, pp. 134-135.
13. Fanning, p. 26.
14. *Ibid.*, pp. 26-27.
15. *Ibid.*, p. 27.
16. "Letter from the Safety Committee in Tryon County to the Safety Committee in Rowan County," July 12, 1776, CR X, pp. 609-610.
17. "Proceedings of the Safety Committee in Rowan County," August 22, 1776, CR X, p. 760; "Journal of the Council of Safety, Begun and Held at Salisbury," September 7, 1776, CR X, p. 827.
18. Fanning, p. 27.
19. *Ibid.*, p. 28. Butler identifies this man as Robert Gilliam of Ninety Six.
20. Fanning, p. 28-30.
21. Howe, p. 5.
22. Butler's footnote, Fanning, p. 19.
23. Fanning, p. 30.

Chapter 5

1. Fanning, p. 30.
2. Seibert, II, pp. 314-315.
3. "Diary of Lieutenant Anthony Allaire of Ferguson's Corps," reproduced in Draper, p. 500, hereinafter cited as "Allaire"; Chesney, p. 18.
4. Fanning, p. 31.
5. *Ibid.*
6. *Ibid.*, pp. 31-32.
7. Bass, p. 193-194.
8. McCrady, Edward, *The History of South Carolina in the Revolution, 1175-1780*, Macmillan, 1902, pp. 580-586.
9. Allaire, p. 504.
10. Draper, p. 104.
11. *Ibid.*
12. Johnson, Joseph, *Traditions and Reminiscences Chiefly of the American Revolution in the South*, Walker & James, 1851, p. 520.
13. Draper, p. 114.
14. *Ibid.*, pp. 109-110.
15. *Ibid.*, pp. 110-111.
16. Lumpkin, Henry, *From Savannah to Yorktown: The American Revolution in the South*, Paragon House Publishers, 1987, p. 88.
17. Fanning, p. 32.
18. Draper, p. 118.
19. Lumpkin, p. 89.
20. McCrady, pp. 580-586.
21. Fanning, p. 33.
22. Allaire, p. 524.
23. Chesney, pp. 18-19.
24. SR XIV, 429, 675-676, 790.
25. Lumpkin, p. 90.

Chapter 6

1. Lumpkin, p. 121.
2. Chesney, p. 22.
3. Fanning, p. 32.
4. Carruthers, p. 36.
5. Fanning, p. 33.
6. Carruthers, pp. 36-37.
7. Laws of North Carolina, 1779, Chapter XXXVIII, SR XXIV, p. 311.
8. Carruthers, pp. 37-38.
9. "Journal of the Provincial Congress of North Carolina," December 13, 1776, CR X, p. 968.
10. Fanning, p. 34.
11. Troxler, George, *Pyle's Massacre*, Alamance County Historical Association, 1973, pp. 1-4; Lee, Henry, *Memoirs of the War in the Southern Department of the United States*, University Pub. Co., New York, 1869, pp. 256-259.
12. Fanning, p. 34.
13. "Declaration of Joseph Graham," June 7, 1832, SR XIX, pp. 961-962.
14. Newlin, Algie, *Battle of New Garden, N.C.*, Friends Historical Society, 1977, p. 48.

15. Fanning, p. 35.
16. Cornwallis to Craig, March 19, 1781, PRO 30/11/85.
17. Stedman, C., *History of the American War*, London, 1794, II, pp. 348-349.
18. Craig to Cornwallis, March 22, 1781, PRO 30/11/69, fols. 19-20.
19. PRO 30/11/76, fol. 47.
20. Fanning, p. 35.
21. *Ibid.*
22. Letter from Greene to Philadelphia, March 20, 1781, quoted in Lt. Col. Banastre Tarleton's *A History of the Campaigns of 1780 and 1781 in the Southern Provinces of North America*, 1787, p. 321.
23. Ramsay to Gov. Burke, April 13, 1781, SR XV, 437.
24. Fanning, p. 35.
25. *Ibid.*, p. 36.
26. *Ibid.*
27. "Greene to Ashe, June 12, 1781," *The Papers of General Nathanael Greene*, Volume VIII, March-July 1781, Dennis Conrad, editor, University of North Carolina Press, 1995, pp. 380-381.
28. Captain Yarborough to General Sumner, May 1, 1781, SR XV, 460.
29. *The Heritage of Randolph County*, 1993, pp. 213-215; Fanning writes of a group of Whigs, "who had attempted to secure the fort of Deep River at Coxes Mill." Since this is the only allusion to a fort, Fanning was probably referring to the "ford" of Deep River, not a fort or stockade. Fanning, p. 49.
30. Fanning, pp. 36-37.
31. General Butler to Wm. O'Neal, March 1, 1782, SR XVI, 211; Fanning, p. 37; good background for the subject of conjurers is Robert Voeks, "African Medicine and Magic in the Americas." *Geographical Review* 83, no. 1 (January 1993): 66-78.
32. Col. Robeson to Col. Ray and Capt. McNeil, July 17, 1781, SR XV, pp. 542-543; James Emmett to Gov. Thomas Burke, July 19, 1781, SR XXII, pp. 584-549; Captain Edward Winston to Gov. Burke, July 20, 1781, SR XXII, pp. 549-550.

Chapter 7

1. Linn, Jo White, *Rowan County, North Carolina Tax Lists 1757-1800*, 1995, p. 141.
2. Carruthers, p. 85.
3. Fanning, pp. 37-38.
4. PRO 30/11/6 fols. 129-131.
5. Stephen, Sir Leslie and Sir Sidney Lee, *Dictionary of National Biography*, IV, pp. 1368-1369.
6. Sprunt, James, *Chronicles of the Cape Fear*, 1916, p. 114.
7. Bunburry, Sir Henry, *Narrative of Some Passages in the Great War Against France*, Peter Davies, London, 1927, p. 182.
8. PRO T1/647/x/j 6385; Hoyt, William (ed.), *The Papers of Archibald D. Murphey*, North Carolina Historical Commission, 1914, II, p. 390, hereinafter cited as "Murphey."
9. Murphey, II, pp. 394-395.
10. Fanning, p. 45.
11. Gen. Ramsay and Others to Gov. Burke, July 22, 1781, SR XXII, pp. 550-551.
12. PRO 30/11/16 fols. 338-339.
13. SR XVII, 399; SR XX 76.
14. MacLeod, Ruairidh, *Flora MacDonald*, Shepheard-Walwyn, 1995, pp. 196-197.
15. Carruthers, p. 44; Fanning, p. 48.
16. Carruthers, p. 44.
17. *Ibid.*
18. Fanning, p. 48.
19. Carruthers, p. 45.
20. Murphey, p. 396.
21. Fanning, p. 47-49; Murphey, II, pp. 395-396.
22. *Ibid.*; Alston's penchant for violence against his opponents, whether Whig or Tory, eventually caught up with him, and he met a violent end, being murdered in bed while sleeping in his cabin along the banks of the Oconee River in Georgia by an unknown assassin on October 28, 1791. He had fled North Carolina to escape justice for the part he played in the murder of a political opponent, Dr. George Glascock, in the summer of 1787. For the most detailed analysis of the Alston/Glascock episode, see George W. Willcox, *A History of the House in the Horseshoe: Her People and Her Deep River Neighbors*, Historical Research Services, 1999, pp. 238-263.
23. Fanning, p. 50.
24. *Ibid.*
25. *Ibid.*
26. *Ibid.*, pp. 50-51.
27. Armand Armstrrong to Gov. Thos. Burke, August 20, 1781, SR XXII, pp. 567-568.
28. Fowler, Malcolm, *Valley of the Scots*,

privately published by Wynona Fowler, 1986, p. 31.
29. Fanning, p. 51; Troxler, Carole, "The Great Man of the Settlement: North Carolina's John Leggett at Country Harbour, Nova Scotia, 1783–1812," *North Carolina Historical Review*, July, 1990, pp. 285–288.
30. Ashe, Samuel A., *History of North Carolina*, Charles Van Nappen, 1925, I, p. 686.
31. Carr, James (ed.), *The Dickson Letters*, Edwards & Broughton, 1901, pp. 17–18, hereinafter cited as "Dickson Letters."
32. Gen. William Caswell to Gov. Thomas Burke, 17 August 1781, SR XXII, 564.
33. SR XV, 121–127.
34. Gen. Wm. Caswell to Gov. Burke, 27 August 1781, SR XV, 627.

Chapter 8

1. Fanning, p. 51.
2. *Ibid.*, p. 52.
3. Dickson Letters, p. 19.
4. "The Battle of Elizabethtown," *Wilmington Weekly Chronicle*, February 1844, as quoted in James Sprunt, *Chronicles of the Cape Fear River*, Edwards & Broughton, 1916, pp. 116–118.
5. *Ibid.*
6. Butler to Burke, September 1, 1781, SR XXII, p. 584.
7. Fanning, p. 53.
8. McLean, Angus, *The Highland Scots of North Carolina*, written in 1919, published by the North Carolina Scottish Heritage Society, 1993, p. 243.
9. *Ibid.*, p. 244.
10. Fanning, p. 53.
11. Murphey, II, p. 390.
12. *Ibid.*, p. 391.
13. Fanning, p. 53.
14. McLean, p. 245.
15. Fanning, p. 53.
16. Murphey, II, p. 392.
17. Fanning, p. 53; Dickson Letters, p. 19.
18. Murphey, II, p. 392–393.
19. Johnson, p. 572.

Chapter 9

1. Col. Hugh Tiner to Gov. Burke, August 28, 1781, SR XXII, pp. 580–581.
2. Waterson, John III, "The Ordeal of Governor Burke," *North Carolina Historical Review*, Spring 1971, p. 104.
3. Fanning, p. 54.
4. *Ibid.*
5. Fanning, p. 54.
6. McDugald's Loyalist Claim, Treasury Papers, 1786. Microfilm on file at the N.C. Department of Archives and History, Raleigh, NC.
7. Fanning, p. 54.
8. General John Butler to Governor Burke, August 10, 1781, SR XXII, p. 557.
9. Fanning, p. 55.
10. Carruthers, p. 49.
11. Margaret Hoffman's *The Granville District of North Carolina, 1748–1763*, Volume II (Roanoke News Co., 1987) contains an entry on p. 285 for a grant of land to Joseph Kirk for "375 acres in Orange County on the S side of Haw River, joining Copelands Island, both sides of Kirks Creek, and the side of the Sd. River." This would place Kirk's farm in the southwestern portion of Chatham County, and in all likelihood under the waters of B. Everett Jordan Lake.
12. Fanning, p. 55; Carruthers, p. 50.
13. "House Journal from April 16, 1782 to May 18, 1782," SR XVI, p. 13.
14. *Ibid.*
15. SR XIX, p. 818; Declaration of William Allen, September 18, 1832, SR XXII, p. 101–102.
16. SR XXII, p. 101–102; Lloyd, Paulina, and Allen Lloyd, *History of the Churches of Hillsborough, N.C., 1766–1962*, 1962, p. 11.
17. Fanning, p. 55.
18. *Ibid.*
19. Carruthers, p. 50.
20. *Ibid.*
21. *Ibid.*, p. 52.
22. Fanning, p. 55.
23. The old roads are still in a remarkable state of preservation as of the winter of 2021, with the various roads along Staffords Branch and Cane Creek just as easily discernible as they had been back in the 1990s. Members of the Braxton and Lindley families, as well as other landowners nearby, have done a remarkable job of preserving the Lindley's Mill Battlefield. With the historical significance of this deadly fight, one wonders why it has never been preserved as an official park.
24. Carruthers, p. 51.

25. Fanning, p. 55.
26. Carruthers, p. 51.
27. *Ibid.*
28. Carruthers, pp. 50–51.
29. Newlin, Algie, *The Battle of Lindley's Mill*, Alamance Historical Association, 1975, p. 11.
30. Carruthers, p. 51.
31. Newlin, 12.
32. *Ibid.*
33. Carruthers, p. 51.
34. Fanning, p. 56.

Chapter 10

1. Carruthers, p. 54.
2. *Ibid.*, p. 55.
3. Wicker, Rassie, *Miscellaneous Ancient Records of Moore County*, Moore County Historical Society, 1971, pp. 380–381. Wicker quotes Connor Dowd's Loyalist Claim dated 12 February 1783.
4. Wicker, p. 214.
5. Carruthers, p. 55.
6. Governor Burke to [unknown], October 17, 1781, SR XV, p. 651.
7. Craig to Balfour, October 22, 1781, PRO 30/11/6.
8. *Ibid.*
9. *Ibid.*
10. Fanning, p. 57.
11. Craig to Balfour, October 22, 1781.
12. *Ibid.*; Clark, Murtric J., *Loyalists of the Southern Campaign, Vol. III*, Baltimore, Genealogical Publishing, 1981, p. 370.
13. Carruthers, p. 55.
14. Shipman, James, National Archives Revolutionary War Pension and Bounty Land Warrant Application File W17810; see also Nash Odom, "The Battle of Brown Marsh," *Bladen Journal*, September 15, 1973.
15. Craig to Balfour, October 22, 1781.
16. Shipman Pension Application. A strong case for placing the site of this battle in the Red Hill community of what is now northwestern Columbus County, see Mrs. J.A. Brown, "Some Early History of Columbus County," in James A. Rogers, *Columbus County, North Carolina*, 1946, p. 13.
17. Fanning, p. 57.
18. To Gov. Burke from Capt. Wm. O'Neal, March 19, 1782, SR XVI, p. 244.
19. Fanning, p. 57.

Chapter 11

1. Carruthers, p. 200; Graham, Major William A., *General Joseph Graham and His Papers on North Carolina Revolutionary History*, Edwards & Broughton, 1901, p. 356.
2. Graham, p. 357.
3. Carruthers, p. 201.
4. Graham, pp. 359–360.
5. Carruthers, p. 202.
6. Graham, pp. 360–361.
7. McLean, pp. 242–243.
8. Craig to Balfour, 22 October 1781, PRO 30/11/6 fol. 11.
9. Graham, pp. 362–363.
10. *Ibid.*
11. Fanning, p. 57; To Gov. Burke from Capt. Wm. O'Neal, March 19, 1782, SR XVI, pp. 244.
12. Fanning, p. 57.
13. *Ibid.* To this day, there is a cave along Brush Creek still pointed out as the place where Fanning hid during his convalescence.
14. Edmund Fanning to David Fanning, PRO T1 647/x/j 6385. A place for Edmund Fanning's letter was made in Colonel Fanning's *Narrative* but it was either lost or forgotten prior to being prepared for the printer and was thus not included.
15. Craig to Balfour, October 22, 1781, PRO 30/11/6, fols. 391–398.
16. Ashe, I, pp. 700–703.

Chapter 12

1. Fanning, p. 60.
2. *Ibid.*, p. 61.
3. *Ibid.*, p. 62.
4. *Ibid.*; CR X, pp. 486, 600, 631, 664, 935, 936, 940, 958.
5. Fanning, p. 63; Carruthers, pp. 56–57; Wicker, pp. 314, 319.
6. Fanning, p. 63.
7. *Ibid.*, p. 64.
8. Murphey, II, pp. 396–397; Fanning, p. 68.
9. Fanning, pp. 67–68.
10. *Ibid.*, p. 71.
11. *Ibid.*
12. *Ibid.*
13. *Ibid.*, p. 72.
14. *Ibid.*
15. Carruthers, p. 79.

16. *Ibid.*, p. 64.
17. *Ibid.*, p. 65.
18. *Ibid.*
19. *Ibid.*, p. 65; Fanning, p. 72.
20. Carruthers, p. 65.
21. *Ibid.*
22. Fanning, p. 72.
23. Carruthers, p. 65.
24. Fanning, p. 72.
25. *Ibid., p.* 73.
26. Fanning, p. 73; Murphey, II.
27. Fanning, p. 73.
28. *Ibid.*, pp. 73–75.
29. *Ibid.*, pp. 75–76.
30. Fanning, pp. 105–108. In the appendix, Butler includes these interesting letters housed in the Library of Congress.
31. Gov. Thos. Burke to Gen. Butler, March 25, 1782, SR XVI, p. 560.
32. SR XVI, p. 559–564.
33. Gov. Thos. Burke to Gen. Butler, March 23, 1782, SR XVI, p. 558–559.
34. For further proof of Williams' desire to be used on clandestine missions, see letter he wrote to Burke on April 8, 1782, offering his services to apprehend Col. Andrews and Maj. Gainey. John Williams to Gov. Thos. Burke, April 8, 1782, SR XVI, p. 586.

It is interesting to note that even though Fanning did not visit town on this occasion, the mere mention of his name was enough to cause pandemonium there. Francis Nash recorded the following story: "So far as known, Fannen appeared but once at Hillsboro, and that was at the capture of Governor Burke, though the terror of his name in 1782 roused members of the general assembly from their beds and made them appear armed upon the streets. It was a false alarm, however, caused by a timid citizen or an unknown practical joker." Nash, Francis, *Hillsboro: Colonial and Revolutionary*, Edwards Broughton, Raleigh, 1903, p. 85.

Chapter 13

1. The identity of Sarah's father is known because of a deed in Randolph County Deed Book 5, dated October 4, 1793, where Joseph Carr gives William a slave, "for love & good will I bear to my Son."
2. Fanning, p. 77.
3. *Ibid.*, pp. 77–78.
4. *Ibid.*, p. 79.

5. Carruthers, p. 67.
6. *Ibid.*
7. Murphey, II, pp. 388–389.
8. Fanning, pp. 79–80.
9. *Ibid.*, p. 80.
10. Gibbes, II, p. 187.
11. *Ibid.*, p. 188.
12. Fanning, p. 82. Dr. Butler identifies this man as Baylor in a footnote on p. 114.
13. Fanning, p. 80.
14. Simms, William Gilmore, *The Life of Francis Marion*, 1846, p. 314.
15. Fanning, p. 80.
16. Gen. Greene to Gen. Marion, July 9, 1782; Gibbes, II, p. 198.
17. McCowen, George Smith, Jr., *The British Occupation of Charleston, 1780–1782*, University of South Carolina Press, Columbia, 1972, pp. 143–144.
18. Barnwell, Joseph, "The Evacuation of Charleston by the British in 1782," *South Carolina Historical and Genealogical Magazine* 11 no. 1, January 1910, pp. 1–26.
19. "Revolutionary Letters," *South Carolina Historical and Genealogical Magazine* 38 no. 1, January 1937.
20. Fanning, pp. 82–83.
21. Fanning, p. 82.
22. Carruthers, p. 69. Faith Rock is currently the focal point of a small park in Franklinville, a town which grew up along the north side of Deep River long after the Revolutionary War.
23. Gregg, Alexander, *History of the Old Cheraws*, New York, Richardson, 1867, p. 396.
24. Fanning, p. 82.

Chapter 14

1. Nelson, William, *The American Tory*, Oxford, Clarendon, 1961, p. 168.
2. DeMond, Robert O., *The Loyalists in North Carolina During the American Revolution*, Durham, Duke University Press, 1940, p. 191.
3. Patrick Tonyn to Lord Shelburne, November 14, 1782, in K.G. Davies, ed., *Documents of the American Revolution, 1770–1783*, Dublin, Irish University Press, 1981, pp. 136–137.
4. Johnston, Elizabeth Lichtenstein, *Recollections of a Georgia Loyalist*, New York, M.F. Mansfield, 1901, p. 74.

5. Savory, Alfred W., ed., *Colonel David Fanning's Narrative*, privately published, 1908, hereinafter cited as Fanning Narrative, p. 38. Savory was the only editor who worked directly with Fanning's original journal to include the portions relating to British East Florida and the Bahamas. Fanning's original manuscript has been lost for more than a century.

6. Schafer, Daniel, "Not So Gay a Town in America as This," in George E. Baker and Jean Parker Waterbury, eds., *The Oldest City: St. Augustine, Saga of Survival*, St. Augustine, FL: St. Augustine Historical Society, 1983, pp. 119–120.

7. Mowat, Charles Loch, *East Florida as a British Province*, Berkeley, University of California Press, 1943, p. 137.

8. Schoepf, Johann David, *Travels in the Confederation*, Philadelphia: William J. Campbell, 1911, pp. 248–249.

9. Fanning Narrative, 38.

10. Gold, Daniel Pleasant, *History of Volusia County, Florida*, DeLand, FL, Painter Print Company, 1927, pp. 25–26.

11. Siebert, Wilbur Henry, *Loyalists in East Florida*, DeLand, Florida State Historical Soceity, 1929, I, pp. 145–147.

12. Fanning Narrative, 38.

13. Wheeler, David, "Recapture of the Bahama Islands," *The Political Magazine and Parliamentary, Naval, Military and Literary Journal*, July 1783, pp. 11–12.

14. Mackenzie, Roderick, *Strictures on Lt. Col. Tarleton's History*, London, R. Jameson, 1787, pp. 167–186; Siebert, pp. 145–147.

15. Mowat, p. 142. The Bahamas and East and West Florida deal was part of the series of peace treaties ending the war between Great Britain, the United States and their allies.

16. Fanning Narrative, p. 39.

17. *Ibid.*

18. *Ibid.*, p. 40.

19. Siebert, p. 144.

20. Fanning Narrative, pp. 40–41.

21. Fraser, Alexander, *United Empire Loyalists: Enquiry Into the Losses and Services in Consequence of Their Loyalty. Second Report of the Bureau of Archives for the Province of Ontario, Part I*, Toronto, Legislative Assembly of Ontario, 1905, pp. 241–242.

22. Clark, Walter, ed. *The State Records of North Carolina*, Goldsboro, NC, Nash Brothers, 1905, pp. XXIV, 489–490.

23. *Ibid.*, pp. XVI, 965–966.

24. Sabine, Lorenzo, *Biographical Sketches of Loyalists of the American Revolution*, Boston, Little, Brown and Company, 1864, I, pp. 165–166.

25. Gilroy, Marion, *Loyalists and Land Settlement in Nova Scotia*, Halifax, Public Archives of Nova Scotia, 1937, p. 76.

26. Fanning Narrative, p. 51.

27. Mowat, p. 144.

28. Fanning Narrative, p. 42.

29. *Ibid.*, p. 43.

30. Howard, Clinton N., "Early Settlers in British West Florida," *The Florida Historical Quarterly* 24, 1945, p. 51.

31. Fanning Narrative, p. 43.

32. *Ibid.*

33. *Ibid.*

34. De Brahm, William Gerard, *The Atlantic Pilot, a Facsimile Reproduction of the 1772 Edition*, Gainesville, University Presses of Florida, 1974, pp. 11–12.

35. Fanning Narrative, p. 43.

36. Brigham, Florence S., "Key Vaca, Part 1," *Tequesta* 17, 1957, pp. 47–68.

37. Audubon, John James, "Three Floridian Episodes," *Tequesta* 5, 1945, p. 54.

38. Fanning Narrative, p. 45.

39. *Ibid.*

40. Wilson, Isaiah, *A Geography and History of the County of Digby, Nova Scotia*, Halifax, NS, Holloway Brothers, 1890, p. 427.

41. Troxler, Carole Waterson, "Loyalist Refugees and the British Evacuation of East Florida, 1783–1785," *The Florida Historical Quarterly*, LX, 1981, p. 22.

42. Wright, James M., "The History of the Bahama Islands with a Special Study of the History of the Abolition of Slavery in the Colony," in George Burbank Shattuck, ed. *The Bahama Islands*, New York, Macmillan, 1905, p. 426.

43. MacKinnon, Neil, *This Unfriendly Soil: The Loyalist Experience in Nova Scotia 1783-1791*, Montreal, McGill-Queen's University Press, 1986, p. 67.

Chapter 15

1. Information on the Bay of Fundy based on personal observations as well as information provided by the staff of Fundy National Park.

2. Rohli, Robert V. and Anthony J.

Vega, *Climatology*, Sudbury, MA, Jones & Bartlett, 2008, p. 184.

3. Martin, R. Montgomery, *History of the British Colonies, Volume III*, London, James Cochrane, 1834, p. 319.

4. DeMond, Robert O. *The Loyalists in North Carolina During the American Revolution*, Duke University Press, 1940, p. 191.

5. Troxler, Carole Waterson, *The Loyalist Experience in North Carolina*, Raleigh, NC Department of Cultural Resources, 1976, pp. 45-46.

6. MacKinnon, Neil, *This Unfriendly Soil: The Loyalist Experience in Nova Scotia 1783-1791*, Montreal, McGill-Queen's University Press, 1986, p. 67.

7. Fanning Narrative, pp. 47-48.

8. Chidsey, Donald Barr, *The Loyalists*, New York, Crown Publishers, 1973, p. 167.

9. Raymond, William O., *The United Empire Loyalists*, Saint Stephen, NB, Saint Croix Printing and Publishing, 1893, 39.

10. Fisher, Peter, *Sketches of New-Brunswick*, Saint John, NB, Chubb & Sears, 1825, pp. 3-4.

11. Howe, Jonas, "Colonel David Fanning: The Career of a Carolina Loyalist of the American Revolution: A Paper Read Before the New Brunswick Historical Society, May 27th, 1890," unpublished manuscript, NBM, p. 10.

12. Deed quoted by Howe, 11.

13. Jonas Howe transcript of David Fanning's Journal, Jonas Howe Papers, NBM.

14. Petition of Thomas Wetmore and Charles Peters, October 4, 1800, Records of the Executive Council, F 6775, 3/1, David Fanning Case, 1800-1802, PANB.

15. *Journal and Votes of the House of Assembly of the Province of New Brunswick*, 1786-1797, Legislative Library, Fredericton, New Brunswick, p. 595.

16. Fanning to Chipman, May 16, 1795, Lawrence Collection, PACO.

17. Howe, pp. 13-14.

18. Fanning to Carleton, November 4, 1801, PANB.

19. Fanning to Odell, October 3, 1799, quoted in Fanning to Carleton, November 4, 1801, PANB.

20. Fanning to Carleton, November 4, 1801, PANB.

21. Fanning to Odell, January 4, 1800, quoted in Fanning to Carleton, November 4, 1801, PANB.

22. Fanning to Carleton, November 4, 1801, PANB.

23. Records of the Executive Council, F6775, 3/1 David Fanning Case, 1800-1802, PANB.

24. *Ibid.*

25. Sarah Fanning Petition, October 9, 1800, PANB.

26. Pardon of David Fanning for a Rape, October 10, 1800, PANB.

27. Fanning to Carleton, November 4, 1801, PANB.

28. Fanning to Carleton, October 31, 1800, PANB.

Chapter 16

1. Hill, Allan Massie, *Some Chapters in the History of Digby County and Its Early Settlers*, McAlpine Publishing Company, Halifax, NS, 1901, reprinted by Longview Press, 1995, Smith's Cove, NS, p. 1.

2. Hill, pp. 6-10.

3. Fanning to Jarvis, December 8, 1800, Jarvis Papers, NBM.

4. Wilson, Isaiah, *A Geography and History of the County of Digby, Nova Scotia*, Halifax, Holloway Brothers, p. 427.

5. Fanning to Jarvis, December 12, 1801, Jarvis Papers, NBM.

6. Fanning to Odell, March 15, 1806, PANS.

7. *Ibid.*

8. *Ibid.*

9. *Ibid.*

10. Fanning to Munson Jarvis, December 1, 1804, Jarvis Papers, NBM.

11. Fanning to Odell, March 15, 1806, PANS.

12. Fanning to Odell, February 9, 1808, Odell Papers, NBM.

13. Fanning to Whitlock, February 15, 1808, Jarvis Papers, NBM.

14. Stephen and Lee, *Dictionary of National Biography*, pp. 1369-1370.

15. Craig to Fanning, April 15, 1808, Odell Papers, NBM.

16. Fanning to Whitlock, November 7, 1808, Jarvis Papers, NBM.

17. Tombstone inscription, Holy Trinity Anglican Church; personal interview with Arnold Trask, May 27, 1996.

18. Wilson, Isaiah, *A Geography and History of the County of Digby, Nova Scotia*, 1890, p. 128.

19. Savary, Alfred, *History of the County of Annapolis*, 1897, p. 285. These stories of raids in the Digby area are corroborated by Joseph Howe, who visited Digby in October of 1828 and penned the following account. "On one occasion the captain and one of the crew of a privateer came into Digby in disguise, to reconnoiter; after their departure, suspicion was awakened and persons sent in pursuit of them: and young Morton, then a lad in his teens, now a member of the assembly, fell in with them, and though they were well armed, forced them both to surrender." Joseph Howe, *Western and Eastern Rambles, Travel Sketches of Nova Scotia*, edited by M.G. Parks, 1973.
20. Wilson, pp. 128–129.
21. Fanning to Jarvis, January 18, 1814, Jarvis Papers, NBM.
22. Jarvis Papers, NBM.
23. Trask interview, May 23, 1996.
24. Hill, p. 53.
25. Trask interview.
26. Wheeler, John, "Introductory Remarks," in Wynne, Thomas H., ed., *Narrative of Colonel David Fanning*, Richmond, 1861, reprinted by the Reprint Company, Spartanburg, SC, 1973, pp. xvii–xviii.
27. "Moore County Will Book A," pp. 182–184, quoted in James Vann Comer, *Descendants of Colonel Archibald McDugald, Sr., and Rebecca Buie*, 1991, p. 9.
28. *Ibid.*
29. Howe, p. 14.
30. Fanning Ledgerbook, Admiral Digby Museum, Digby, Nova Scotia.
31. Will of Colonel David Fanning.
32. Wilson, p. 369.
33. Fanning Ledgerbook.
34. Trask interview.

Bibliography

Abbreviations used for archival sources quoted in the Endnotes: NBM—New Brunswick Museum, St. John, New Brunswick; PACO—Public Archives of Canada, Ottawa; PANB—Provincial Archives of New Brunswick, Fredericton, New Brunswick; PANS—Public Archives of Nova Scotia, Halifax, Nova Scotia

Anonymous, *Journal and Votes of the House of Assembly of the Province of New Brunswick*, Legislative Library, Fredericton, New Brunswick, 1786-1797.

———. "Papers of the First Council of Safety of the Revolutionary War Party in South Carolina," *South Carolina Genealogical Magazine*, January 1900.

———. "Revolutionary Letters," *South Carolina Historical and Genealogical Magazine*, January 1937.

Ashe, Samuel A., *History of North Carolina*, 1925.

Barnwell, Joseph, "The Evacuation of Charleston by the British in 1782," *South Carolina Historical and Genealogical Magazine*, January 1910.

Bass, Robert, *Ninety Six: The Struggle for the South Carolina Backcountry, 1700-1781*, 1978.

Bizzell, Virginia, and Bizzell, Oscar M., *Revolutionary War Records, Duplin and Sampson Counties, North Carolina*, 1997.

Brigham, Florence, "Key Vaca," *Tequesta* 17, 1957.

Bunbury, Sir Henry, *Narrative of Some Passages in the Great War with France*, 1927.

Butler, Lindley (ed.), *The Narrative of Colonel David Fanning*, 1981.

Calnek, W.A., *History of the County of Annapolis*, Toronto: William Briggs, 1897.

Cann, Marvin, *Old Ninety-Six in the South Carolina Backcountry, 1700-1781*, 1996.

Carr, James, *The Dickson Letters*, 1901.

Carruthers, Eli, *Interesting Revolutionary Incidents and Sketches of Character, Chiefly in the Old North State in 1776*, 1856. Greensboro, NC: Reprinted by the Guilford County Genealogical Society, 1985.

Cashion, Edward, *The King's Ranger: Thomas Brown and the American Revolution on the Southern Frontier*, 1989.

Chidsey, Donald Barr, *The Loyalists*, New York: Crown Publishers, 1973.

Clark, Murtric J., *Loyalists of the Southern Campaign, Vol. III*, Baltimore, MD: Genealogical Publishing, 1981.

Comer, James Vann, *Descendants of Colonel Archibald McDugald, Sr., and Rebecca Buie*, 1991.

Conrad, Dennis (ed.), *The Papers of General Nathanael Greene*, 1995.

Davies, K.G. (ed.), *Documents of the American Revolution, 1770-1783*, Dublin: Irish University Press, 1981.

DeMond, Robert O., *The Loyalists in North Carolina During the American Revolution*, Durham, NC: Duke University Press, 1940.

Draper, Lyman C., *King's Mountain and Its Heroes*, 1881. Reprinted by Genealogical Publishing, 1989.

Drayton, John, *Memoirs of the American Revolution*, 1821.

Fisher, Peter, *Sketches of New-Brunswick*, Saint John, NB: Chubb & Sears, 1825.

Fowler, Malcolm, *Valley of the Scots*, 1986.

Fox, William Tilbury, "On the Identity of Parasitic Fungi Affecting the Human Surface," *Lancet* 2 no. 12, July 1859: 5-7.

Fraser, Alexander, *United Empire Loyalists, Second Annual Report of the Bureau of Archives for the Province of Ontario*, 1905. Reprinted by Genealogical Publishing, 1994.

Gibbes, Robert, *Documentary History of the American Revolution*, 1855.

Gold, Pleasant Daniel, *History of Volusia County, Florida*, 1927.

Graham, William A., *General Joseph Graham and His Papers on North Carolina Revolutionary History*, 1901.

Gregg, Alexander, *History of the Old Cheraws*, 1867.

Hartzell, Milton, *Diseases of the Skin; Their Pathology and Treatment*, 1917.

Hill, Allan Massie, *Some Chapters in the History of Digby County and Its Early Settlers*, 1901. Reprinted by Longview, 1995.

Hoffman, Margaret, *The Granville District of North Carolina 1748-1763*, 1987.

Howe, Jonas, "Colonel David Fanning: The Career of a Carolina Loyalist of the American Revolution; a Paper Read Before the New Brunswick Historical Society May 27th, 1890." Unpublished manuscript.

Howe, Joseph, *Western and Eastern Rambles: Travel Sketches of Nova Scotia*, edited by M.G. Parks, 1973.

Hoyt, William (ed.), *The Papers of Archibald D. Murphey*, 1914.

Johnson, Joseph, *Traditions and Reminiscences Chiefly of the American Revolution in the South*, 1851.

Johnson, Todd, "David Fanning: Revolutionary War Soldier," *Smithfield Herald*, July 27, 1993.

Johnston, Elizabeth Lichtenstein, *Recollections of a Georgia Loyalist*, New York: M.F. Mansfield, 1901.

Jones, Alfred E., "The Journal of Alexander Chesney," *Ohio State University Bulletin* 26, no. 40.

Lee, Henry, *Memoirs of the War in the Southern Department of the United States*, 1869.

Linn, Jo White, *Rowan County, North Carolina Tax Lists 1757-1800*, 1995.

Lloyd, Paulina, and Lloyd, Allen, *History of the Churches of Hillsborough, N.C., 1766-1962*, 1962.

Logan, John, *History of the Upper Country of South Carolina*, 1859.

Lumpkin, Henry, *From Savanah to Yorktown: The American Revolution in the South*, 1987.

MacKenzie, Roderick, *Strictures on Lt. Col. Tarleton's History*, 1787.

MacKinnon, Neil, *This Unfriendly Soil: The Loyalist Experience in Nova Scotia 1783-1791*, Montreal: McGill-Queen's University Press, 1986.

MacLeod, Ruairidh, *Flora MacDonald*, 1995.

Marryat, Thomas, *Therapeutics; or the Art of Healing*, Bristol: W. Sheppard, 1805.

Martin, R. Montgomery, *History of the British Colonies, Volume III*, London: James Cochrane, 1834.

McCrady, Edward, *The History of South Carolina in the Revolution, 1775-1780*, 1902.

McGowen, George Smith, Jr., *The British Occupation of Charleston, 1780-1782*, 1972.

McLean, Angus, *The Highland Scots of North Carolina*, 1919. Reprinted by the North Carolina Scottish Heritage Society, 1993.

Mowat, Charles Loch, *East Florida as a British Province*, Berkeley, CA: University of California Press, 1943.

Nelson, William, *The American Tory*, Oxford: Clarendon, 1961.

Newlin, Algie, *The Battle of Lindley's Mill*, 1975.

_____, *Battle of New Garden*, 1977.

Odum, Nash, "The Battle of Brown Marsh," *Bladen Journal*, September 15, 1973.

Powell, William (ed.), *The Correspondence of William Tryon*, 1981.

Quain, Richard, *A Dictionary of Medicine*, 1885.

Raymond, William O., *The United Empire Loyalists*, Saint Stephen, NB: Saint Croix, 1893.

Rogers, James A., *Columbus County, North Carolina*, Whiteville, NC: The News Reporter, 1946.

Rohli, Robert V., and Vega, Anthony J., *Climatology*, Sudbury, MA: Jones & Bartlett, 2008.

Ross, Elizabeth., "William and Needham Bryan," *Heritage of Johnston County*,

Bibliography

North Carolina, Smithfield: Johnston County Genealogical Society, 1985.

Savary, Alfred W., *History of the County of Annapolis*, 1897.

―――― (ed.), *Colonel David Fanning's Narrative*, reprinted from the *Canadian Magazine*, 1908.

Schafer, Daniel, "...not So Gay a Town in America as This...." in George E. Baker and Jean Parker Waterbury, eds., *The Oldest City: St. Augustine, Saga of Survival*, St. Augustine, FL: St. Augustine Historical Society, 1983.

Schoepf, Johann David, *Travels in the Confederation*, Philadelphia: William J. Campbell, 1911.

Shipman, James, "National Archives Revolutionary War Pension and Bounty Land Warrant Application File W17810," February 1833.

Siebert, Wilbur Henry, *Loyalists in East Florida, 1774-1785*. DeLand: Florida State Historical Society, 1929.

Simms, William Gilmore, *The Life of Francis Marion*, 1846.

Sprunt, James, *Chronicles of the Cape Fear*, 1916.

Stedman, C., *History of the American War*, 1794.

Stephen, Sir Leslie and Lee, Sir Sidney (eds.), *Dictionary of National Biography*, 1917.

Tabeau, Carleton, *The Story of Florida*, 1971.

Tarleton, Banastre, *A History of the Campaigns of 1780 and 1781 in the Southern Provinces of North America*, 1787.

Troxler, Carole Waterson, "The Great Man of the Settlement: North Carolina's John Leggett at Country Harbour, Nova Scotia, 1783-1812," *North Carolina Historical Review*, July 1990.

―――― , *The Loyalist Experience in North Carolina*, Raleigh: NC Department of Cultural Resources, 1976.

―――― , "'To Git Out of a Troublesome Neighborhood': Colonel David Fanning in New Brunswick," *North Carolina Historical Review*, October 1979.

Troxler, George, *Pyle's Massacre*, 1973.

Voeks, Robert, "African Medicine and Magic in the Americas." *Geographical Review* 83 no. 1, January 1993: 66-78.

Waterbury, Jean Parker (ed.), *The Oldest City*, 1983.

Waterson, John III, "The Ordeal of Governor Burke," *North Carolina Historical Review*, Spring 1971.

Wheeler, David, "Recapture of the Bahama Islands," *The Political Magazine and Parliamentary, Naval, Military and Literary Journal*, July 1783: 11-12.

Wicker, Rassie, *Miscellaneous Ancient Records of Moore County, N.C.*, 1971.

Willcox, George W. *A History of the House in the Horseshoe: Her People and Her Deep River Neighbors*, Historical Research Services, 1999.

Wilson, Isaiah, *A Geography and History of the County of Digby, Nova Scotia*, 1890.

Wynne, Thomas H. (ed.), *Narrative of Colonel David Fanning*, 1861. Reprinted by Reprint Company, 1973.

Index

Abaco 135
Act of Pardon and Oblivion 138–139
Admiral Digby Museum 169
Alaire, Anthony 40
Alamance, Creek, Battle of 7–8
Alligator Creek, Battle of 32
Alston, Phillip 68–74, 100, 175–176
Alston, Temperance 71–72, 175
Alston House *see* House in the Horseshoe
Anastasia Island 133–134
Andrews, Captain 71
Andrews, Samuel 139
Annapolis Royal, N.S. 150, 159, 162, 166
Asheboro Regional Airport 117
Avera, Alexander 74–75

Baldwin's Old Field *see* Brown Marsh
Balfour, Margaret 121
Balfour, Nisbet 64–65
Balfour, Thomas 58, 61, 73, 114, 117, 120–121
Balfour Cemetery 117
Baptist, Captain 144–146
Barbecue Church 56
Baylor, George 129
Beach Swamp, Va. 6
Beatti's Bridge, Battle of 80–83, 88, 106
Bell, Jacob 148
Bethune, David 111
Bickerstaff's 47–48
Birdsong, John 68
Birmingham, James 21
Black, Kenneth 69–71, 176
Blackstock's Ford 50
Bonnell, William 161
Boyd, James 38
Brown, Sam 32–33
Brown, Thomas 15–16, 31
Brown Marsh, Battle of 104–107, 112
Brown's Cave on the Catawba 33

Bryan, Needham 7–8
Buchan, John 71
Budd, Elisha 161
Buffalo Ford 51, 59, 131
Buie, Daniel 168
Bunch, William 146–147
Burke, Thomas 67, 73–74, 76, 86–89, 100, 102–103, 107–109, 114, 120, 123–124, 139
Butler, John 86–88, 92–94, 96–97, 102–108, 110, 112, 119–120, 124

Camden, Battle of 46, 86, 108, 117
Cameron's Hill 109, 168
Cane Creek, Battle of *see* Lindley's Mill
Cape Sable 143–146
Carleton, Guy 156–159
Carleton, Thomas 17–18
Carr, Joseph 125
Carr, William 125
Charles Town 11–12, 15, 17, 25, 27, 29, 39, 41, 52, 68, 75, 90, 108, 120, 123, 125–126, 128–134, 141, 151
Charlotte, NC 60
Chatham Court House 56, 64, 67–68, 70, 86–87, 93
Cherokee Ford on the Savannah 32
Cherokee Path 10–11
Clifton, Daniel 123
Clutsam, Samuel 146–147
Collier, John 58–59, 61, 122
Collins, John 122
Colville, Maturine 79
conjurer 61
Cook, Charles 168
Cornwallis, Charles 5, 41–42, 46–47, 50–57, 63–65, 101, 108, 114, 129
Cotter, Moses 17–18
Cowan's Ford 14
Cowpens, Battle of 50–52
Cox, Harmon 60
Cox, John 118

Index

Cox, Robert 118
Cox, William 60
Cox's Mill 59–61, 66–67, 73, 84, 87–88, 92–93, 99, 107, 117, 120, 130–131
Craig, James H. 56–57, 64–68, 72–73, 75–77, 84, 87, 99, 102–106, 108–109, 113–114, 119, 127, 163–164, 175
Cross Creek 55–57, 59–60, 74–77, 86, 103, 109
Cross Hill 69
Cruger, John Harris 41
Cunningham, John 30
Cunningham, Patrick 14–15, 17–18, 21, 23–25, 39
Cunningham, Robert 14-15, 17–18, 52
Cunningham, William "Bloody Bill" 39–40

dePeyster, Abraham 46–47
Deveaux, Andrew 135–136
Dickerson's Ford 71
Dickson, William 79
Digby, N.S. 1, 38, 160–162, 164–167, 169–172, 177–178
Digby, Robert 160
Digby Gut 159–161, 167
Dixon's Mill 55–56
Dougan, Thomas 84–85, 123
Dowd, Connor 73, 99–101, 107
Dowd, Owen 101
Drayton, William 15–17
Dudley, Guilford 59–60

East Florida 2, 31–32, 35, 125, 132–141, 143, 147–149, 151
Edwards, Edward 89
Edwards, Richard 74–75, 88–89
Elizabethtown, Battle of 77–80
Elrod, William 63, 84–85, 110

Faith Rock 126–131
Fannen Ledge 177–178
Fanning, Bryan 6
Fanning, David, Sr. 6–7
Fanning, David William 164–165
Fanning, Elizabeth 7
Fanning, Feribee 154, 157
Fanning, Ross Currie Carr 9, 170
Fanning, Sarah Carr 125, 157, 171, 173
Fanning Lake 177
Fanning Mountain 177
Fanning's Brook 155, 177
Fanning's Grave 171–172
Fanning's Narrative 154
Fanning's Rocks 152, 177
Ferebee and Phoebe 147

Ferguson, Patrick 39, 42–43
Fletchall, Thomas 13–19, 22, 34
Florida Everglades 144–146
Fort Charlotte 14–15, 39
Fort Howe 31

Gagetown, N.B. 157
Gainey, Micajah 119, 128–129
Gilbert Town 46–47
Glascock, George 176
Glasscock's Old Field 56
Goling, John 155–158
Goodwin, Uriah 17
Goudy, Robert 11–13
Graham, Joseph 54–55, 109
Graham, William 109–112
Great Cane Brake, Battle of 23–24
Greene, Nathanael 51, 55–60, 65, 90, 114, 129–130
Guiggy, John 166
Guilford Courthouse, Battle of 55, 86–87

Halifax, N.C. 60, 86, 117, 120
Halifax, N.S. 152, 163, 165
Halifax River, Fl. 135–136, 149, 152
Hamilton, John 52, 63, 138
Hammond's Store, Battle of 50
Hanford, Thomas 157
Hart, Oliver 15
Hayes, Joseph 50
Herndon, James 68
Hickory Mountain 99
Hillsborough, N.C. 51, 53–54, 57–60, 74, 86–92, 95, 97, 104
Hine, Joseph 68
Hooker, William 113, 125
House in the Horseshoe (Alston House) 70–72, 100, 175–176
Howe, Robert 31–32
Hunter, Andrew 127–128, 130–131

Innes, Alexander 41
Isaacs, Elijah 117–119
Island Ford on the Saluda 16, 19, 33

Jackson, David 117–118
Jarvis, Munson 160–162, 166
Johnson, James 8
Johnston, Elizabeth Lichtenstein 133
Jones, Matthew 68

Kellet, Joseph 10
Kennedy, Thomas 116
Kershaw, Joseph 15
Kettle Creek, Ga., Battle of 38, 60
Key Biscayne 142–143

Index 195

Key West 142–144
King's Mountain, Battle of 47–48
Kirkland, Moses 14–15
Kirk's Farm, Battle of 88–89

Lee, Henry 54–55, 57, 114
Leech, T. 7
Leslie, Alexander 126, 129–130
Lewis, Samuel 30

Lindley, James 13–14, 38, 60
Lindley, William 119–120
Lindley's Fort 25–27
Lindley's Mill, Battle of 73, 93–98, 101, 103, 107–109, 112–113, 119–120
Locke, Francis 41
London, Sarah 157–158, 173
Long Reach, NB 154
Lopp, John 116
Lord Dunsmore Proclamation of 1775 61
Lytle, Archibald 89–90

Magaherty 119–120
Mallett, Peter 139
Manson, Daniel 104–107
Marion, Francis 39, 57, 112, 119, 128–130
Mayson, James 14–15, 18–21
McBryde, Archibald 8, 167–168
McDonald, Flora 69
McDugald, Archibald 74, 88, 93, 95–99, 102–104, 107, 109–110, 128, 168
McLean, Sober John 90, 93–96, 99–100
McNeill, Daniel 138
McNeill, Elder Hector 81–83, 87–90, 93–95, 98, 106, 109–110
McNeill, One Eyed Hector 109–110, 119
McPhaul's Mill 62, 67, 77–80, 99, 102, 104, 106, 110
McRae 102
Millikan, William 121
Mills, Ambrose 34–35, 47–48
Mine Creek, S.C. 17–18
Mitchell Mountain 93
Moore, James 41–42
Morgan, Daniel 39, 50–51
Murphey, Archibald 71–73, 123, 167
Musgrove's Mill, Battle of 40–46

Nassau 136, 146
Natchez, M.S. 141
Negro Head Road 112
New Blessing 132–133
New Brunswick Provincial Assembly 154
New Providence 135–136, 143–14, 156
Ninety-Six, S.C. 10–12, 14–22, 28, 30, 33–34, 36–43, 45–47, 50, 54, 60

Odell, Jonathan 156, 162–164
O'Deniell, John 8–10
O'Deniell, William 10
O'Neal, Henry 15

Pearis, Richard 18, 22, 26, 29–30, 40, 41, 47
Perkins, Thomas 176
Peters, Charles 157
Pyle, John 53–55, 117
Pyle's Hacking Match 54–55

Raft Swamp, Battle of 110–112
Rains, John 52, 73, 88, 98, 113, 126
Ramseur's Mill, Battle of 101
Ramsey, Herndon 68
Ramsey, Matthew 68, 119
Ramsey's Mill 56, 86–88
Randolph County Scourge 121–123
Rapely, Richard 15
Ray, Duncan 62, 74–75, 77, 102–106, 110
Red Doe 127–128, 130–131
Regulator Uprising 8, 11, 60, 114
Ritchie, William 26, 39–40
Rutherford, Griffith 41, 108–112, 114–117

Saaz, Claraco 136
Salisbury, N.C. 36, 60, 74, 123
Salvador, Frances 15
Savary, Alfred 5, 166
Schoepf, David 134
Scoby, Robert 120
Seely, Ebeneezer 156
Shearing, Charles 53
Shipman, James 106
Slingsby, John 74–75, 77–80, 84, 97
Smalley, Fanning 38
Smith, Robert 112
Smith, William 146–147
Smith's Ferry on the Neuse 7
Snow Campaign 24–25
Squires, Talmon 161–162
St. Augustine, Fl. 35, 108, 131, 13–134, 136–141, 143, 149, 168
Stewart, John 161–162

Tarleton, Banastre 46, 48, 50, 54–55
Taylor, Thomas 68, 69, 176
Terrell, Simon 68
tetter-worm 8–10
Thompson, Balaam 120
Thompson, John 119
Tonyn, Patrick 133, 136–137, 139–140
Tory Hole 78–79
Trask, Arnold 165, 167, 172
Trask, Barbara 30

Trinity Anglican Church 169–172
Tryon, William 7–8
Tyson, Cornelius 53

Upper Saluda Militia Regiment 13–14
Uwharrie Mountains 62, 109, 125

Vaca Key 144
Veits, Roger 167
Velasco, Vincente 137

Waddell's Ferry 112
Walker, Adam 161
Walker, Stephen 118
War of 1812 165–166

Washington, William 50
West Florida 2, 29–30, 40, 136, 138, 141, 146
Wetmore, Thomas 157
Wheeler, Thomas 135–136
White, William 119–120
Wilcox Iron Works 120
Williams, Benjamin 176
Williams' Fort 50
Williamson, Andrew 17–23, 27, 41
Wilmington, N.C. 56–57, 64–68, 70–77, 79, 84–85, 92–93, 99, 101–109, 111–116, 118–119, 139, 163, 175
Woody's Ford 92–93

York, John 31–32, 38

www.ingramcontent.com/pod-product-compliance
Lightning Source LLC
Chambersburg PA
CBHW032044300426
44117CB00009B/1189